Reading Medieval Ruins

The Japanese provincial city of Ichijōdani was destroyed in the civil wars of the late sixteenth century but never rebuilt. Archaeological excavations have since uncovered the most detailed late medieval urban site in the country. Drawing on analysis of specific excavated objects and decades of archaeological evidence to study daily life in Ichijōdani, *Reading Medieval Ruins* illuminates the city's layout, the possessions and houses of its residents, its politics and experience of war, and religious and cultural networks. Morgan Pitelka demonstrates how provincial centers could be dynamic and vibrant nodes of industrial, cultural, economic, and political entrepreneurship and sophistication. In this study a new and vital understanding of late medieval society is revealed, one in which Ichijōdani played a central role in the vibrant age of Japan's sixteenth century.

MORGAN PITELKA is Professor of History and Asian Studies at the University of North Carolina-Chapel Hill.

T0382141

Reading Medieval Ruins

Urban Life and Destruction
in Sixteenth-Century Japan

Morgan Pitelka

University of North Carolina–Chapel Hill

CAMBRIDGE
UNIVERSITY PRESS

CAMBRIDGE
UNIVERSITY PRESS

Shaftesbury Road, Cambridge CB2 8EA, United Kingdom

One Liberty Plaza, 20th Floor, New York, NY 10006, USA

477 Williamstown Road, Port Melbourne, VIC 3207, Australia

314–321, 3rd Floor, Plot 3, Splendor Forum, Jasola District Centre, New Delhi – 110025, India

103 Penang Road, #05–06/07, Visioncrest Commercial, Singapore 238467

Cambridge University Press is part of Cambridge University Press & Assessment, a department of the University of Cambridge.

We share the University's mission to contribute to society through the pursuit of education, learning and research at the highest international levels of excellence.

www.cambridge.org
Information on this title: www.cambridge.org/9781009069977

DOI: 10.1017/9781009071703

© Morgan Pitelka 2022

This publication is in copyright. Subject to statutory exception and to the provisions of relevant collective licensing agreements, no reproduction of any part may take place without the written permission of Cambridge University Press & Assessment.

First published 2022
First paperback edition 2023

A catalogue record for this publication is available from the British Library

Library of Congress Cataloging-in-Publication data
Names: Pitelka, Morgan, 1972– author.
Title: Reading medieval ruins : urban life and destruction in sixteenth-century Japan / Morgan Pitelka, University of North Carolina–Chapel Hill
Other titles: Urban life and destruction in sixteenth-century Japan.
Description: Cambridge, United Kingdom ; New York : Cambridge University Press, 2022. | Includes bibliographical references and index.
Identifiers: LCCN 2021051125 (print) | LCCN 2021051126 (ebook) | ISBN 9781316513064 (hardback) | ISBN 9781009069977 (paperback) | ISBN 9781009071703 (epub)
Subjects: LCSH: Ichijōdani (Japan)–History. | Ichijōdani (Japan)–Social life and customs. | Asakura family. | Fukui-ken (Japan)–History–16th Century. | BISAC: HISTORY / Asia / General
Classification: LCC DS897.I245 P58 2022 (print) | LCC DS897.I245 (ebook) | DDC 952.155–dc23/eng/20211020
LC record available at https://lccn.loc.gov/2021051125
LC ebook record available at https://lccn.loc.gov/2021051126

ISBN   978-1-316-51306-4   Hardback
ISBN   978-1-009-06997-7   Paperback

Cambridge University Press & Assessment has no responsibility for the persistence or accuracy of URLs for external or third-party internet websites referred to in this publication and does not guarantee that any content on such websites is, or will remain, accurate or appropriate.

Contents

Figures

Maps

Tables

Acknowledgments

I first became interested in the city of Ichijōdani, the focus of this book, while I was a graduate student and looking for case studies of the significance of ceramics in premodern Japanese society. Louise Cort, Curator for Asian Ceramics at the Freer and Sackler Galleries, suggested in 1996 that I investigate the site as a possible dissertation topic. I visited for the first time that summer, and though I chose different topics for my first and second research projects, I have been returning to Ichijōdani whenever possible ever since.

I have benefited from the generosity of numerous scholars and staff associated with the Fukui Prefectural Ichijōdani Asakura Family History Museum over the years, and extend my thanks for their openness and support. In particular, I offer my thanks to Ono Masatoshi and Satō Kei, two scholars who conducted pioneering research on Ichijōdani and wrote voluminous studies of the city and its relevance in the larger flow of Japanese history. Both also met with me, shared resources, and supported my research, for which I am endlessly grateful. Thank you also to Ishikawa Miho and Watanabe Hiroaki, curators at the museum, for their generosity and scholarship.

Two fellowships helped to make the research for this book possible. I was lucky enough to be a fellow at the National Humanities Center from 2011 to 2012, which allowed me to make progress in researching Ichijōdani. From 2017 to 2018, I had a semester of research leave in the fall and was a fellow at the Institute for Arts and Humanities at UNC-Chapel Hill in the spring, which allowed me to draft several chapters and benefit from the wisdom and advice of a remarkable group of writing peers. Thanks to Sam Amago, Deborah Gerhardt, Cara McComish, Dave Pier, Dan Sherman, Beverly Taylor, Meenu Tewari, Gabe Trop, Lien Truong, and Molly Worthen, as well as our beloved leader Michele Berger, for a transformative semester as IAH Faculty Fellows.

Libraries around the world have been key to the research for this volume. I couldn't begin to name all of the professional librarians who assisted me, though I do want to mention Kristina Troost of Duke

University, who helped to acquire so many important medieval Japanese materials over the years. Thanks also to the UNC library, the Diet National Library, the Kyoto Prefectural Library and Archives, the Fukui Prefectural Library, and the Princeton University East Asian Library.

I presented versions of my research at several symposia and conferences and offer my sincere gratitude to the organizers for the opportunities to receive feedback on work in progress. I offer my appreciation to Peter Shapinsky, David Spafford, and Suzanne Gay for their involvement in the 2014 panel at the Association for Asian Studies Annual Meeting, "Beyond Unification," where I presented on Ichijōdani for the first time. Similarly, I extend my thanks to fellow panelists on "Merits of the Mundane," from the 2017 AAS Annual Meeting: Michelle Damian, Sachiko Kawai, and Tristan Grunow. In 2018, I was invited to present on Ichijōdani at the University of Southern California, and thank the assembled faculty and graduate students for a range of helpful comments. In 2020, I enjoyed the chance to present at the University of Michigan on the near-completed draft of the manuscript, and benefited enormously from the questions and advice of faculty and students there.

This project was also shaped by a fortuitous encounter with a historian of medieval Europe that led to a multiyear international collaboration. In 2016, I gave a talk at Durham University's Institute for Medieval and Early Modern Studies, where I fell into a fruitful conversation with the historian of medieval Europe David Rollason. Together we planned a series of panels and conferences to explore the comparative history of the palace city in Europe, the Middle East, and East Asia. We held multiple sessions at the 2017 International Medieval Conference at the University of Leeds, which served as a wonderful launch for the project. This was followed in 2019 by an international conference cohosted by the Japan Foundation Budapest and the Sainsbury Institute for Japanese Arts and Cultures, with funding from the Toshiba International Foundation, held at multiple medieval sites in Hungary including Budapest Castle, the Royal Palace at Visegrád, and the HNM Castle Museum in Esztergom. Traveling, presenting, and learning with the assembled scholars from all over the world was a remarkable experience. I offer my gratitude to Simon Kaner, Tada Sanae, Charlotte Horlyck, Beatrix Mecsi, Zsolt Vágner, Orsolya Mészáros, Károly Magyar, Katalin Szende, Meredith Cohen, Oka Yōichirō, Brian Ayers, Alastair Northedge, Lina Ktheifan, Maria Cristina Carile, Adrienn Papp, Philip Garrett, and Senda Yoshihiro.

At UNC-Chapel Hill, I offer my thanks and appreciation to all of my colleagues in the departments of History and Asian Studies, at the

Carolina Asia Center, and in various units throughout the college. Thanks also to colleagues at Duke University and at North Carolina State University who make the Triangle such a vibrant area for scholarship on Japan. Thank you also to the various graduate students who taught me so much during the years when I worked on this book, including Zach Smith, Laurel Foote-Hudson, Magdalena Kolodziej, Daniele Lauro, Drisana Misra, Dalvin Tsay, and Megan McClory.

At the very end of the process, this manuscript benefited enormously from careful reads and countless constructive comments by David Spafford, James Dobbins, Suzanne Gay, Halle O'Neal, and Brian Ayers, as well as two erudite and anonymous reviewers through Cambridge University Press. I cannot thank them enough, although I have undoubtedly failed to successfully integrate all of their suggestions.

I offer my sincere thanks to my editors at Cambridge University Press, Lucy Rhymer and Rachael Blaifeder. Thanks also to Dr. Gabriel Moss, who produced all of the maps in this book, some based on data from the Ichijōdani Asakura Family History Museum.

Thank you always to Brenda, Ravi, Luca, Vince, and Linda.

Note on the Text

Terminology: Like most Japanese history books published in English, this volume records Japanese names in the East Asian order, with the surname first and the given name last. In a slight departure, however, this book avoids most Japanese terms, apart from a few globalized words such as "samurai" and "shogun." Readers, particularly students, are frequently bewildered by the plethora of specialized Japanese terms that appear on the pages of English-language books. Even words such as *bakufu* (military government), *daimyō* (warlord), and *hatamoto* (direct retainers or bannermen), which historians often assume are widely understood in English, can sow confusion. This book therefore attempts to use English translations of almost all specialized Japanese terms, with the Japanese provided in italics, and to translate the titles of Japanese books and documents when mentioned in the main text.

Calendars and dates: On January 1, 1873, Japan began using the Gregorian calendar, but prior to that time, the official Japanese calendar was lunar. To make the lunar calendar correspond with the length of the year (in other words, with the solar calendar), premodern Japanese officials added a thirteenth month (known as an intercalary month) during some years, which could appear at any point during the year. Months were numbered rather than named, so it was not uncommon for a fourth month to be followed by a fourth intercalary month, or a tenth month to be followed by a tenth intercalary month.

Dates in premodern Japan are named by year, month, and day of the month. Years were usually numbered according to an era (*nengo*). So, for example, Asakura Yoshikage, one of the main characters in the sixth chapter of this book, was born in the second year of the Tenbun era in the ninth month on the twenty-fourth day: or Tenbun 2/9/24. Most of the second year of Tenbun corresponds to the Gregorian calendar's year 1533, so it is also common for historians of Japan who are writing in

English to record this date as 1533/9/24, and I follow that practice in this book. (A complete translation to the Gregorian calendar would yield the date October 12, 1533, but I avoid such conversions to make it easier for my colleagues in Japanese studies to find entries in diaries and other documents that I am referencing.)

Prologue

Yo no naka wa
Ashiki yamaji ni
Noru koma no
Fumi mo sadamenu
Mi ni koso arikere.

Our lot in life is
Like that of the horse that climbs
Rough mountain pathways,
Where it finds no sure footing,
Only peril at each step.

—Sōgi, *Record of the Road to Tsukushi* (1480)[1]

It is midday in the medieval city of Ichijōdani, a community of roughly 10,000 people nestled in a valley in the northern region of Echizen Province, Japan. A doctor welcomes a patient into his large residential and clinical complex situated among temples and capacious warrior homes. The patient, who walked hours from her village south of the city, looks around with wide eyes at the large gate, the grand buildings, and the impressive decorated interior. The structures are larger even than the homes of the wealthiest village elders in her community. Then again, she is in the capital city, home to the lord of the province. She describes her symptoms to the doctor, who listens carefully and makes notes: pain and vomiting in the morning, bad enough that she has found it difficult to work. She is worried that she may be dying, and other than her husband, she has no one in her village to turn to, as she was raised in a different region. The doctor reassures her that her symptoms are consistent with morning sickness. It seems she is pregnant; she expresses relief.[2] His assistant serves the patient tea while the doctor consults his most prized possession: an imported Chinese *materia medica* with encyclopedic explanations of ingredients and their effects. While perusing the text,

---

[1] Eileen Katō, "Pilgrimage to Dazaifu: Sōgi's *Tsukushi no michi no ki*," *Monumenta Nipponica* 34.3 (Autumn, 1979): 351.

[2] See Anne Walthall, "The Life Cycle of Farm Women in Tokugawa Japan," in *Recreating Japanese Women 1600–1945*, ed. Gail Lee Bernstein (University of California Press, 1991), 45–46. On East Asian doctors' treatment of morning sickness, see Andrew Edmund Goble, *Confluences of Medicine in Medieval Japan: Buddhist Healing, Chinese Knowledge, Islamic Formulas, and Wounds of War* (University of Hawai'i Press, 2011), 42–43.

1

he thinks of his large store of medical materials. Is it licorice (*ganzō*) that he needs in this case? No. Perhaps rhubarb root (*daiō*)? No, not that. Then he finds it: pinellia rhizome (*hange*), the tuber of the plant *Pinellia ternata*, good for the suppression of nausea. He retrieves the dried ingredient from another imported Chinese treasure, a lidded porcelain bowl, places it in his druggist's mortar (*yagen*), and asks his assistant to grind it into a powder. He then uses a copper spoon to mix the ingredient and administer it to the patient, and also gives her a small packet of additional medicine to use until the morning sickness passes. She drinks the concoction, thanks him profusely, pays him a small fee (taken from her own modest dowry), and departs. He discusses the case with his assistant while drinking a bowl of tea, waiting for his next patient.

The above scenario is speculative, as the city of Ichijōdani was almost entirely destroyed by the armies of the warlord Oda Nobunaga in 1573. The people who lived in this thriving urban center fled or were ruthlessly killed, washing the streets of the provincial capital in blood. Written records of the lives of the residents were completely lost, with the exception, of course, of documents about Ichijōdani held in other locations, which are few. The elimination of Ichijōdani and its residents was so thorough, in fact, that it was never resettled as an urban hub, but returned to a kind of originary state as an isolated and pastoral valley, dotted here and there by material remains of the agglomeration that had once made it the most important city in the province. These ruins stood largely untouched, until modern archaeologists became interested in the site as a potential source of information about medieval Japan. Preliminary digging occurred in the early twentieth century, and thorough, scientific excavations began in the 1960s and continue at the time of the publication of this book. As a result, although the passage above is in one sense notional, in another it is based on tangible, material evidence. Archaeologists carefully unearthed the doctor's residential and clinical complex with a remarkable degree of granularity, and the tools of his trade as I describe them are based on real excavated objects that the doctor used in the pursuit of his profession. Even the description of the Chinese medical text is based on the rare find of fragments of a book that scholars were able to analyze and identify.

The range of surviving material evidence in Ichijōdani is startling: from domestically produced and imported ceramics to stone religious sculptures; from wood and metal tools to the remains of vegetable, marine, and animal foodstuffs. More than fifty years of excavations have revealed Ichijōdani's stone foundations, roads and bridges, city gates, palace walls, cemeteries, tea houses, gardens, wells, and toilets. This panoply of material remains, which archaeologists have assiduously mapped and reconstructed, endures as a conspicuous archive of a historical community that is now lost. Many aspects of life in Ichijōdani are legible in these excavated edifices. Seemingly inconsequential objects such as broken earthenware dishes reveal patterns of ritual behavior. Widely dispersed stone Buddha statues suggest the scope and depth of religious practices. Excavated Chinese and Korean ceramics point to patterns of trade and elite consumption of goods. The unearthed materials from Ichijōdani, particularly as interpreted by archaeologists and then situated against a range of documentary and visual evidence, transcend their seemingly static and passive state as artifacts. Instead, we can read them as constituent elements of the city of Ichijōdani, agents in the production of a space and a community that prospered for a century.

The thriving city of Ichijōdani is the subject of this book, which considers daily life in this provincial urban center in a period usually associated only with political incohesion and endemic warfare. The chapters that follow examine the archaeological evidence from Ichijōdani, often in conversation with excavated materials from other urban sites in Japan, in order to illuminate the rhythms and logic of life and death for the many medieval Japanese who lived in urban agglomerates other than the capital city of Kyoto. The book is also concerned with the destruction of this provincial city and the meaning of that erasure for our understanding of both the period in which it took place and the larger flow of Japanese history. According to standard treatments of premodern Japanese history, this chaotic and violent period of provincial wars known as Sengoku (literally, "warring states" after the earlier Chinese era) was brought to an end only by the actions of three warlords, sometimes known as the Three Heroes of the Age of Unification: Oda Nobunaga (1534–1582), Toyotomi Hideyoshi (1536–1598), and Tokugawa Ieyasu (1543–1616). In an incremental process of war, alliance building, and cultural patronage, these men unified the nation and set the platform for the unfolding of the early modern age, which in turn prepared Japan – as much in the failures of supposed isolationism as in the success of national networks of travel, communication, and trade – for its entry into the modern world in the second half of the nineteenth century.

I have argued elsewhere that the "three heroes" historiography is overly teleological, too focused on the actions of a few individuals, and insufficiently attentive to the role of early modern hagiography and historical reinvention in producing the history of the Age of Unification in a dramatic and highly mythologized fashion.[3] In the present volume

[3] See Morgan Pitelka, *Handmade Culture: Raku Potters, Patrons, and Tea Practitioners in Japan* (University of Hawai'i Press, 2005), particularly 14–17, and *Spectacular*

I seek to consider the Age of Unification from a different vantage point, of those who were lost in the wars of the late sixteenth century and have been left out of the story of the progress of the nation. Although the canonical narrative of Japanese history is populated by a lively cast of celebrated losers, ranging from the Taira in the twelfth century to the forty-seven rōnin in the eighteenth century,[4] the massive destruction and loss of life of the second half of the sixteenth century has usually been elided in English writings to make way for rather triumphalist accounts of unification.

Focusing on provincial communities like Ichijōdani affords a profoundly different view of the final century of the medieval period. The Ōnin War of 1467–1477, a violent conflict over succession disputes that spilled destructively into the provinces, is usually identified as the beginning of a tragic period of political instability in the history of Japan, the Sengoku, or "Age of Warring States." Yet for many it was a moment of rebirth, an opportunity to build new settlements and form new alliances. International trade increased in the late fifteenth and early sixteenth centuries, bringing, for example, more Chinese ceramics into provincial centers than ever before. The relative political volatility of Kyoto was a boon of sorts for regional communities, as performing arts troops, artists, and poets traveled across Japan, stimulating cultural production in provincial cities and leading to a more balanced relationship between Japan's center and its peripheries. Many of these regional hegemons actively resisted the unification efforts of Nobunaga and Hideyoshi.

This book uses one of the most significant examples, the Asakura house of warlords, to zoom in on the city that functioned as their headquarters, Ichijōdani.[5] The Asakura served the Shiba, governors of

---

Accumulation: Material Culture, Tokugawa Ieyasu, and Samurai Sociability (University of Hawaiʻi Press, 2016).

[4] See Michael Wert, *Meiji Restoration Losers: Memory and Tokugawa Supporters in Modern Japan* (Harvard University Asia Center, 2013), and Mikael S. Adolphson and Anne Commons, eds., *Lovable Losers: The Heike in Action and Memory* (University of Hawaiʻi Press, 2015), for two recent examples.

[5] The Asakura were a multigenerational house (*ie*) of samurai warriors; they controlled a large samurai organization, or what many authors would refer to in English as a "war band." This organization included the main Asakura line, led by a chieftain who for the main period of this book was a *daimyō* or warlord; collateral lines located outside the capital city, placed strategically throughout the province of Echizen; and a range of allies and vassals inside and outside Ichijōdani who reported to the main line. For more detail on the naming conventions and organization of warrior families in the late medieval period, see John Whitney Hall's formative essay "Foundations of the Modern Japanese Daimyo," *The Journal of Asian Studies* 20.3 (May 1961): 317–329. More recently, David Spafford examines these issues in "The Language and Contours of Familial Obligation in Fifteenth- and Sixteenth-Century Japan," in *What Is a Family? Answers from Early Modern*

a large territory including Echizen Province, from at least the early fourteenth century. During the Ōnin War, which hinged in part on a conflict over the succession of the headship of the Shiba house, the Asakura switched sides and effectively displaced their masters as rulers of Echizen. For five generations the Asakura governed the province from the provincial city of Ichijōdani, safely nestled in a valley about 20 miles inland, while also maintaining regular contact with cultural and political institutions in Kyoto about 100 miles to the south. The Sengoku period, it turns out, was for the Asakura and their subjects an age defined less by war and destruction than by stability and prosperity. It was instead the rise of Nobunaga and his grandiose attempts to pacify the realm, which involved breaking up alliances as often as forming them, that led to the destruction of Ichijōdani. The Asakura were killed, the city itself was destroyed, and the valley of Ichijōdani became a deserted site. Unfortunately, the focus of historians here has almost universally pivoted quickly from the moment of destruction to the ostensible world-building of Nobunaga and his peers as a kind of historical inevitability. The meaningful lives and sudden deaths of tens of thousands of urban inhabitants over multiple generations are subsumed into the larger narrative of progress toward the modern as "unification" – a seemingly necessary precondition for early modernity and thereafter the creation of imperial Japan – unfolds.

Thinking about the flow of Japanese history, it is hard to resist the urge to leap forward from the destruction of the Asakura in 1573 to Nobunaga's subsequent string of victories such as his defeat of the Takeda in 1582, the rise of Hideyoshi and his inexorable pacification of the entire archipelago, the Japanese assault on Korea in 1592, the victory of Tokugawa Ieyasu at Sekighara in 1600, and so on. Few periods contain more drama on an epic scale than the sixteenth century. Yet what if we counter the teleological pressure to rush forward through this story of "unification" and instead allow our thoughts to linger on the rhythms of daily life in Ichijōdani before its destruction? What would result from careful consideration of the archaeological evidence to investigate the landscape of the city, the relations among its residents, the deployment of power over the agglomeration by the Asakura, the city's religious and cultural practices, and ultimately the untimely end of the community? It is not, of course, an empty gesture to scrutinize a community that is now gone; quite the opposite, it is the very purpose of the

Japan, ed. Mary Elizabeth Berry and Marcia Yonemoto (University of California Press, 2019), 23–46.

discipline of history to recover lost subjects, to read the experiences of people who lived before us from the ruins they left behind. This book pursues this purpose by proposing first that the material remains in Ichijōdani contain a deep and profound message regarding life in late medieval Japan, which I read and interpret in stages over the course of each chapter. Second, this book argues that mainstream historical narratives of premodern Japan are compromised by their failure to take seriously the diversity of experiences in provincial cities. Rehabilitating the worldview of the residents of Ichijōdani and incorporating it into our understanding of the Japanese medieval is a vital step in resisting the normalization of an anachronistic and monolithic vision of Japanese national identity. The unification of Japan in the late sixteenth century was not preordained, but both contingent and contested.

Urban Life

The mention of urban life in medieval Japan immediately evokes images of Kamakura, the headquarters of the first warrior government from 1192 to 1333, and of course Kyoto, the imperial capital since 794 and the headquarters of the second warrior government after 1336. These were unquestionably the largest and the most significant cities in medieval Japan, yet their prominence has perhaps been exaggerated by the tendency even of contemporaneous writers to use them as signifiers of the larger polities they harbored. Medieval authors substituted place names for institutions, a habit that is revealing in terms of the power relations that inhere in linguistic practices but that produces a documentary record that overemphasizes these two cities. We tend to think of whole swaths of Japanese history in reductionist geographical terms, so that our imagination of the Heian period (794–1185) rarely strays beyond the boundaries of the city of Heian-kyō (Kyoto), and our perception of the diarchy of shared power between the imperial court and first warrior government during the Kamakura period concentrates on activities in the cities of Kyoto and Kamakura. I do not mean to suggest that we lack scholarship in English on parts of medieval Japan other than Kyoto and Kamakura. From John Whitney Hall's foundational work on Bizen Province to Peter Shapinsky's work on the sea lords of the Inland Sea to David Spafford's writing on the Kantō region, historians have been appropriately attentive to the interplay between capital and province, the fundamental reliance of urban elites on estates in the provinces and on religious institutions located outside urban centers, and the agency of nonstate actors from provincial regions. Rather, I want to suggest that in the English-language field of medieval *urban history*, our gaze has rarely wandered far from Kyoto and Kamakura.[6]

The Japanese scholarship on medieval urban centers, by contrast, is extremely robust, and the development of the field is worth following in some detail. At the end of the nineteenth century, historians in Japan began to turn their attention to the impressive monolithic structures at the heart of cities across the archipelago, and the study of castles (*shiro*) – including medieval structures – emerged as a distinct scholarly field.[7] As Japan pursued its aggressive course of growing its national wealth and strengthening its military (*fukoku kyōhei*), highlighting the role of these military fortresses in early modern urbanization was a natural trend. After the war, by contrast, historians shifted their attention to the urban settlements that developed around castles and particularly to the complex social and economic relationship between urbanization and warrior rule. The historian Toyoda Takeshi foregrounded the emergence of professional groups (*za*) in medieval villages and urban centers,[8] ultimately offering the Marxist analysis that Japan's urban growth had been dependent on the exploitative power of feudal proprietors.[9] Toyoda also articulated the typology of urban centers that had become widely accepted by the 1950s: historical capitals, temple towns, post-station towns, port towns, and castle towns (including centers like Ichijōdani, though I have chosen to label this a provincial palace city rather than a castle town, for reasons explained below).[10] Of most interest to Toyoda and many of his peers was the tension between the emerging activities of workers and merchants, who displayed flashes of collectivism, the increasing stratification of urban elites into distinct classes, and the ongoing dominance of military leaders over other social groups. The emergence of "free cities" such as Sakai, which allowed comparison with

---

[6] I know of two exceptions. First, Mimi Hall Yiengpruksawan's *Hiraizumi: Buddhist Art and Regional Politics in Twelfth-Century Japan* (Harvard University Asia Center, 1998) is a marvelous study of a northern city and its art and architecture. The book focuses on an aristocratic family (the Northern Fujiwara) at the height of their pomp and power at the tail end of the Heian Period and doesn't engage with the Japanese literature on medieval cities. Second is Bruce Batten's *Gateway to Japan: Hakata in War and Peace, 500–1300* (University of Hawai'i Press, 2006), which is overwhelmingly focused on the history of the port city of Hakata before the medieval period. Its concluding chapter does introduce archaeological evidence from the medieval period, and was extremely useful as I prepared my own study of Ichijōdani.

[7] Two of the earliest publications were *Nihon jōkaku shi* in 1899, followed by *Jōkaku no kenkyū* in 1915, and the survey of early archaeological work on castles, *Buke jidai no jōkaku to shiro ato* in 1930.

[8] Toyoda Takeshi, *Toshi oyobi za no hattatsu* (Chūō Kōronsha, 1948).

[9] Toyoda Takeshi, *Nihon no hōken toshi* (Iwanami Shoten, 1952).

[10] Toyoda, *Nihon no hōken toshi*, 17–36.

Weberian notions of urbanization from European history, was also a topic of significant debate, though Toyoda and his contemporary Harada Tomohiko seem to agree that this ostensible freedom was in fact quite constrained by a weak economic system and the power of samurai landholders.[11] John Whitney Hall summarizes these debates well in an early article, writing, "In Japan of the sixteenth century the truly significant institutional development was not the free city nor the rising merchant community, but rather the maturation of a new type of feudal ruler, the daimyo."[12] Most of these studies of medieval urbanization were primarily interested in the early modern urban landscape, and thus read the medieval period with a teleological urgency that had as its objective the explanation of the large cities and vibrant urban marketplaces of the Tokugawa period.

In the 1960s, the sociologist Takeo Yazaki provided a sweeping study of Japanese urbanization that appeared in two English translations: an abbreviated summary, in 1964, and a full translation of the 487-page monograph in 1968. In the chapters that consider pre-Tokugawa urbanization, the author examines organizational structures of villages and towns, the rise of new political structures in the medieval period that led to increased urbanization, and the aforementioned tension between urban autonomy and the increasing concentration of power in the hands of warlords. On the rise of castle towns after the Ōnin War of 1467–1477, he writes that "to facilitate the integrative functions of the castle in controlling political, economic, and social life throughout each domain, the castles were sometimes located at already established towns such as temple towns, highway stations, port and market towns."[13] Yazaki also notes that

castle and town were not fully united in the Middle Ages and, when wars broke out, the town's houses were often burned to the ground to obstruct the enemy's advance or cut off his supply routes. The sacrificed towns were rebuilt only when the integrative functions of economy and transportation were resumed. Castle towns built solely for political aims tended, if destroyed, not to be restored, having had only an unstable basis to begin with.[14]

---

[11] Harada Tomohiko, *Nihon hōken toshi kenkyū* (Tokyo Daigaku Shuppankai, 1957), 27–51.

[12] John Whitney Hall, "The Castle Town and Japan's Modern Urbanization," in *Studies in the Institutional History of Early Modern Japan*, ed. John Whitney Hall and Marius B. Jansen (Princeton University Press, 1968), 173, originally published in *Far Eastern Quarterly* 15.1 (November 1955).

[13] Takeo Yazaki, *Social Change and the City in Japan: From Earliest Times through the Industrial Revolution*, trans. David Swain (Japan Publications, 1968), 105.

[14] Yazaki, *Social Change*, 106.

The author details the forms of stratification that occurred in castle towns, the rise of markets and regional trade centered on these towns, and the increasing integration between market activities and the power of the warlord; it is worth noting, for the purposes of this study of Ichijōdani, that Yazaki sees 1572 as the key moment in the development of the early modern urban form.

Some historians in the 1970s began to focus on *provincial cities* as sites of significant political consolidation. Matsuyama Hiroshi employed historical documents to look at the activities of the medieval warrior leaders known as governors (*shugo*) who often established early urban centers referred to in the Japanese literature as "governors' residences" (*shugosho*), an appellation for the fortress, palace, or early castle of the ruler of a province.[15] Likewise, the historian Ishii Susumu – who would become one of the most influential scholars of medieval cities, as we shall see below – began to consider urban locations as sites of significant political activity, examining the ways in which medieval warrior authority and organization were rooted in residency in a particular place, bringing a kind of geographic, spatial dimension to the analysis of the intersection of warrior history and politics.[16] The governors were ostensibly empowered by their assignment to a bureaucratically determined parcel of territory, but over time this responsibility was trumped by the need to have direct control over vassals and their parcels of land, which led to the emergence of the warlords of the Sengoku period. Only with reunification and the establishment of the Tokugawa shogunate did this political geography change, in a shift that we might identify as part of the movement from medieval to early modern, and in the return to a top-down system of state-sanctioned control. In the same period, John Whitney Hall commented in his seminal study of Bizen Province on the particular situation of the Sengoku rulers like the Asakura: "In actual practice, therefore, the domains of the Sengoku lords formed from the inside out, not as administratively defined subdivisions of the state. Their shape conformed, in other words, to the territorial limits of the combined holdings of the vassals over which they exercised control, not to the abstract boundaries of provinces or districts."[17]

The historian Amino Yoshihiko, one of the most original voices in the study of premodern Japanese social history in the postwar era, turned his

---

[15] Matsuyama's 1973 book *Nihon chūsei toshi no kenkyū* and his 1982 book *Shugo jōkamachi no kenkyū* are prominent examples.

[16] Ishii Susumu, *Chūsei bushi dan* (Shōgakkan, 1974).

[17] John Whitney Hall, *Government and Local Power in Japan, 500 to 1700: A Study Based on Bizen Province* (Princeton University Press, 1966), 247.

attention to cities with increasing frequency beginning in the late 1970s, making the first attempt to provide an overview of the trends in the field of Japanese medieval urban studies.[18] He noted that two main scholarly schools have been prominent: Marxist approaches, which focused on theories regarding the authority of feudal lords and their relationship to the land that they occupied; and the *kenmon taisei* approach, which looked at three power blocks in medieval Japanese society: temples, the court, and the warrior class.[19] He began to articulate a new theory of urban space in medieval Japan, one that was dependent not on warrior authority but on integrated networks of trade. Amino's method was characteristically innovative; he cautioned against looking only for the usual markers of a "city" such as the concentration of political power in a single site or the density of the population. Instead, he advocated scouring available sources for evidence of horizontal trading activities and associations, not only in large communities but even in rural sites that would usually be considered towns or villages, to reveal the diverse forms of urban space that were produced by medieval itinerants, agriculturalists, artisans, and workers.

The field of medieval urban studies in Japan underwent a transformative *material turn* in the 1980s, when a wave of new archaeological research (initiated in the 1960s and 1970s) washed across Japan, and excavations of medieval urban sites increased dramatically.[20] Initially, the two most important sites were Kusado Sengen, a commercial town located near the Ashida River in Fukuyama, Hiroshima Prefecture; and Ichijōdani, the subject of this book. Excavations of many other sites soon followed, allowing research that integrated archaeological materials with documentary study to advance. Port towns such as Hakata in Kyushu, Sakai near present-day Osaka, and Tosa Minato at the northern tip of

---

[18] Amino Yoshihiko, *Chūsei toshi ron* (1976; reprint, Iwanami Shoten, 2007).

[19] Amino reiterates this point in various state of the field essays he has published over the years. See, for example, *Amino Yoshihiko chōsakushū, vol. 13: Chūsei toshi ron* (Iwanami Shoten, 2007), 3–5. On the *kenmon taisei* in English, see Suzanne Gay, "Muromachi Bakufu Rule in Kyoto: Administrative and Judicial Aspects," in *The Bakufu in Japanese History*, ed. Jeffrey P. Mass and William P. Hauser (Stanford University Press, 1985), 49–65; Hitomi Tonomura, *Community and Commerce in Late Medieval Japan: Corporate Villages of Tokuchin-ho* (Stanford University Press, 1986), 251; and James C. Dobbins, "Editor's Introduction: Kuroda Toshio and His Scholarship," *Japanese Journal of Religious Studies* 23.3–4 (1996): 217–232, as well as the other articles in that special issue.

[20] An early commentary on this shift that clearly expresses the excitement and enthusiasm of researchers is Murata Shūzō's article from 1980, "Jō ato chōsa to Sengoku shi kenkyū," originally published in *Nihonshi kenkyū* 211 (3/1980) but also available as a chapter *Tenbō Nihon rekishi, vol. 12: Sengoku shakai*, ed. Ikegami Hiroko and Inaba Tsuguharu (Tōkyōdō Shuppan, 2010), 246–266.

Honshu, near Aomori, were thoroughly researched, revealing extensive trade networks across medieval Japan and the circulation of large quantities of imported goods. Even the big cities like Kamakura, Kyoto, and Nara – all well understood because of documentary research – were now reexamined with the aid of archaeological evidence.[21]

In 1984, Komazawa University hosted an event related to urban history titled the "National Castle Research Seminar," which became an annual conference that additionally published proceedings in an influential journal.[22] Themes ranged widely from methodology to the depiction of castles in medieval paintings, with a fundamentally multidisciplinary approach and openness to a variety of methods. More broadly, this established a framework for researchers from different parts of Japan – historians, archaeologists, folklorists, and others – to come together to engage in comparative analysis of the castle as a national phenomenon. This trend continued in 1993 when the Japanese Archaeology Association held a symposium on national excavation results.[23] By contrast, in 1988, a landmark symposium was held in Nagoya on the results of the excavation of Kiyosu castle, which started the trend of holding scholarly gatherings to focus on the archaeological research of a particular castle site or a specific region within Japan.[24] Important late medieval archaeological sites have held similar events since this symposium. In little more than a decade, therefore, two streams of scholarship on medieval urbanization emerged in Japan: broad, multidisciplinary, synthetic approaches that established the larger

---

[21] Of course, many scholars continued to examine Japan's urban history primarily using documentary sources, such as the pioneering historian Wakita Haruko. Wakita presented a more nuanced view of the types of urban communities found in medieval documents, dividing cities into metropolises such as Kyoto, port or entrepot cities such as Sakai and Hakata, country towns that grew out of village marketplaces such as Tondabayashi near present-day Osaka, and castle towns, which she argues often absorbed preexisting port or country towns. She focused on collectivism in medieval villages, towns, and cities: the emergence of guilds or professional associations (*za*), urban communal associations (*kyōdōtai*), ward and neighborhood administrations, and perhaps most significantly, the degree to which any of these organizations enabled self-governance. For a helpful English articulation of her work, see Wakita Haruko with Susan B. Hanley, "Dimensions of Development: Cities in Fifteenth- and Sixteenth-Century Japan," in *Japan before Tokugawa: Political Consolidation and Economic Growth, 1500–1650*, ed. S. Hall, Nagahara Keiji, and Kozo Yamamura (Princeton University Press, 1981), 325–326. In Japanese, see Wakita Haruko, *Nihon chūsei toshiron* (Tokyo Daigaku Shuppankai, 1981).
[22] "Chūsei jōkaku kenkyū," based at Komazawa University: www.komazawa-u.ac.jp/~kazov/chujoken/books/.
[23] The book that resulted is Nihon Kōkogaku Kyōkai, ed., *Shugosho kara Sengoku jōka e* (Meicho Shuppan, 1994).
[24] Tōkai Maizō Bunkazai Kenkyūkai, *Kiyosu: Shokuhōki no shiro to toshi* (Tōkai Maizō Bunkazai Kenkyūkai, 1988).

context, and deep explorations of specific sites that teased out the nuances of individual locations.

Between 1988 and 1994, Amino Yoshihiko, Ishii Susumu, and Fukuda Tomohiko organized a new series of multiauthored books that sought to explore and promote the emerging vision of medieval Japan informed by the plethora of new archaeological excavations. Written to appeal to a general audience, with generous pictures and maps, but including essays by some of the top scholars active in the field, *Restoring the Medieval* (*Yomigaeru chūsei*) helped elevate the status of medieval archaeology, a heretofore minor field compared with prehistoric and ancient archaeology. The preface notes that "medieval and early modern sites have been discovered and investigated across the country. And although this information will not become big news like the discovery of Kofun or ancient imperial sites, for modern people these sites are closer to us and can teach us matters of importance."[25] The organizers stressed the significance of the material culture recovered from excavated sites, arguing that what we might call "the affect of things" could potentially create powerful associations for modern viewers of archaeological evidence. Beginning in the first volume with the port city of Hakata and the notion that Japan was not an isolated archipelago but part of a vibrant, northeast Asian maritime community, the books successively used the regional archaeological evidence to challenge tropes about Japan as a monolithic, unified nation while still highlighting topics of great interest to general readers, such as the vibrancy of Kamakura as the first warriors' capital. Key sites from the 1970s to 1980s medieval excavation boom like Kusado Sengen and Ichijōdani received their own volumes, and have helped shape my thinking about this project.[26]

---

[25] Amino Yoshihiko, Ishii Susumu, and Fukuda Tomohiko, "Kankō ni atatte," in *Yomigaeru chūsei, vol. 1: Jitsuzō no Sengoku jōkamachi Echizen Ichijiodani*, ed. Ono Masatoshi and Suitō Makoto (Heibonsha, 1990), 1.

[26] The collaboration between Amino and Ishii led to a larger series of cooperative efforts that married the new archaeological evidence with the field of historical research on Japan's medieval period, with particular focus on urban sites. Ishii began organizing symposia at Teikyō University, which resulted in a series of multiauthor anthologies, including *Kōkogaku to chūseishi kenkyū* (1991) and *Chūsei toshi to shōnin shokunin* (1991). Amino and Ishii collaborated with the archaeologist Ōmiwa Tatsuhiko to found the *Chūsei Toshi Kenkyūkai* in 1993, which has held annual meetings and published rich proceedings every year up to the present day, focusing on themes such as "urban space," "cities and religion," and "methods in urban studies." The early volumes in particular explicitly attempted to constitute and shape a new, multidisciplinary field, asking what the goals and methods should be when studying medieval Japanese urban sites. www.hi .u-tokyo.ac.jp/personal/shinichi/toshiken-kiroku.htm.

Another influential publication was Amino's and Ishii's seven-volume series titled *Reading the Landscape of the Medieval* (*Chūsei no fūkei o yomu*), which inspired the title of this book. The goal of this series, which was less explicitly about the study of archaeological evidence but which still adopted a multidisciplinary approach, was to emphasize the rich diversity of medieval Japan and its relationship with the Asian continent, and to explicate five main themes overall: cities, villages, belief, trade, and artisans. Volumes such as *People Who Live in the Boundary and the Countryside* (*Kyōkai to hina ni ikiru hitobito*), *The Evolution of Japan Sea Exchange* (*Nihonkai kōtsū no tenkai*), and *Living with Belief and Freedom* (*Shinkō to jiyū ni ikiru*) were important in the researching and writing of this book.

By the 1990s, therefore, the field of medieval urban history was well established, and was built on the foundations of social history (à la Amino and Ishii) with its interest in diversity, regionalism, and regional context, and of archaeology, with its focus on site-specific research and the richness of material evidence. Even scholars of early modern and modern cities were increasingly paying attention to medieval urban studies, seen, for example, in the inclusion of a number of significant chapters on the medieval in the otherwise early modern and modern-focused series *Introduction to Japanese Cities* (*Nihon toshi nyūmon*, 1989–1990). Across Japan, archaeological research centers continued to produce high-quality excavation reports, collaborative symposium volumes, and large-scale data collections that allowed both local/regional research and comparative, national research to prosper.[27] Much of the resulting publications of the past two decades can be found in the citations in this book, and I will sometimes refer to the work of Ono Masatoshi, Kojima Michihiro, Fujiki Hisashi, Mizuno Kazuo, and Sukigara Toshio, among others, in the pages that follow.[28]

Ichijōdani as a Palace City Rather than a Castle Town

The material evidence from Ichijōdani provides a glimpse of the depth and complexity of Japan's medieval urbanism, but the available terminology to classify urban agglomerations in the Japanese context obscures

---

[27] Kokuritsu Rekishi Minzoku Hakubutsukan, *Nihon shutsudo no bōeki tōji*, 5 vols. (Kokuritsu Rekishi Minzoku Hakubutsukan, 1994)

[28] For a helpful summary of research on medieval towns in Japan, see Simon Kaner, Brian Ayers, Richard Pearson, and Oscar Wrenn, eds., *The Archaeology of Medieval Towns: Case Studies from Japan and Europe* (Archaeopress, 2020). This volume includes a translation by Richard Pearson of some of the older work of Ōno Masatoshi, under the title "Ichijōdani: the Archaeology of a Medieval Japanese Town," 27–41.

significant distinctions between sites. Ichijōdani has been held up not just as a good example of a castle town but as an ideal model, seen, for example, in the titles of two books by the archaeologist Ono Masatoshi: *Actual Conditions of a Sengoku Castle Town: Echizen Ichijōdani (Jitsuzō no Sengoku jōkamachi: Echizen Ichijōdani)* and *Warring States Castle Town Archaeology: Messages from Ichijōdani (Sengoku jōkamachi no kōkogaku: Ichijōdani kara no messe-ji)*. I would like to posit that we could more profitably analyze Ichijōdani by discarding the term "castle town," which is misleading and inadequate in this instance. Part of the problem emerges not from the secondary scholarship in Japanese but from the clumsiness of this English translation. The Japanese term *jōkamachi* 城下町 literally means "neighborhoods beneath the castle," but the usual English translation as "castle town" elides the spatial separation between these two entities. Furthermore, the actual character for castle in this phrase, 城 (*jō* or *shiro* in Japanese, *chéng* in Chinese), originally signified not a distinct fortress but rather a fortified (i.e., walled) urban agglomeration.[29] The phrase "castle town" in English is useful for the discussion of certain urban sites such as Oda Nobunaga's headquarters, Azuchi, or the domainal capitals of the early modern period, seen in James McClain's scholarship on Kanazawa,[30] but it fails to capture the nuances of sites like late medieval Ichijōdani. In the words of the archaeologist Matthew Johnson, we need to look *behind the castle gate* to the urban communities they protected.[31]

I argue in this study that the significance of Ichijōdani is found not in its relationship to the distant, mountaintop castle but rather in the dynamic and diverse lives of its residents.[32] Indeed, the hub of the town by any measure is the central residence of the Asakura, which is often mistakenly described as a castle but which is clearly in fact a palace, making Ichijōdani a good example of a completely different kind of urban

---

[29] See the entry for *chéng* in Morohashi, *Daikanwa jiten* (Taishukan Shoten, 1955) vol. 3, 2455 (no. 5120).

[30] James L. McClain, "Castle Towns and Daimyo Authority: Kanazawa in the Years 1583–1630," *The Journal of Japanese Studies* 6.2 (Summer, 1980): 267–299, and James L. McClain, *Kanazawa: A Seventeenth-Century Japanese Castle Town* (Yale University Press, 1982).

[31] Matthew Johnson, *Behind the Castle Gate: From Medieval to Renaissance* (Routledge, 2002).

[32] See Spafford's explorations of warrior headquarters, cities, and castles in *A Sense of Place*. See also two recent English-language studies of castles in Japanese history that significantly expand our understanding of these vital structures: Mark Karl Erdmann, "Azuchi Castle: Architectural Innovation and Political Legitimation in Sixteenth-Century Japan" (PhD dissertation, Harvard University, 2016), and Oleg Benesch and Ran Zwigenberg, *Japan's Castles: Citadels of Modernity in War and Peace* (Cambridge University Press, 2019).

agglomeration, found in various other locales throughout the medieval world: a palace city.[33] The social and cultural life of the palace shaped the city in complex ways, and defies the notion that what matters about Ichijōdani was its semi-fortified nature or its putative dependence on warrior authority. In fact, the dialectical relationship between elite warrior consumption and ritual activity, on the one hand, and urban commoner production and trade, on the other, is messy and layered but also well captured in the archaeological evidence, allowing a reading of the material culture that helps us to see beyond the constraining tropes of samurai power in the Age of Warring States.[34] The focus of this volume is therefore on the rhythms and material textures of *urban life* in a provincial palace city in the late medieval period.[35]

Material History

The study of medieval urban life in Japan is largely reliant on analysis of objects and their material contexts in collaboration with careful reading of the sparse available documentary evidence. And the study of things as a form of historical evidence has its own tangled history that informs this project. Some of the earliest work on material culture that influenced my approach is found in American folklore studies, wherein scholars such as Henry Glassie beginning in the 1960s and Bernard "Bernie" Herman beginning in the 1980s investigated the vernacular architecture, quilting politics, music and food cultures, and other distinctive products and practices of specific North American peoples and locales, associated

---

[33] The literature on the phenomenon of the "palace city" is wide and varied, though much attention has focused on the Islamic palace city, particularly the two examples of the Alhambra and Madina al-Zahra in Spain, though the term is also used for sites in Europe, Asia, and the Middle East. See George Michell, Richard Eaton, and Richard Maxwell Eaton, *Firuzabad: Palace City of the Deccan* (Oxford University Press, 1991), and Glaire Anderson, *The Islamic Villa in Early Medieval Iberia: Architecture and Court Culture in Umayyad Córdoba* (Ashgate, 2013). April L. Najjaj defines the palace city in her dissertation, "The Alhambra in Comparative Perspective: Towards a Definition of Palace-Cities" (Boston University, 2005), as follows (p. iv): "multiple residences, gardens, baths, religious spaces, market, and bureaucratic offices, all enclosed by walls that limits [*sic*] access to the site while affording the residents access to an adjacent urban area beyond its walls." This applies well to the case of Ichijōdani, as we shall see.

[34] Niki Hiroshi's work on similar topics has informed my research. See his *Mura to machi no katachi* (Yamakawa Shuppansha, 2004) and *Kyōto no toshi kyōdōtai to kenryoku* (Shibunkaku Shuppan, 2010).

[35] For an English-language summary of the state of the field, see Suzanne Gay, "Commerce and Towns in Medieval Japan," in *Routledge Handbook of Premodern Japanese History*, ed. Karl Friday (Routledge, 2017), 390–401.

sometimes with historical preservation movements.[36] Herman is a particularly eloquent advocate for the linked study of materiality and particular places:

Events take place. Place matters. The substance of experience matters. The story of urban houses begins in the spaces between buildings and how people designed, occupied, and viewed their houses and those of others. That space, however, is not simply the material reflection of everyday life – it is also where the commonplace achieves the currency of symbolic language .... The connotative quality of objects, their semiotic ambiguity, is what makes their ability to convey sense and significance at once situational, provisional, and performative.[37]

Concurrently, American historians such as Thomas Schlereth came to the study of things through their determination to apprehend the material culture of American homes and more broadly the changing consumption habits of diverse US populations, part of the emergence of American studies as a multidisciplinary field in the postwar era.[38] Some American art historians, too, added to the growing scholarship on material culture through their analysis of the social history of the decorative arts, such as Barbara Carson's study of the decorative program of the Virginia governor's palatial residence.[39] A distinct stream of material culture studies emerged in the United Kingdom in anthropology and archaeology, best represented by the work of the anthropologist Daniel Miller on the relationship between material culture and consumption and the archaeologist Christopher Tilley on phenomenology and subjectivity in the study of sites and things; both were trained at the University of Cambridge and taught for decades at University College London, which became a center for British scholarship on things.[40] Material culture studies thus is startlingly diverse, with a transdisciplinary assortment of

---

[36] See, for example, Henry Glassie, *Pattern in the Material Folk Culture of the Eastern United States* (University of Pennsylvania Press, 1969) and *Folk Housing in Middle Virginia: Structural Analysis of Historic Artifacts* (University of Tennessee Press, 1975), and Bernard L. Herman, *Architecture and Rural Life in Central Delaware, 1700–1900* (University of Tennessee Press, 1987).

[37] Bernard L. Herman, *Town House: Architecture and Material Life in the Early American City, 1780–1830* (University of North Carolina Press, 2005), 262.

[38] See, for example, Thomas J. Schlereth, *Artifacts and the American Past* (American Association for State and Local History, 1980) and *Material Culture: A Research Guide* (University Press of Kansas, 1985).

[39] Barbara Carson, *The Governor's Palace: The Williamsburg Residence of Virginia's Royal Governor* (Colonial Williamsburg Foundation, 1987).

[40] Voluminous studies of material culture have been published by scholars associated with UCL, including a dozen books authored or edited by Miller, culminating perhaps in his 2007 book *Stuff* (Polity Press, 2009); *The Journal of Material Culture*, established in 1996; and the volume *Thinking through Things: Theorising Artefacts Ethnographically*, ed. Amiria Henare, Martin Holbraad, and Sari Wastell (Routledge, 2007).

methods and objectives. Yet several themes overlap in these variegated investigations: seemingly banal things are both symbolically informative and historically significant; the relationship between functional and decorative elements is powerful and often political; and the exuberant specificity of places is legible in the materiality of their buildings, the details of their things, and the analysis of their human relations.

Influenced by this first wave of scholarship on material culture, research on things has proliferated and permutated in every field of the humanities and qualitative social sciences.[41] Perhaps most influential in terms of the writing of this book is the work of scholars taking part in the early twenty-first-century ontological turn in anthropology and the environmental historical turn in my own field of history. We might think of these related scholarly divergences as shifting from a focus exclusively on epistemology, or systems of knowing the world, to ontology, or systems of being in the world; a more reductive phrasing is to say that these recent approaches are more interested in reality than in representation. My schematic reading of this complex literature is that it makes clear that framing the study of a given historical moment or society in terms of its material and environmental conditions and constraints is a productive approach.[42] Likewise, the practices and performances of the members of a society, bounded by their material and environmental context, express an understanding of reality that is logical and legible. Focusing on materiality reveals what historian of science and technology studies Andrew Pickering calls "the dance of agency," which refers to the political formations that emerge from the interactions between people, architecture, things, animals, and the environment.[43] The dance of agency is

[41] This includes, at long last, Japanese studies, where volumes such as Pamela D. Winfield and Steven Heine, ed., *Zen and Material Culture* (Oxford University Press, 2017), and Karen M. Gerhart, ed., *Women, Rites, and Ritual Objects in Premodern Japan* (Brill, 2018), have demonstrated the insights that material culture approaches bring to the study of Japanese history and culture. Also significant are two volumes associated with the acquisition and exhibition of a historically significant ceramic tea jar by the Smithsonian Institution: Louise Allison Cort and Andrew M. Watsky, eds., *Chigusa and the Art of Tea* (Smithsonian Institution, 2014), and Dora C. Y. Ching, Louise Allison Cort, and Andrew M. Watsky, eds., *Around Chigusa: Tea and the Arts of Sixteenth-Century Japan* (Princeton University Press, 2017).
[42] See, for example, Arturo Escobar, "Postconstructivist Political Ecologies," in *The International Handbook of Environmental Sociology*, 2nd ed., ed. Michael Redclift and Graham Woodgate (Edward Elgar Publishing, 2010), 91–105, and Bruno Latour, *Reassembling the Social* (Oxford: Oxford University Press, 2007);
[43] Andrew Pickering, "Material Culture and the Dance of Agency," in *The Oxford Handbook of Material Culture Studies*, ed. Dan Hicks and Mary C. Beaudry (Oxford University Press, 2010), 191–208.

particularly vibrant in the densely social and material context of a provincial palace city like Ichijōdani.

One of the goals of this study of the dance of agency in Ichijōdani is to demonstrate the unique encounters, moments, and events that unfolded in this particular provincial palace city in the particular period of the sixteenth century. Anthropologist Miho Ishii provides some useful analytical tools in her study of the "contingent coactions of persons and things."[44] She proposes that it is the process of acting *through* things that results in the creation of unique and meaningful experiences. When a person uses a tool or produces a product for the community or market, a process of both self-making and expansion of the social network occurs that is mediated by things. Furthermore, Ishii argues that in some moments of instability and contingency, encounters between people and things can result in the co-creation of what she calls "divine worlds." Her examples include idol creation and spirit possession, but her insights are applicable to a range of ritual practices in Ichijōdani, including cultural rituals that use objects to mediate the social encounter as well as communal funding and installation of religious icons.[45] The notion that people and things collaboratively create "divine worlds" in moments of crisis is useful for thinking through the response of the Ichijōdani community to war and its aftereffects, particularly the irruption of death in daily life, as I will explore in Chapters 4 and 6.

One relevant example of localized practices in which Ichijōdani residents coacted with objects and the environment is the practice of flower viewing, particularly organized outings to enjoy the blossoming of cherry trees in the spring, which today is intrinsically associated with Japanese culture. Yet this practice was largely limited to elites until the sixteenth century. It was only with the relative social and cultural experimentation that accompanied late medieval political destabilization that commoners began to embrace the pattern established by elites. Flower viewing, and indeed variations of the practice of arranging flowers, became

[44] Miho Ishii, "Acting with Things: Self-Poiesis, Actuality, and Contingency in the Formation of Divine Worlds," *HAU: Journal of Ethnographic Theory* 2.2 (2012): 371–388.

[45] Catherine Bell, a specialist in Chinese religions, was a prodigious scholar of ritual who provides a comprehensive overview of definitions germane to the East Asian context in *Ritual Theory, Ritual Practice* (Oxford University Press, 1992), 69–93. Bell argues that "ritualization" refers to strategic activities that are "rooted in the body, specifically, the interaction of the social body within a symbolically constituted spatial and temporal environment" (93). I have also relied on Futaki Ken'ichi's voluminous scholarship on rituals, particularly those enacted by members of the warrior class, including *Chūsei buke girei no kenkyū* (Yoshikawa Kōbunkan, 1985) and *Buke girei kakushiki no kenkyū* (Yoshikawa Kōbunkan, 2003).

increasingly widespread.[46] Urban residents owned ceramic flower vases in a huge range of styles and originating in various kilns not only in Japan but around Asia. Consider, for example, one example of an object excavated from Ichijōdani: a Chinese celadon bottle, used in Japan as a flower container, made during the Yuan Dynasty. The piece has what is sometimes called a garlic-head shape, with a large bulbous lower body, and is decorated with a few spots of iron pigment underneath a translucent, greenish celadon glaze. As the cracks and signs of repair indicate, the bottle was shattered in the destruction of Ichijōdani, and recovered in the hundredth survey of the excavation site. Specifically, archaeologists unearthed the piece from a parcel of land associated with the Kawai house of retainers to the Asakura, a higher-ranking warrior family that was still significantly lower in status and wealth than the rulers of the province.

What does the piece mean? How can we read an excavated object of this sort that comes with no box inscription, no certificate of authentication, no name or biography like so many tea utensils of Chinese origin that passed in and out of warrior collections before arriving in modern museums? One obvious context is the culture of flower appreciation among warrior elites. The origins of the culture of displaying flowers in the decorative alcove (*tokonoma*) is found in the Buddhist practice of using flowers as part of ritual offerings. In the palatial residences of the Ashikaga shoguns, arrangements of flowers were deployed in gatherings of elite warriors that served to reify hierarchy, allow gift exchange, and cement bonds of loyalty. Flowers in the halls of the Ashikaga were prominently displayed alongside hanging scrolls, usually paintings or works of calligraphy imported from China or brushed by Japanese Zen priests. The flower containers themselves were relatively modest, often Chinese ceramics as in this example, or in some cases wooden or metal vessels. The flowers functioned in the salons, tea gatherings, and linked verse sessions as seasonal markers and as general representations of the natural world. This object therefore points to the ritualized culture of arranging, observing, and celebrating flowers as examples of the ephemerality of life and as objects of beauty.

Another way to contextualize this flower container is in the circulation of continental objects throughout Japan in the medieval period, a major theme of this volume. Consideration of the abundant variety of objects made in China, Korea, and parts of Southeast Asia in late medieval urban centers helps to complicate our vision of Japan as an enclosed

---

[46] Haruo Shirane, *Japan and the Culture of the Four Seasons: Nature, Literature, and the Arts* (Columbia University Press, 2012), 169.

national entity, an isolated and culturally homogenous state with its own unique history. Japan as we know it of course didn't exist in the sixteenth century, and its residents – not only its elites but many commoners as well – frequently came into contact with imported works of material culture. Chinese objects played a role in the daily life of urban residents in late medieval Japan, appearing in rituals of flower arrangement, exchanged in acts of sociability, and appreciated in the larger context of what Haruo Shirane has called Japan's powerful "culture of the four seasons." And as we shall see in the pages of this book, a small population of Chinese merchants and artisans formed a key part of the larger community of Ichijōdani.

Also key in our study of excavated materials and daily life is the relationship between affect and material evidence, particularly in a project like this one that deals with stories of loss, of ruins, of forgetting, and of the power of these forces to potentially problematize the master narrative of the formation of the Japanese nation. By "affect" I mean the intensity of the impact of material things on our perception of the past, the feeling of wonder – or perhaps we might turn to Benjamin's notion of the aura of precapitalist forms of cultural production – that old things inspire, and the ways in which this reaction might be further intensified when the objects in question are not mediated by the editorial vagaries of the archive, the private collection, the modern museum. How does the seemingly scientific process of reclaiming these bits and pieces of the past, the excavation of the earth that makes the medieval present in the present, reveal historical relations in a different way, and indeed create different relations between historians and evidence? What are the "forces of encounter" (a useful definition of affect) that both are revealed by the objects excavated in this medieval urban site and are potentially created through their examination?

The answer lies in an analysis of material evidence as objects of power, and a consideration of the politics of the relationality between people and things that takes seriously the possibility that objects can affect society because of the values, properties, and forces attributed to them. In the case of Ichijōdani, the proximity of Chinese ceramics to the ashes of burnt wooden tools in the excavation pits of the castle town, or the intermixing of the collapsed foundations of Buddhist temples with the stone markers of graves, can be used to map the modalities of power in late sixteenth-century Japan; the accrual of so much force over so many objects and subjects by the warlords of that period is symptomatic of the larger political process whereby a single family at the apex of a small social group came to ruthlessly dominate with the threat of violence the varied populations of the archipelago.

Destruction and the Production of Ruins

A study of urban life in sixteenth-century Japan will necessarily attend to the experience of war. In fact, this book posits that the determination of certain warlords to push back against the pressure to join "the realm" of Oda Nobunaga represents a movement away from "unification" – not a romantic resistance to central governance, per se, but rather a focus on rooting one's authority in local rule, particularly the agglomeration of power in a provincial palace city. This decision led, inexorably perhaps, to conflict with the unifiers and to violent encounters for urban residents with the massive armies of the age. Anglophone scholars have not been inattentive to the topic of the impact of war on urban residents in medieval Japan. Many thousands of urban residents lost their lives over the course of the long sixteenth century, as Ashikaga authority collapsed, and no new Japan-wide structure emerged to replace it. Indeed, from 1467 to 1477, the Ōnin War ravaged the city of Kyoto and its environs, destroying much of the landscape of the capital and inflicting terror on its residents. Mary Elizabeth Berry, in *The Culture of Civil War in Kyoto*, quotes from an aristocratic resident of the city, writing in his diary: "Yakushiji Yoichi Motoichi, the deputy governor of the province of Settsu ... has rebelled against Masamoto and turned enemy. He is marching toward Yodo in our province. All of Kyoto is in an uproar over these events; the exodus of residents carrying their valuables is shocking, people say."[47] Her book examines Kyoto in this period and beyond, when war in and around the capital was normalized, a period that she claims, somewhat controversially, is defined by "convulsion itself."[48] She considers the acts of violence that caused widespread fear, the attempts of residents to use demonstration and legal discourse to assert control, as well as how they leaned on cultural practices and neighborly associations to stay sane. Likewise, Matthew Stavros, in *Kyoto*, discuss the widespread destruction that took place in Kyoto during and after the Ōnin War, noting that many of the key sites for the performance of classical aristocratic rituals were destroyed. Both authors also discuss the increasingly visible role of commoners in this city long dominated by aristocratic and military elites, as active agents of change, as during the Hokke movement of 1532–1536. By contrast, Suzanne Gay, in her careful study of the moneylenders of late medieval Kyoto, examines the lives of a distinct

---

[47] Mary Elizabeth Berry, *The Culture of Civil War in Kyoto* (University of California Press, 1994), 1.
[48] Berry, *The Culture of Civil War in Kyoto*, xvi.

class of influential urban commoners in the wake of the Ōnin War.[49] She finds that the worst violence of the period was relatively brief and that the entrepreneurial merchants quickly recovered despite the political incohesion around them. The capital city was thus the site of warfare and the characteristic political instability of this Age of Warring States, yet at the same demonstrated ample signs of bottom-up regeneration through community organizing and economic activity.

Yet the focus of these volumes on the capital city alone belies the much larger scope of the conflict of this era that spread out across Japan throughout the sixteenth century. Likewise, many historians of late medieval Japan treat the rise of the unifiers as a stabilizing force, as they focused much of their energy on the consolidation of power in Kyoto (particularly Hideyoshi) and thus helped to buttress the political structures that had been in disrepair for a century. The optics of this focus on the center obscure, however, the disruptions in the provinces that were made worse by the actions of the unifiers. The very act of unification – what Berry in *Hideyoshi* calls "conquest and conciliation" – included invasion, siege, looting, sexual violence, human trafficking, and widespread demolition. For many warlords, vassals, and urban commoner populations, the story of the age of unification was not one of increased stability or the notion of progress toward a more rational early modernity, but rather a story of complete destruction. Michel-Rolph Trouillot argues that "any historical narrative is a particular bundle of silences, the result of a unique process," and this book will seek to clarify, drawing on documentary and archaeological sources, the silences that have buried the story of provincial city life and its destruction in the sixteenth century. It will also attempt to wrestle with what the anthropologist of the afterlives of colonial regimes, Ann Stoler, called "the less perceptible effects" of imperial intervention and "their settling into the social and material ecologies in which people live and survive."[50] In this instance, rather than query the ruins produced by colonialism, we must interrogate the largely unexamined tendencies produced by the hyper-violent pacification of Japan in the late sixteenth and early seventeenth century. What was the inheritance of this tyrannical unification process for the early modern era it produced? And how has the memory, or perhaps more accurately the misremembering, of the destruction of communities like Ichijōdani haunted modern Japan's struggles with national identity, with

---

[49] Suzanne Gay, *The Moneylenders of Late Medieval Kyoto* (University of Hawai'i Press, 2001), 166–171.
[50] Ann Laura Stoler, *Imperial Debris: On Ruins and Ruination* (Duke University Press, 2013), 4.

the legacy of samurai violence, and with the nuances of its relationship between war and stability in its own history?

A visit to the valley of Ichijōdani today is an exercise in pastoral wandering. From Fukui Station, a major stop on the networks of the West Japan Railway Company (JR West) and the private, local company Echizen Railway, visitors can board a bus, take a local train, or hire a taxi to traverse the eleven-kilometer distance. The valley is tucked in the hills to the southeast of the urban sprawl of Fukui City, the prefectural capital, and is largely devoid of signs that it was, in the late medieval period, a thriving urban center. The Ichijōdani Asakura Family Museum (Fukui Kenritsu Ichijōdani Asakura Shi Iseki Shiryōkan) is located in a neighborhood just outside the valley, along the Asuwa River. Turning south from the Asuwa River into the valley, a narrow road follows the Ichijō River, past the remains of the old city gates, past a range of excavated sites, farmhouses, and rice paddies, until the "center" of the historic city is reached. On the left, across the river and beyond a green, grassy field, are the ruins of the main gate of the Asakura palace. (This gate is itself an Edo-period reconstruction.) On the right is one of several parking lots and entrances to the sprawling "Reconstructed Town" (*fukugen machinami*) of Ichijōdani, a kind of historical theme park that contains new constructions of warrior and urban commoner townhouses in the style of late sixteenth-century residences. Further along the road are more modern homes, some official town buildings including the Ichijō Elementary School, some temples, a famous waterfall, and a handful of additional archaeological sites. The town is sleepy and calm even at the height of the summer tourist season, as crowds of visitors dissipate across the valley, following maps, looking at stone markers, hiking trails into the hills, and generally searching out the dilapidated stone edifices of a medieval city that is almost impossible to envision.

Globally, the idea of historical ruins tends to be associated with nostalgic romanticism. Ichijōdani largely fits this archetype, particularly as configured today: a crumbling historical site, propped up by some new constructions, that allows for genteel contemplation of the apolitical urban life of bygone eras. Yet as Stoler has pointed out, the verbal form "to ruin" means nothing less than the infliction of disaster, the destruction of agency, and the creation of poverty and demoralization. Ichijōdani was ruined at a particular historical moment for particular social, political, and cultural reasons. This was, to be sure, a world-ending disaster for most of its residents, who lost their homes and livelihoods if not their lives. The few survivors fled to nearby Echizen-Fuchū if they were lucky; those who were captured by the soldiers of Oda Nobunaga, as I discuss in Chapter 6, suffered terrible fates. This aspect of the history of Ichijōdani, it is no exaggeration to say, is almost entirely elided in the presentation of its ruins today, not only at the historical site itself, but in a range of museological displays and exhibitions.

The scholarly and exhibitionary treatment of Ichijōdani contrasts starkly with the memorialization of other conflict sites in both Japanese history and more broadly in East Asia. The ruination caused by modern wars, in particular, is core to the complex ways in which Japanese intellectuals have wrestled with the articulation of national identity in the postwar era, revealed in countless studies of the "perilous memories" of the Pacific War.[51] More broadly, the ruination caused by East Asia's encounter with the West and the trials of imperialism and colonialism in the region has been explored thoroughly in a huge range of critical and insightful Anglophone literature, such as Tobie Meyer-Fong's study of China's Taiping civil war, *What Remains? Coming to Terms with Civil War in Nineteenth-Century Century China*, and Wu Hung's examination of the emergence of ruins as an artistic theme after China's disastrous encounter with the West, *A Story of Ruins: Presence and Absence in Chinese Art and Visual Culture*. Both works delve deep into the resonance between material remains, psychological trauma, the effects of war and social disruption on human bodies, and the unwanted memories – a different kind of ruins – that populations wrestled with for generations.

The profusion of good scholarship on ruins in modern East Asia does not mean, of course, that there is some kind of consensus on how these conflicts should be framed and remembered. Indeed, certain key sites – from Yasukuni Shrine to the battlefields of Okinawa to Nanjing's Zhongshan Gate – are defined in a sense by disputes over their meaning. Rather, it is the very vocal and contentious nature of discourses about and representations of these sites that stands as evidence of their instrumentality, their role as what Michel Foucault called "heterotopias" that are significant precisely because they are useful, but in varied ways to different collectives and at distinct historical moments. As Caitlin DeSilvey and Tim Edensor have noted, "ruins are used to do particular kinds of cultural and aesthetic work, producing different meanings and modes of encounter," as well as being "conscripted to do certain kinds of intellectual labour."[52]

This raises a question that in some sense animates this book: What is Ichijōdani good for? As a significant historical site that contains complex

---

[51] T. Fujitani, Geoffrey M. White, and Lisa Yoneyama, eds., *Perilous Memories: The Asia-Pacific War(s)* (Duke University Press, 2001), is an excellent example.

[52] Caitlin DeSilvey and Tim Edensor, "Reckoning with Ruins," *Progress in Human Geography* 37.4 (2012): 467.

meanings, how is it currently being deployed, by archaeologists and historians, by Fukui prefecture, by regional and national museums, and how might we imagine a different framing of its significance? This book attempts an answer by reading the ruins of Ichijōdani to critique the teleological and nationalist meta-narrative of Japanese history in which the sixteenth-century unification of Japan is generative rather than destructive. By foregrounding the political and cultural processes that led to the destruction of Ichijōdani, we can in effect remember a vital chapter in Japanese history that has been allowed to atrophy. This study also posits that analyzing excavated material evidence, in conversation with documentary and visual sources, allows a reexamination of the lived experience – the ontology – of urban residents in late medieval Japan that differs from the insights offered by reading textual evidence in isolation.

Summary of Chapters

The book begins with an examination of the space of Ichijōdani, a relatively rural valley with the burnt foundations of a whole city buried beneath its rice fields and farmhouses. Chapter 1, "A Provincial Palace City as an Urban Space," examines the layout of the city, its neighborhoods, its interior and exterior, and its relationship to the natural environment that framed and constrained its growth. Chapter 2, "The Material Culture of Urban Life," digs into the stuff of the city, examining the range of objects excavated from homes, garbage pits, moats, and even toilets to try to imagine the rhythms and character of daily life for the residents of Ichijōdani. Chapter 3, "Late Medieval Warlords and the Agglomeration of Power," traces the rise of the Asakura clan from mid-ranking warriors to warlords of the province of Echizen, and the emergence of Ichijōdani as the thriving capital of the region for a century. It considers the construction of a palatial residence near a fortified castle, and the resulting growth of a city around this pairing, as one of many forms of elite warrior politics in late medieval Japan. Chapter 4, "The Material Foundations of Faith," explores the excavated evidence of religious institutions and diverse faith-based practices across the city, revealing a bare and unvarnished set of concerns and habits focused on the commemoration of death and ritual use of objects. Chapter 5, "Culture and Sociability in the Provinces," lays out the vibrant social networks and rich cultural activities of the elite residents of Ichijōdani, pushing back against the derivative claim that provincial capitals were mere "Little Kyotos." Chapter 6, "Urban Destruction in Late Medieval Japan," examines the chain of events that led to the utter ruination of Ichijōdani in 1573, arguing that the Asakura were not mere roadblocks to the glorious process of unification, but central political actors exploring an alternative vision of prosperous, provincial rule. Their decimation at the command of Oda Nobunaga, part of his larger campaign of tyrannical violence, meant more than the elimination of a warlord family or even a provincial city. In that act of destruction, a "small universe" of meaningful lives, unique spaces, and powerful creations that is key to understanding the rich diversity of medieval Japan was erased. The Epilogue, "The Excavated Nation on Display," moves from the museumification of Ichijōdani as a prefectural heritage site to the display of medieval urban archaeological materials in general. The excavation, analysis, and display of material culture from Ichijōdani provides us with an opportunity to rethink how we tell the story of medieval Japan and its relationship to modern history, particularly around issues of war, community, and national identity.

1   A Provincial Palace City as an Urban Space

Every society – and hence every mode of production with its subvariants (i.e. all those societies which exemplify the general concept) – produces a space, its own space.   —Henri Lefebvre, *The Production of Space* (31)

This chapter explores the logic and grammar of the city of Ichijōdani, capital of the Asakura warlords who ruled Echizen province, as an urban space. The tradition of warrior urban centers overlaps with the emergence of the warrior class as a distinct political force. The establishment of a Provincial Office (*kokufu*) in what was in effect the regional capital, as well as a fortified Governor's Residence (*shugosho*) that was sometimes located separately from the capital, can be found throughout the Kamakura period (1184–1333) with intensification during eras of political instability, such as the long transition between the Kamakura shogunate and the Ashikaga shogunate. Provincial Offices and Governor's Residences were often surrounded by the residences of high-ranking vassals, important temples and shrines, and, eventually, some markets and commoner neighborhoods. These regional urban conglomerations were relatively unplanned, however, and geographically varied.[1]

In Echizen Province, home to the Asakura, the Provincial Office was located in Echizen-Fuchū (present-day city of Echizen, about twenty kilometers to the southwest of Ichijōdani), and this served as the primary political center of the region as well as an important trading hub because of the intersection of several major roads and a nearby port to the Sea of Japan (see Map 1.1). Previous political leaders of Echizen had maintained both residences and governmental offices in Echizen-Fuchū,

---

[1] Political leaders constructed multifunctional palace cities in Japan as early as the Heian Period (794–1185), seen in sites such as Shirakawa, Toba, Rokuhara, and Fukuhara, though none has received attention as an urban center in English-language scholarship. On the relationship between urbanization and warrior power during the first half of the medieval age, with particular focus on the Kamakura period, see the works of Takahashi Shin'ichirō, including *Chūsei no toshi to bushi* (Yoshikawa Kōbunkan, 1996), *Buke no koto, Kamakura* (Yamakawa Shuppansha, 2005), and *Chūsei toshi no chikara: Kyō, Kamakura, to jisha* (Kōshi Shoin, 2010).

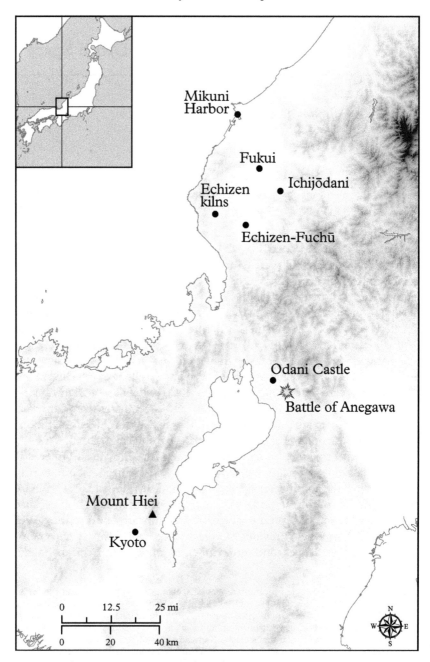

Map 1.1 From Ichijōdani to Kyoto.
By Gabriel Moss.

including the Shiba and the Kai. The province was also home to a
number of trading towns (*machiba*), such as Kanazu (present-day
Awara City), long known as a stop along the Northern Highway
(Hokurikudō) that stretched from Wakasa Province to Echigo Province.
In addition, the province was home to multiple fortified structures that its
leaders used as military bases. Somayama Castle, for example, was first
built in the early Kamakura period to the south of the Provincial Office as
a mountain stronghold. It was occupied and refurbished numerous times
throughout the medieval period, sometimes as a residence but primarily
in times of military necessity.[2] Another well-known mountaintop fort was
Kanegasaki Castle (present-day Tsuruga City), built by the Taira in the
twelfth century and famous for its role in the conflict between the
Ashikaga, the Nitta, and Emperor Godaigo in 1337. It also played a role
in the conflict between the Asakura and Oda Nobunaga (see Chapter 6).

The Asakura therefore had a range of options for their headquarters
when they received the appointment to the position of Governor of
Echizen after their political flip-flop in the Ōnin War and their successful
military assault on the Shiba. They may have hoped to avoid the concentration of power that the Shiba and their vassals the Kai had attained in
Echizen-Fuchū after more than a century of rule; likewise, though a
mountaintop fortress such as Somayama Castle or Kanegasaki Castle
would have allowed the prioritization of defense, it would have made the
mobilization of vassals, the regulation of trade, and the patronage of the
arts more difficult because of the requisite geographic isolation. The
Asakura had maintained a residence in Ichijōdani since at least 1450;
the Asakura's land holdings may have been located nearby as well,
though the documentary evidence is unclear on this point. One final
force that may have drawn the Asakura to choose to use the valley of
Ichijōdani as the headquarters of their rule was the existence of production and mercantile networks along the Asuwa River and even in the
Ichijō valley, as we shall see below. For these and surely other reasons,
the Asakura made Ichijōdani their capital for a century, and the city that
developed around their residence resulted from this political calculation,
and like many instances of urban agglomeration, it had unforeseen
consequences in the layout and structure of the settlement as it
developed over time.[3]

---

[2] See the summary in *Nihon jōkaku taikei*, vol. 1, 108. Also, Minami Echizen Machi, "Koku
   shitei shiseki Somayama jōato" (2013; accessed November 7, 2016, www.town
   .minamiechizen.lg.jp/kurasi/103/128/p001165.html).
[3] One comparable site is the castle and castle town of Katsuno (in the hills near present-day
   Tosu City), which was the headquarters of the Chikushi clan, who vied with other warrior
   powers for control of northwestern Kyushu. See Ishibashi Shinji, "Katsuno jōkamachi

What, we might begin by asking, was urban about the space of Ichijōdani? The location today is relatively rural. Ichijō is itself the name of a valley, about five kilometers in length, that is framed by mountains in the Ryōhaku range. To the east is the modest Mt. Ichijō (436 meters); to the southwest is Toishiyama, and Shiroyama is located to the west. Beyond Shiroyama is the beginning of the flood plain of the Kuzuryū River, long an agricultural basin but today the site of Fukui City, the capital of Fukui Prefecture, as well as Sabae City and Echizen City, which form a modern urban corridor that extends along the Echizen Basin to the Sea of Japan. Water acts here as a connector; the Ichijōdani River that runs through the valley empties into the Asuwa River, which in turn is a tributary of the Kuzuryū River, which empties into the Sea of Japan. Thus, although the pastoral valley of Ichijō appears to be an entirely isolated site, it is geographically close to the historic urban center of the province in Fuchū and was connected by rivers not only to the trading zone of the Echizen Basin but to the larger regional and international maritime matrix of commerce and travel. Interconnectedness is a theme that will come up repeatedly throughout this book, as both a sign of the desire of the Asakura and the residents of Ichijōdani to have access to the larger world around them, and as evidence of the vulnerability of this community to the political and military tides of late medieval Japan.

This interconnected geography was the platform for Ichijōdani's growth; as the town expanded over time it developed an increasingly urban character, what Amino Yoshihiko defined as the quality of integration into networks of exchange and circulation.[4] The center of the town was built deliberately around the Asakura palace and came to occupy a flat area of approximately 100,000 square meters (or nearly 25 acres). This central area was defined by structures that marked it as urban space: the lower city gate in the north and an upper city gate to the south, linked together by a system of interlocking roads, known to us today through extensive archaeological excavations. As we shall see in the analysis of the town layout below, the urban character of Ichijōdani is largely framed and also defined by this structure that is predicated on the

iseki ni okeru Sengoku ki jōkan no shoyōsō," in *Kōwan toshi to taiga kōeki*, ed. Ōba Kōji et al. (Shinjinbutsu Ōraisha, 2004), 130–164. See also Niki Hiroshi and Ishii Nobuo, *Shugosho/Sengoku jōkamachi no kōzō to shakai: Awa no kuni Shōzui* (Shibunkaku Shuppan, 2017), on the history and archaeological remains of Shōzui Castle, an important governor's residence that evolved into the castle headquarters of a Sengoku warlord.
4 Amino Yoshihiko, *Nihon chūsei toshi no sekai* (Chikuma Shobō, 1996). See Alan S. Christy's helpful summary of Amino's evolving view on this point in "Translator's Introduction: A Map to Amino Yoshihiko's Historical World," in Amino Yoshihiko, *Rethinking Japanese History* (University of Michigan Center for Japanese Studies, 2012), xviii.

need to move people and things from place to place within the agglomeration as well as into and out of the valley itself.

Ichijōdani's urban area was also, however, demarcated by military defenses, a reminder that although the geography of the valley and the river outlet to a larger network of waterways and roads created regional integration, the site was also chosen for its strategic location and natural protection. The eastern peak was home to the Asakura's mountaintop fortress (see Map 1.6 below), a common feature for Sengoku warlords who lived in a well-protected city but desired an additional site for occasional residence that could of course also be used in times of war. This fortress, about 400 meters above sea level, was surrounded by moats, angled trenches, and earthen walls, and was thus thoroughly protected and also separated by both space and fortifications from the town below. It was significant in scope, with numerous structures built on large foundation stones scattered across an area that stretched 500 meters in length and 300 meters in width. Access to the keep was gated by three enclosures – sannomaru, ninomaru, and ichinomaru – allowing multiple points of defense. The main keep included a residence, a family shrine, a guardhouse, a watchtower, and other structures (at the time of this writing excavation was still ongoing).[5] This stronghold was the linchpin in a series of fortresses that surrounded the valley. Jōganji Castle was located across the Asuwa River on the northern bank, protecting the entrance to Ichijōdani from access via the river's floodplain. Tōgōmakiyama Castle watched over the town from Shiroyama to the west, while Mitsumine Castle protected access to the valley from the southwest. In addition, fortifications of various kinds, including earthen walls and ditches, protected the town itself. In short, the town was circumscribed by geography that supported both its urban-commercial function and its military-political function.

Roads were of course the basic framework of Ichijōdani's urban development until its destruction in 1573. Excavations of the central region of the town have revealed roughly thirty roads, which vary by width (see Maps 1.2 and 1.5).[6] The widest thoroughfares were between 7.4 and 7.6 meters in width, had bridges, and appear in documentary records as "roads" (dōri). These appear most often in the districts that contained

---

[5] Ono, Jitsuzō no Sengoku jōkamachi, 45–46.

[6] Ono Masatoshi claims that more than fifty roads have been excavated in his 1997 book Sengoku jōkamachi no kōkogaku: Ichijōdani kara no meseiji (Kōdansha, 1997), 37, but I will use the more conservative number provided by Yoshioka Yasuhide in his essay from 2002, "Ichijōdani no toshi kōzō," in Sengoku daimyo Asakura shi to Ichijōdani, ed. Mizuno Kazuo and Satō Kei (Kōshi Shoin, 2002), 66–67.

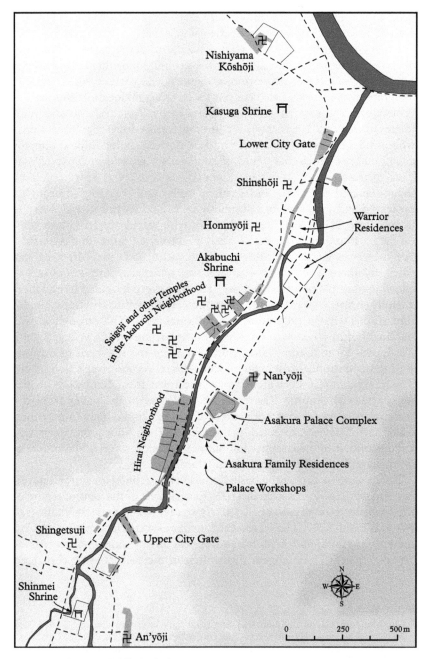

Map 1.2 Ichijōdani city.
By Gabriel Moss.

larger warrior residences and temple complexes. Thoroughfares of medium width, ranging from 3 meters to around 5 or 6 meters, were referred to as "narrow streets" (*kōji*) and lacked bridges, and thus did not extend from one side of the river to the other. The smallest thoroughfares discovered were mere alleys, unmentioned in the documentary record, and only 1.2–2.1 meters in width, which allowed traversal between properties or through the less-developed districts of the town. This complex of roads, streets, and alleys, primarily arranged along the cardinal directions and in line with the Ichijōdani River, structured the arrangement of buildings, the transportation of goods, and indeed the lived experiences of the residence of this city. And, as the archaeologist Ono Masatoshi has noted, the arrangement of the roads in Ichijōdani, particularly in the two widest categories of thoroughfares, indicate clear planning.[7] This was not an urban space that developed haphazardly, through a natural process of incremental settlement and centripetal urbanization, but rather a deliberate result of the political intentionality of the Asakura family, their vassals, and the many constituencies that worked for and with them.[8] The axis of the human settlement was undoubtedly the river, channeled by the contours of the mountains that framed the valley, but the articulation of that urban agglomeration is an expression of cultural and political necessities that we can read from the historic and archaeological record.

How does Ichijōdani's urban space compare with the layout of similar cities? One useful comparator is the city of Funai (present-day Oita city in Oita prefecture) in the province of Bungo, usually referred to as Bungo Funai, which served as the capital of the province and the headquarters of the Ōtomo family of warlords for most of the medieval period. As a port city on the southernmost island of Kyushu that faced toward the Seto Inland Sea, Funai was ideally situated to engage in trade with other ports along the inland sea as well as with Chinese merchants and, in the second half of the sixteenth century, with European visitors to Japan. It was also a castle town and a functioning military base. The ruling warlord in this period, Ōtomo Yoshishige (1530–1587), better known as Sōrin, effectively expanded the dominion of his family and the influence of Funai as an entrepot city and a center for various religious activities. Although Sōrin successfully allied himself with Hideyoshi and his family's position seemed secure when he died in 1587, the next generation

[7] Ono, *Sengoku jōkamachi*, 31.
[8] On the role of roads and commoner residences in defining the urban space of Kyoto, see Yamamoto Masakazu, "Chūsei Kyōto no gairo to machiya," in *Chūsei no naka no Kyōto*, ed. Takahashi Yasuo (Shinjinbutsu Ōraisha, 2006), 180–200.

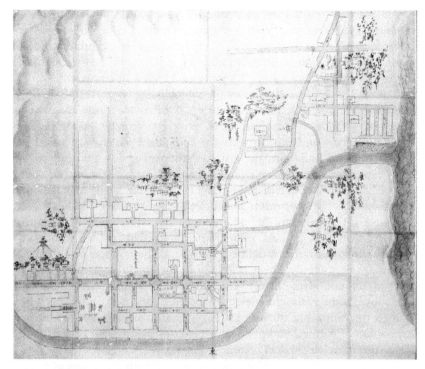

Figure 1.1 "Old Map of Funai."
Used with permission of the Oita City History Museum.

comprehensively failed to protect the Ōtomo legacy and the line was extinguished in 1605. Abundant documentary research as well as archaeological excavations of the Ōtomo castle residence, markets, churches, temples, and other urban sites in Funai have greatly advanced our understanding of this significant provincial city. Several historic maps of Bungo Funai are extant, mostly late Tokugawa-period copies, but one map (Figure 1.1) known simply as "Old Map of Funai" (*Funai kozu*) appears to date to the late sixteenth century.[9]

The map focuses on the residence of the Ōtomo warlords, and in addition shows five primary east–west roads and four primary north–south roads dividing the center into blocks. The Oita River demarcates the eastern edge of the town, while hilly areas form the western edge. The residence of the Ōtomo is found in the western block, with a

---

[9] Tamanaga Mitsuhiro and Sakamoto Yoshihiro, *Ōtomo Sōrin no Sengoku toshi, Bungo Funai* (Shinsensha, 2009), 8–13.

mountaintop fortress known as Uehara no Yakata located to the southwest. Archaeological excavations have shown that the largest road in the town ran from north to south along the edge of the Ōtomo residence, along one border of the large Rinzai Zen temple complex Manjuji, and along several mercantile districts. This avenue was approximately 11 meters in width, making it larger than any main artery in Ichijōdani. This road was unusual, however; other north–south arteries were narrower, approximately 6 meters in width, comparable to the middle group of roads in Ichijōdani. It appears that the centrality of this road as well as the fact that it traversed the most important institutions in Funai required, or allowed, it to be exceptionally wide and thus particularly useful for mercantile and political purposes.

Other provincial urban centers from the sixteenth century appear to have possessed similar spatial demarcations and road networks, though Ichijōdani's excavations have revealed an unusual quantity of roads large and small. The eastern headquarters of the Hōjō family, Odawara, for example, possessed similar groupings of roads to both Ichijōdani and Bungo Funai. The narrowest lanes were just 2 meters in width, the middle group of roads were 5–6 meters in width, and one larger avenue was 8 meters wide.[10] It is worth noting that in most contemporary road systems, a single lane (to be traversed by one automobile) is 3.25–3.7 meters in width. The largest avenues in these sixteenth-century castle towns were thus comparable in width to modern two-lane roads. The road network of Ichijōdani was thus typical of provincial cities that developed as agglomerations around warlord residences in the sense that the types and sizes of roads match other known examples; the shape of Ichijōdani, however, as a long and narrow city that hewed closely to the serpentine contour of the river in the center of the valley and the mountains on either side of the valley, is quite distinct.

Additional built features that defined the urban space of Ichijōdani included the gates that marked entry and exit, bridges that enabled traversal of the river, and moats and ditches found around and throughout the town that helped direct water runoff and protected against flooding. These features helped to define different neighborhoods and districts of provincial cities like Ichijōdani, and these neighborhoods in turn appear to have contained populations that were varied in terms of status: warrior neighborhoods and urban commoner neighborhoods. Indeed, roads alone do not constitute a town or city; it is the presence of a relatively dense population of residents, the built environment of

---

[10] Sasaki Kensaku, "Chūsei Odawara no machiwari to keikan," in *Chūsei no michi to hashi*, ed. Fujiwara Yoshiaki (Kōshi Shoin, 2005), 182.

their shops and homes, and the "place of power" at the core that make the conveyance of people and goods into and out of a site like Ichijōdani meaningful. But Amino's insistence that it is the ability to engage in production and consumption in a networked fashion that allows a town to be both independent and integrated into a region highlights the significance of roads and waterways – routes of conveyance –in the making of medieval urban space.[11] Roads allowed provincial urban centers to balance their autonomy with their interconnectedness, and they are useful to historians today as a tool that makes the political logic of medieval regional cities legible.[12]

The Asakura Palace

The central feature of Ichijōdani was the residence of the Asakura, which was located on the eastern side of the Ichijō valley approximately 1,500 meters south of the confluence with the Asuwa River (see Map 1.2). We know little about the evolution of this structure over time; instead, data from the six-year excavation of the site has illuminated the size, layout, and use of the structure at the time of the destruction of Ichijōdani in 1573, when Asakura Yoshikage was lord of the domain. His political machinations, which ultimately led to the elimination of the family, also resulted in new uses for the structure as a site of both daily life and political pageantry. The structure itself helps clarify the work of the Asakura as independent, regional warlords who were interested in resisting the tides of unification and buttressing their own authority, a process that ironically required that they appeal to medieval notions of central authority and traditional ritual practices.[13]

The Asakura palace was situated on the eastern bank of the Ichijōdani River with the Ichijō Mountain at its back, to the southeast. Each of the walls was approximately 90 meters in length, making the area of the complex roughly 8,100 square meters (or roughly 2 acres). Access to

---

[11] See Amino's discussion of "urbanizable spaces" or "toshi no dekiru basho" in "Toshi no kigen," in Amino Yoshihiko, *Amino Yoshihiko chōsakushu, vol. 13: Chūsei toshi ron* (Iwanami Shoten, 2007), 427–429.

[12] Iimura Hitoshi, "Jobun: Ikō to shite no 'michi,' 'michi' kare mieru iseki," in Fujiwara, ed., *Chūsei no michi to hashi*, 16–17.

[13] Excavation of this site has understandably been one of the primary foci of archaeological activities in Ichijōdani, and in fact some see the excavations of the palace gardens in the late 1960s as the origin of the field of medieval archaeology in Japan. The Asakura palace – also known as "Asakura Yoshikage's residence" – has been excavated many times, notably between 1968 and 1969 in the first (unnumbered) excavations, and then as part of the more organized, sequential excavations nos. 1–3 in 1971; 5 in 1972; 9 in 1973; 67 in 1989; 95 in 1995; 99 in 1996; and 109 in 2000.

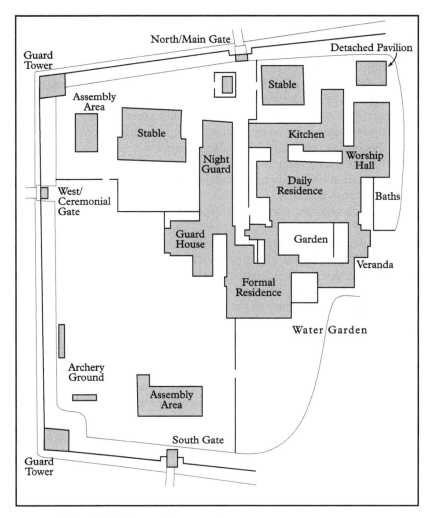

Map 1.3 Asakura palace complex.
By Gabriel Moss.

the palace was tightly controlled by three portals (see Map 1.3). The palace complex was lightly defended, with a substantial moat surrounding the front and both the northeastern and southwestern sides, while the southeastern quadrant of the complex melded into the steep slope of the hillside. Large earthen walls provided an additional barrier just inside the moat. Each of the western-facing corners of the complex was home to a guard tower, which maintained watch over the walls, the moat, and the three entrances to the structure. The southeastern sector of the complex represented the interior of the residence, and allowed access to paths that led to the mountaintop fortress above. The northern wall of the complex was home to the "front gate" (*omote mon*) of the structure. The western wall of the complex was home to an ornate Chinese-style gate. The southern wall of the complex was home to the third gate. The complex circumscribed and protected by these walls contained approximately sixteen buildings and a range of planned, open spaces. Some structures and spaces can be clearly identified based on their archaeological remains, while historians and archaeologists have deduced the functions of others based on comparison with contemporaneous sites and use of documentary evidence.

The three separate entrances to the palace complex serve as useful markers of the three different types of populations who accessed the distinct spaces of the interior. The northern or main gate was likely used for deliveries and by the lower-status daily laborers who kept the palace running but did not reside within. The exact structure of the gate is unknown, but looking at extant paintings of similar warrior palaces from the period, it seems likely to have been a relatively simple rectangular gate with a flat roof of unpainted wood, signifying its everyday usage.

Walking through this gate, a five-bay stable was located on the left and a miniature shrine (*hokora*) could be found on the right. Moving left past the stable, several interconnected structures are found, including a storage building and what was most likely the kitchen for the palace, evidenced by the excavation of the remains of a large hearth used for cooking. In the northeast was what appears to be a worship hall next to the palace bathhouse, which had a view of the lake garden to the south. Slightly separate from the other structures, at the very corner of the complex, was a small detached pavilion (*hanare zashiki*). This space may have been used for isolated study or private retreat. All of these areas that were easily accessed by the main gate represented the interior of the palace complex, largely hidden from the gaze of visitors and reserved for the more private and everyday (known in Japanese as *ke*) activities.

By contrast the southern gate opened to immediately face an assembly area in which guards would have been stationed and military equipment stored; this may also have allowed samurai visitors to store weapons and other belongings before entering the complex. After arriving at this gate, a mid-ranking warrior visitor – perhaps an Asakura relative or a retainer whose estate was located across the river – would then proceed through a wide, open space. These open areas were commonly found in imperial and warrior palaces in medieval Kyoto, as seen in a range of panoramic painted screens from the late sixteenth century.[14] This southern gate was likely used for relatively routine visits by warriors, and therefore the open grounds would probably have been largely empty. Perhaps a few soldiers would have been training in the western part of the grounds, aiming arrows at targets or engaging in other forms of martial practice.[15] Trainers might have been working with some of the horses from the large, seven-bay stable on the northern edge of the expanse, and archers might have been practicing in formation on the western edge of the compound. Regardless, the visitors would cross from the southern gate to the main Asakura residence under the watchful eyes of soldiers from the substantial attached guardhouse before being admitted to attend to business. The process of passing, physically, from the gate to the mansion was itself an embodiment of the politics of the palace. The area between the entrance and the destination emphasizes, spatially, the lofty status of the lord and the relative lower rank of the visitor.

The third gate to the west was reserved for grander occasions, such as the formal visitation ceremonies (*onari*) held when another elite warrior or a courtier from Kyoto called on the Asakura lord. The gate itself was an impressive, Chinese-style structure with a curving, tiled roof, an architectural signifier of the increased ritual significance of its usage. Entering the grounds, the stable was immediately to the left, the guardhouse directly in front (effectively blocking the visitor's view of the official residence hall), and the grounds would have been filled with the lord's vassals, seated on cushions and observing the entourage of the visiting dignitary. The horses would have been led to the stables, belongings left in the storehouse, hands washed of the dust of the road at the well nearby, and then the visitors would proceed toward the formal residence.

The official residence of the Asakura was in fact part of an interconnected network of buildings that included a range of carefully constructed and curated spaces for the political work of successful provincial rulers. This structure – the palace – consisted of higher-status space with both private areas for rest, contemplation, and daily life, and semi-public gathering spaces for banquets, tea gatherings, and other social rituals (see Maps 1.3 and 1.4 for details). The buildings consisted of multiroom, rectangular structures that could be reconfigured for various cultural and social purposes. The southwest corner of the building (the "Formal Residence" on the maps) served as a site for the initial

[14] See Matthew Philip McKelway, *Capitalscapes: Folding Screens and Political Imagination in Late Medieval Kyoto* (University of Hawai'i Press, 2006), Plates 12 and 13.
[15] See Saitō Shin'ichi's discussion of such areas in warrior residences in *Chūsei bushi no shiro* (Yoshikawa Kōbunkan, 2006), 83.

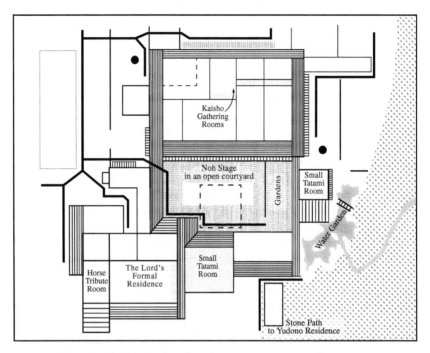

Map 1.4 Asakura palace interior.
By Gabriel Moss.

meeting with visitors, and contained a room for the reception of gifts, which in the late sixteenth century frequently included horses (the "Horse Tribute Room"). This sizable, six-bay room would have had dirt floors, large doors, and ample space for the lord or his emissary to observe as visitors presented and received offerings in the elaborate rituals of exchange that helped glue warrior society together. In 1568, for example, when the heir to the shogunate Ashikaga Yoshiaki visited the Asakura lord's official residence in perhaps the most famous cultural ritual in Ichijōdani's history, the Asakura offered numerous horses to Yoshiaki; at one point in the exchange, the lord's son brought a rare palomino horse from the gardens for Yoshiaki to inspect and accept. This likely happened in this gift-reception room.[16] The building also includes a storage room – likely a space in which gifts that would soon be offered or that had just been received could be set aside – as well as a large, fifteen-bay room in

---

[16] The entire event is recorded in Fukui Shi, "Asakura Yoshikage tei onari-ki," 808–814.

which other sociable rituals, such as the ritual of three cups (*sankon no gi*), in which the hosts and guests exchanged multiple rounds of sake and food, were performed as part of the initial sequence of the formal reception of visitors. (More on these rituals in Chapters 5 and 6.)

Beyond this reception area, in the inner quarters of the palace, a wide range of flexible spaces ("Kaisho Gathering Rooms") allowed for meetings, Noh performances, banquets, and tea gatherings. The foundation of a stage was excavated from a courtyard that also housed several segmented gardens. Archaeologists discovered the remnants of a "fountain pavilion" (*izumidono*) on the southern side of the palace, a room in which natural flowing water has been routed to be visible as an architectural feature. A small room with a veranda faced the eastern hills, and would have afforded those seated – perhaps taking part in a tea gathering – with a lovely view of both the forested peaks and the water garden to the southeast of the palace. These spaces were key to the political work of the Asakura, providing both the location and the ritual labor for networking, alliance-building, planning, and general governance to occur.

The Asakura residential complex contains many elements of the elite homes and palaces of Kyoto, and in that sense it gestures in the direction of the very central authority that some Sengoku warlords seemed intent to defy. Ashikaga Yoshiteru's castle residence in Kyoto, for example, contained many of the same structures and features: separate residential and gathering/reception halls, as well as a tea room, bathhouse, storehouse, stables, and an open area for horse riding.[17] Historians have commented on the military preparedness of this structure, noting its walls and moat and the fact that entrance was limited to just three gates through the walls, a similar layout to the Asakura residence. More broadly, the gardens and spaces for contemplation were an important feature of cultural and political structures for elite warriors going back to the palatial constructions of the shoguns Ashikaga Yoshimitsu (seen in the reconstructed Golden Pavilion today) and Ashikaga Yoshimasa (seen in the extant structures of the Silver Pavilion). This Ashikaga tradition in Kyoto, though it proved to be politically untenable in the long term, provided a clear model for rulers in the provinces who adapted the structures and rituals of the political center (which had already been appropriated from the older and more established

---

[17] Takahashi Yasuo with Matthew Stavros, "Castles in Kyoto at the Close of the Age of Warring States: The Urban Fortresses of the Ashikaga Shoguns Yoshiteru and Yoshiaki," in *Japanese Capitals in Historical Perspective: Place, Power and Memory in Kyoto, Edo and Tokyo*, ed. Nicolas Fiévé and Paul Waley (RoutledgeCurzon, 2003), 41–66 (50).

practices of the imperial court) to cement their own hegemony as independent, regional rulers.[18]

Similar features can be found in other provincial cities of the age. The lower residence of the Ema family of warriors in Kamioka (present-day Hida City, Gifu Prefecture), for example, grew in the late fifteenth and early sixteenth centuries into a sizable residential complex. The site has been largely excavated and has revealed large walls and a moat surrounding a rectangular space that contained multiple residential and social buildings, a rock and water garden, and open spaces (*hiroba*) that served multiple performative and military functions. Like the Asakura residence, the Ema residence was built against a mountain that was the site of a more easily defended military fortress. Also like the Asakura residence, the Ema complex balances spaces for the public performance of political authority and military dominance with more private spaces in which social rituals could be held with smaller groups of vassals and visiting dignitaries. Like the Asakura, the Ema did not survive the wars of unification, but were eliminated in 1582 in the turbulence following the assassination of Nobunaga.[19]

Another example is the residence of the Ōtomo in Bungo Funai, which was likewise the central feature of the urban community in the late sixteenth century, with a history going back at least 200 years. The Ōtomo residential complex expanded significantly between the mid-fifteenth and mid-sixteenth centuries, as it was transformed from a governor's residence into a larger Sengoku warlord residence, with more vassal homes in the vicinity and larger spaces for social and political gatherings, as well as significant expansion in the defenses, seen in deeper and wider moats around strengthened walls.[20] The rock and water garden installed in the early sixteenth century was enlarged as well. These changes allowed the Ōtomo to use the residence as a site for the complex politics of clarifying and maintaining the relationships of their warrior organization. Documentary evidence indicates that banquets for as many as 200 warrior vassals could be held in the gathering hall, followed by performances of Noh or Sarugaku on a stage in the complex. Also included on the grounds were guardhouses, a storehouse, an audience chamber, a kitchen, a secretary's office, and a bathhouse.[21] Like the Asakura residential complex, the home of the Ōtomo was also the center

---

[18] See Matthew Stavros, "Building Warrior Legitimacy in Medieval Kyoto," *East Asian History* 31 (June 2006): 1–28.

[19] Ono, *Sengoku jōkamachi*, 87–89.

[20] Sakamoto Yoshihiro, "Bungo Funai no tatemono ikō," in *Ōuchi to Ōtomo: cūsei Nishi Nihon no nidai daimyō*, ed. Kage Toshio (Bensei Shuppan, 2013), 219–225.

[21] Tamanaga and Sakamoto, *Ōtomo Sōrin no Sengoku toshi*, 25–33.

of a large military organization that relied on cultural practices and social rituals to perpetuate the relationships that maintained the power of the regional ruler.

The Asakura residential complex is clearly modeled on the aristocratic and warrior palaces of Kyoto. The palace is an articulation of a notion of "lordship" in the relationship between its structures and its environment, making it a provincial example of a *designed medieval landscape*.[22] Although it gestures in the direction of the imperial capital and its traditional institutions, it is not a derivative urban site or a "pretentious 'little Kyoto'" in the words of one eminent historian of Japan.[23] Particularly in light of the flow of aristocratic, cultural, and even political elites in and out of Ichijōdani throughout the sixteenth century (as detailed in Chapter 5), the Asakura palace needed to accomplish more in the political, cultural, and social playbook of its provincial rulers than simply replicating the structures of Kyoto. Instead, the careful placement of semi-public and largely private spaces for rituals of sociability, performance areas, gardens, and other features of fifteenth- and sixteenth-century lordship illustrate the instrumentality of the Asakura palace as the key "place of power" in Echizen Province.

Social Status and Urban Space

Scholars view Ichijōdani as perhaps the best-preserved example of a late medieval provincial city.[24] One reason is the fact that the site was largely abandoned as a political center after its destruction in 1573, with light agricultural activity continuing but none of the large-scale early modern and modern building efforts that can hamper attempts to excavate urban sites like Bungo Funai, or an even more urban location such as Kyoto. Excavations have proceeded continually in Ichijōdani since 1967, which is unusual for any urban archaeological site in Japan (though many districts remain unexamined). In addition, the settlement possessed the classic elements of a regional urban agglomeration for its period, making it useful as a kind of table of contents to the cities of the age: a mountain-top castle nearby; a palatial hub of the ruler's residence, as discussed

---

[22] This term is borrowed from scholarship on British medieval archaeology. See, for example, Oliver Creighton, "Overview: Castles and Elite Landscapes," in *The Oxford Handbook of Later Medieval Archaeology in Britain*, ed. Christopher Gerrard and Alejandra Gutiérrez (Oxford University Press, 2018), p. 1 of the PDF.

[23] Conrad Totman, *A History of Japan* (Blackwell Publishers, 2000), 238.

[24] Ichijōdani is, for example, the first case explored in the issue of *Nihon no bijutsu* dedicated to castles and castle towns. See Kamei Nobuo, ed., *Shiro to jōkamachi*, no. 402 in the series *Nihon no Bijutsu* (Tōbundō, 1999).

above; multiple temple complexes, as we will see in Chapter 4; and distinct neighborhoods that help illuminate social distinctions and understandings of community. It is this last element that will be the focus of this final section of the chapter.

The overall structure of Ichijōdani as a city included distinct neighborhoods but does not appear to have had set restrictions on building and location by occupation as was true in many castle towns under the Tokugawa system. The Asuwa River and the regional roads beyond the valley represented the outside world and the network of trade, politics, and military activity that the Asakura constructed Ichijōdani to protect against but also to control access to. The mountaintop fortress of the Asakura pointed to the source of the authority of the family to accrue power in this settlement but also to their duty, in the Confucian sense, to protect it. As discussed above, the Asakura palace was walled off from the main community, flanked by the closest members of the warrior elite, and functioned as the political center of the community. To the north were the homes of the highest-ranking vassals of the Asakura as well as a Buddhist temple, and to the south were the residences of Asakura family members, as well as additional vassal residences. Across the river, on the western side of the town, were more warrior residences, commoner shops and residences, and multiple temple complexes. This entire complex was bounded by the lower city gate in the north and the upper city gate in the south, but the urban space of Ichijōdani extended beyond these formal borders (Map 1.6 below). Additional temple complexes were located in the valley beyond the gates at both ends of the community, and agricultural settlements and a market were likewise found outside the walls. In addition, the growth of the town necessitated the development of new neighborhoods, such as "Eastern New Town" (Higashi Shinmachi) and "Western New Town" (Nishi Shinmachi) south of the upper gate and the Abaka district north of the lower gate, abutting the Asuwa River.

One notable example of the high-status residences of Asakura family members (see Map 1.2) is found just to the south of the outer wall of the palace, home to the last Asakura lord's mother, Kōtokuin.[25] The placement of this residence, Nakanogoten, immediately adjacent to the main Asakura palace speaks to the important political role of the often-hidden Asakura women in the administration of the province, and in fact the structure is believed to have predated Kōtokuin's residence there.

---

[25] Sites 4 and 13: see Fukui Kenritsu Ichijōdani Asakura Shi Iseki Shiryōkan, *Tokubetsu shiseki Ichijōdani Asakura shi iseki hakkutsu chōsa hōkoku III: dai 4/13 ji, dai 20 ji chōsa* (1990).

Kōtokuin was born into the Wakasa Takeda family of warlords, who ruled the small but strategically significant province of Wakasa just to the south of Echizen. She married Asakura Takakage (1493–1548) before he became the fourth lord of the province in what must have been a politically significant union that further strengthened the alliance between Wakasa and Echizen, though this relationship later broke down due to succession disputes within Wakasa. Although Kōtokuin's year of birth is unknown, historians hypothesize that she may have been significantly younger than her husband, and thus easily outlived him and continued to advise her son Yoshikage up until the destruction of their family. We do know that visitors to Ichijōdani treated her with the utmost respect, referring to her as "your highness," or *uedono*.[26] Additionally, during the long visit of Ashikaga Yoshiaki in the period before the destruction of Ichijōdani, she received the elevated status of "second-ranked nun" (*ni-i no ama*). The historian Matsubara Nobuyuki in fact speculates that she was the highest-ranking woman in all of Ichijōdani, and as the mother of the provincial lord, occupied a truly unique political position.[27] This is reflected in the excavation of her residence, which consisted of at least five separate but interconnected structures built on a flat zone surrounded by low earthen walls, with an impressive garden and pond in the southern corner of the compound.[28] Like the Asakura residential complex, this arrangement of private and semi-public spaces would have played an important role as a stage for cultural and social rituals that were key to the grammar of sixteenth-century politics. The density of these ritual activities is legible through the distribution of ceramic shards across the site, with particularly intense concentrations around the two structures that are believed to have served as the residential quarters and the gathering quarters of the complex.

The Asakura residential complex and the elite warrior residences that surrounded it were serviced by a remarkable pair of artisanal studios that archaeologists have located to the south of Kōtokuin's residence (see Map 1.2). A metalsmith was certainly in operation here, evidenced by excavation of various materials including a crucible, casting remains, a pouring ladle, and the remains of a furnace. Based on the materials discovered, this workshop focused on production of sword fittings. In addition, archaeologists have excavated the remnants of a glass

---

[26] Matsubara Nobuyuki, "Asakura Yoshikage no seiko Kōtokuin to Wakasa Takeda-shi," in *Asakura Yoshikage no subtete*, 129.
[27] Matsubara, "Asakura Yoshikage no seiko Kōtokuin to Wakasa Takeda shi," 130–131.
[28] Fukui, *Tokubetsu shiseki Ichijōdani Asakura shi iseki hakkutsu chōsa hōkoku III: dai 4/13 ji, dai 20 ji chōsa*, 40.

manufacturing studio; this is an extremely rare and unusual find, as most glass in Japan during the medieval period appears to have been imported from China. The only other artisanal glass facilities discovered in medieval Japan come from excavation of the Yamashina Honganji site, which was the headquarters of the Ikkō sectarians in Kyoto until its destruction in 1532. These studios thus seem to have served the Asakura directly, another indication of the high level of artistic patronage that a provincial urban ruler could provide.[29]

On the other side of the valley, one thoroughly excavated neighborhood is the Hirai neighborhood (see Map 1.2). Strictly speaking, we do not know the name of this district during the sixteenth century. Instead, archaeologists sometimes use the names of the residents of certain properties, identified through text on excavated objects or in some cases from supplementary documentary evidence, as a shorthand name for the district. In this case, three names are associated with this neighborhood: Hirai, Kawai, and Saitō. Hirai seems to be the name used most often in Japanese publications about Ichijōdani, so I have opted to use it here, but this is a helpful reminder that using material evidence to reconstruct the structures of a premodern city involves, and indeed requires, a great deal of guesswork.

In Hirai, more than 30,000 square meters of land have been excavated in a long but narrow strip along the river, 100 meters wide in the north where the largest residences are located, and narrower to the south, where there is less flat land between the river and the mountains.[30] Broadly, the district had seven main roads and was divided into roughly three blocks.[31] This district was well planned, with many individual properties that were protected by earthen fortifications with access controlled by a main gate, mimicking the structure of the Asakura residence on a smaller scale. More than a dozen large residences have been excavated, eight of which are most likely large warrior homes, while the others may have been commoner townhouses (*machiya*) or smaller warrior residences.[32] The largest are located to the north, closer to the Asakura complex, and are notable for their rectangular compounds with multiple

---

[29] From 2007 and 2008 excavations of the Yonezu site. See Fukui, *Tokubetsu shiseki Ichijōdani Asakura shi iseki hakkutsu chōsa hōkoku 15.*

[30] Excavations nos. 10, 11, 15, 24, 25, 29, 30, 54, 57, 58, and 83. Refer to the map in Fukui, *Tokubetsu shiseki: Ichijōdani Asakura shi iseki hakkutsu chōsa hōkoku* VI (1997), 31, to see the labels for each excavation on a map of the neighborhood. This report also contains helpful photographs of the sites during excavation.

[31] Yoshioka, "Ichijōdani no toshi kōzō," 68–70.

[32] Scholars differ in their interpretations of the excavated evidence, and opinions continue to evolve. See Ono, *Sengoku jōkamachi*, 32–33, and Ono Masatoshi and Suitō Makoto, eds., *Jitsuzō no Sengoku jōkamachi, Echizen Ichijōdani* (Heibonsha, 1990), 52.

buildings and inner gardens. These properties also yielded large ceramic pots (*kame*) used for storing foodstuffs, as well as a range of high-status goods that I will discuss in the next chapter. What is most notable about these warrior compounds is simply their size: they range from 1,000 to 2,500 square meters, and are thus roughly ten to twenty-five times larger than their commoner counterparts, which tend to be significantly less than 100 square meters, as we shall see below.[33] The warrior residences are not as large as the compounds of members of the Asakura family located closer to the palace, which could be larger than 3,000 square meters, but they do allow us to map the hierarchical distinctions between the status groups.[34]

Another significant neighborhood in Ichijōdani was Akabuchi (see Map 1.5), located to the north of Hirai. This district was more variegated than the largely residential neighborhood of Hirai, with a greater range of differently sized warrior compounds and commoner townhouses, as well as a variety of identifiable shops and ateliers. It also was home to multiple Buddhist complexes along the base of the mountain, including the well-documented Saigō temple, which I will consider further in Chapter 4. The district was wide and long, bisected by one central road running parallel to the river in the direction of the lower gate, with multiple crossroads. This was the main thoroughfare of the town, and the small, narrow townhouses that faced it were likely the homes and shops of various merchants and artisans; such shops were also found on the road leading to Saigō temple. Scattered behind these mercantile homes were some larger warrior compounds interspersed with some smaller properties.

One notable storefront and workshop on this main road was that of a maker of Buddhist beads (*juzu*), typically used for counting prayers or pressed during ritual services (Map 1.5). The small, combined home and workshop (37 square meters)[35] was built on a stone foundation and included an entry door, a well, and a dirt-floor working space. Beyond this was a living space with a wooden floor and a toilet with a dirt floor. The work room yielded a range of materials associated with the production of prayer beads, including glass and stone beads and large fragments of a grinding stone,[36] indicating that this space functioned as the production site, the shop, and the residence of the bead maker. We can

---

[33] Ono, *Sengoku jōkamachi*, 121.   [34] Ono and Suitō, *Jitsuzō no Sengoku jōkamachi*, 53.
[35] This is similar in size to an apartment with two bedrooms and a living room (a "2LDK") in modern Tokyo.
[36] Site no. 36, excavated in 1983. See summary in Ono, *Sengoku jōkamachi*, 123–124, as well as Fukui Kenritsu Ichijōdani Asakura Shi Iseki Shiryōkan, *Waza: shutsudo ibutsu ni miru chūsei tekōgei no sekai* (Fukui Kenritsu Ichijōdani Asakura Shi Iseki Shiryōkan, 2007), 31.

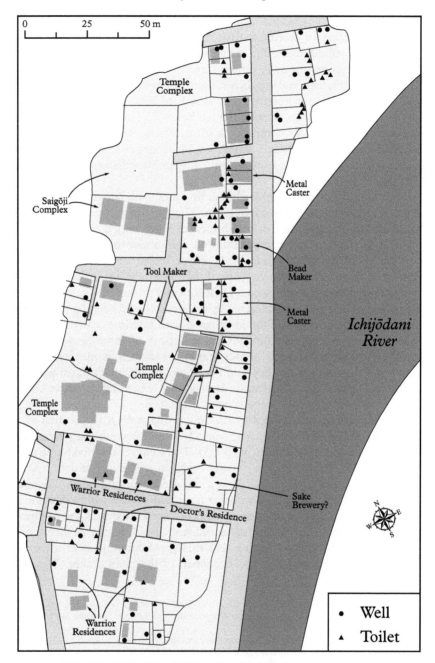

Map 1.5 Akabuchi neighborhood, Ichijōdani.
By Gabriel Moss.

imagine a visitor to Ichijōdani arriving at the lower gate in the north, progressing down the main road into town, and stopping at this shop to purchase a string of beads, perhaps a mixture of round, clear, glass beads and opaque stone ones as were found in the excavations. The traveler would then turn the corner and walk away from the river, entering the southern gate of the temple (Saigōji) located at the base of the mountains to offer prayers and perhaps take part in particular rituals.

A similar residence and shop was that of a metal tools caster (*imonoshi* or *imoji*), found to the north of the bead shop on the main road. This property was narrow but also longer than the bead shop, roughly 6 meters in width and 12 meters in length, allowing space for five rooms and an outside garden and toilet. The entrance was not on the main street but down a narrow side alley on the right side of the building. Entering the shop, visitors crossed into a large, dirt-floored showroom that likely showcased the metal wares on offer. To the left of the entrance was the workshop, which included a furnace used to melt metals that were then poured into a cast to create the desired shapes. Portions of the furnace and a large ceramic jar that may have been used to hold water were recovered in the excavations of the property. Straight ahead of the showroom was a dirt-floored kitchen that had its own well. An elevated area in the kitchen served as the entrance to the interior portion of the home, which had two rooms with raised, wooden floors. A similar caster's property was found south along the main road, with a slightly larger floor plan at 9.5 × 13.5 meters. Archaeologists excavated a crucible and copper slag here in addition to the furnace. At least four additional likely caster's shops have been identified; together, these properties paint a lively picture of the work of the metal caster in late medieval society.[37]

Townhouses that also functioned as shops and production sites are scattered around the town. One common type was the textile dyer. An example found tucked among the warrior residential compounds of the Hirai district, for example, was considerably smaller than its neighboring properties across the road, taking up just 66 square meters. The entrance was at the front of the property, and this led into a dirt room with a well that may have functioned both as the reception room and as the kitchen. Forward from the kitchen/reception room was another dirt-floored room which seems to have served as the workshop space; archaeologists excavated the bases of four large ceramic jars here, likely used to hold different liquid agents in the dying process. To the right was a room with a raised wooden floor that held eight large jars. At the front of the property was a

---

[37] Ono, *Sengoku jōkamachi*, 124–125.

narrow strip of land and at the back was a wider strip as well as an outdoor toilet. These exterior spaces were likely used for drying cloth after dying.[38] Another dyer's shop and residence, excavated in a less studied northern neighborhood closer to the lower gate at the entrance to town, was a similar but larger operation that took up approximately 145 square meters.[39] This property had a large, dirt-floored room that traversed the entire building, from the entrance on the street to the exit to the garden at the rear. The room included a well and an area for washing cloth. The left side of the structure consisted of three rooms with raised wooden floors, one of which included a hearth, and a wooden veranda looking out at the back garden. This exterior garden contained a large storage jar as well as a separate structure that was in turn home to fifteen large ceramic jars, implying that the dyer here was capable of a wider range of possible dye colors and textile treatments. Several additional dyer's shops were found throughout Ichijōdani, a reminder that textile sales and maintenance were vital to the functioning of a society in which one's status and rank were indicated externally, through dress among other markers of identity and group belonging.

Archaeologists have identified other workshops in the town, including those of two lacquerers, a plaster-wall (*nurikabe*) specialist, an earthenware potter, and a cypress woodworker. Perhaps most interesting, however, is the home and shop of a doctor found in the lively neighborhood of Akabuchi.[40] This residence was located down a large, north–south street that turned off the main road in the last block of the Akabuchi district. Turning onto this street from the main road, a series of medium-sized warrior properties were located on the right, with large earthen walls and the impressive gates that distinguished samurai compounds from those owned by commoners. On the left side of the street were a series of townhouses, surrounded only by ditches and perhaps wooden fences. The sole exception was the rather large residential compound of the doctor, which had one earthen wall at the front facing the street and another running down the left (north) edge facing a side alley. Based on excavation of the stone and wood remains at the entrance, it seems that this property was marked by a large and distinctive Doctor's Gate (*yakuimon*), a style that became popular for samurai entrances in the early modern period, but which in the late medieval period was actually used for, and associated with, doctors' properties such as this one. With a

---

[38] Site no. 62.   [39] Site no. 54.
[40] Excavations 51 and 52: see Fukui Kenritsu Ichijōdani Asakura Shi Iseki Shiryōkan, *Tokubetsu shiseki Ichijōdani Asakura shi iseki hakkutsu chōsa hōkoku X: dai 51/52 ji chōsa* (2010).

distinctive decorative style, in which one main roof covers the two primary pillars and the two support pillars, this gate advertised to all traversing the street that the resident of the property was a medical professional.[41]

The compound contained at least four structures as well as various usable exterior spaces. On the left after entering through the Doctor's Gate was the largest building on the property, roughly 120 square meters in area. Visitors and patients entered this building by leaving their shoes on a stone stand and stepping up onto the raised wooden floor of the veranda. Inside was a large room that may have been the examination space, which was connected to another room that may have functioned as a treatment space. Archaeologists excavated an impressive range of porcelain and celadon dishes here that could have been used for holding or dispensing medicinal concoctions. Between this building and the earthen wall facing the street was a garden with a well at the southern end. Beyond this large building on the southern side of the property was a small, newer structure, though its purpose is unknown. It appears to have been an expansion to the original property of the doctor, suggesting that the business was successful.

Archaeologists located another medium-sized building in the middle of the property. Three large Echizen-ware jars were excavated here, as well as a stone mortar used for grinding ingredients, denoting that this may have functioned as a storeroom for medical materials. This space also yielded fragments of the medical text *Materia Medica of Decoctions* (*Tangye Bencao*, 湯液本草), by the Chinese doctor Wang Haogu (1200–1308). It is extremely unusual to find remnants of a book in an archaeological site, where only the most durable materials, such as ceramics and stone, tend to survive the depredations of time, weather, and natural decomposition. Yet in this case archaeologists recovered legible fragments of text from inside of a large, buried jar, along with a range of other high-quality items, including a Chinese blue and white porcelain bottle, celadon plates, copper coins, and fragments from an armor set. All were partially burned, indicating that they, and indeed the surrounding structures, were ruined in the fires that wracked Ichijōdani when it was destroyed in 1573. The surviving fragments of *Materia Medica* were clustered together in a clump and were initially illegible. After separating and preserving the thirty pieces, words became legible but the specific,

---

[41] See the photos of the excavated site in Fukui, *Tokubetsu shiseki: Ichijōdani Asakura shi iseki hakkutsu chōsa hōkoku X*, 3–4; the diagram of the layout of site 51 on p. 12; and the diagram of the layout of site 52 on p. 36. More broadly, see Shinmura Taku, ed., *Nihon iryōshi* (Yoshikawa Kōbunkan, 2006).

original text was unclear because these were shards of each page and, in the words of the research director at the time, "not full sentences that could be understood."[42] Further study of the text, which seemed to contain numerous medical terms, eventually led researchers to the conclusion that it was a Chinese medical pamphlet. After this preliminary information was published, an expert in East Asian medical history was able to help the archaeologists definitively identify the original text. The comparison with the original clarified that the fragments showed slices of information from a detailed examination of medical ingredients: a *Materia Medica*.

How did this text come to reside in a doctor's shop in a provincial palace city? Andrew Goble explains in his study of medieval Japanese medical history that a pharmaceutical Silk Road, what he calls "a multi-stage maritime trade network," delivered transported ingredients and practices from the Indian Ocean and the Arabian Peninsula to India, Southeast Asia, China, the Ryukyu Islands, and ultimately Japan.[43] Chinese merchants traded medical materials and products throughout the East Asian region, with Buddhist temples among the most frequent and determined purchasers of these valuable and expensive products. Despite occasional interruptions to the flow of materials from China at certain moments in the medieval period, the supply largely became more abundant over time and indeed the demand only increased as knowledge about new medical practices was disseminated. Texts such as *Materia Medica of Decoctions* were of course the vehicle for that dispersion of knowledge. Block-printed texts authored by Song- and early Yuan-dynasty doctors in China, built on generations of study of Chinese as well as global practices (including Arabic and Islamic medical sources),[44] were widely disseminated in East Asia and often focused on explanation of the proper usage of the various ingredients and concoctions available through regional trade. Some of these books were printed at the behest of the Northern Song Imperial Court, while others from the Southern Song were commissioned and published by scholar-officials or even the doctors themselves; as a result, a startling breadth and range of medical knowledge is contained in these texts produced in varied institutional contexts.[45]

[42] Fukui, *Ichijōdani no ishi*, 5.   [43] Goble, *Confluences*, 46.
[44] Goble, *Confluences*, 56–66.
[45] Kosoto Hiroshi, "Volumes of Knowledge: Observations on Song-Period Printed Medical Text," in *Tools of Culture: Japan's Cultural, Intellectual, Medical, and Technological Contacts in East Asia, 1000s–1500s* (Association for Asian Studies, 2009), 212–227.

These Chinese medical books were thus widely distributed throughout the region and were highly valued by elites in Japan, but that still perhaps does not adequately explain the size of Ichijōdani's doctor's compound or the existence of a text like *Materia Medica of Decoctions*. It may be that Ichijōdani was unusual, and the book and its owner resided in the Asakura capital precisely because of the patronage of the ruling family. It turns out that *Materia Medica of Decoctions* is not the only medical text associated with Ichijōdani or the Asakura. In fact, the second medical book known to have been printed in Japan, a 1536 edition of *Wutingzi sujie bashiyi nanjing (Master Wuting's Explanation in Common Language of the Eighty-One Critical Questions about the Nei-jing)* by Xiong Zongli (1409–1481), was printed in Ichijōdani by the doctor Tanino Ippaku. Ippaku, a monk trained in Nara, had traveled to China to study medicine and on his return became well known as a scholar and medical practitioner. In 1529, the penultimate lord of Echizen, Asakura Takakage, invited Ippaku to relocate to Ichijōdani. We can imagine that Takakage wanted a medical professional in his capital city because of his own personal concern for health and long life, or simply because of the needs of a growing population that included men who often returned to Ichijōdani from battle with a range of medical needs. A doctor with both religious and medical training was ideal. As Edward Drott has noted, "theories about longevity and the aging process were based on fundamental beliefs about both the structure of bodies and the nature of the spiritual forces thought to animate them,"[46] and Ippaku had the profile to minister to the residents of Ichijōdani in both the spiritual and embodied realms. Ippaku accepted Takakage's invitation, and lived the remainder of his life in Echizen's capital, passing down his tradition of medicine to the Misaki family (who still live in Fukui and who possess an original printing of the 1536 book).[47] We have no evidence to link Ippaku's followers to the excavated doctor's house, but at the least the story of Ippaku's patronage by Asakura Takakage and his printing of a canonical Chinese medical text provides a kind of genealogy for the city as both a center of medieval medical practice and a place where scholarship – including the collection of books – thrived.

The excavated textual fragments of *Materia Medica of Decoctions* in Ichijōdani mention a wide range of ingredients – some available locally but many imported from China or other locales – that illustrate the

---

[46] Edward R. Drott, "Gods, Buddhas, and Organs: Buddhist Physicians and Theories of Longevity in Early Medieval Japan," *Japanese Journal of Religious Studies* 37.2 (2010): 247–273 (248).
[47] Fukui, *Ichijōdani no ishi*, 22.

concept of the pharmaceutical Silk Road and substantiate the larger point that this network extended into provincial Japan. The fragments mention licorice (*ganzō*), *Cynanchum stauntonii* (*byakuzen*, a kind of vine), aucklandia root (*mokkō*), anemarrhena rhizome (*chimo*), scutellaria root (*ōgon*), goldenthread rhizome (*ōren*), rhubarb root (*daiō*), forsythia fruit (*rengyō*), ginseng root (*ninjin*), and pinellia rhizome (*hange*), among others.[48] When we consider the knowledge provided by this text alongside a range of medical artifacts excavated from Ichijōdani, particularly the existence of ten whole or partial ceramic druggist's mortars (*yagen*) and ten copper spoons (for administering concoctions), it is clear that both processing materials such as those mentioned in *Materia Medica* and giving doses to patients were vital practices in the maintenance of the health of the community.[49]

The excavation of this imported Chinese medical text is in and of itself a remarkable discovery, but the discovery of both *Materia Medica of Decoctions* and the specific examples of material culture used in the doctor's shop allows us to push further in our consideration of the spatial configuration of the city and, more importantly, the lives of Ichijōdani residents. A glimpse of the actual lived experiences of the doctor and his assistants as medical practitioners and patients who must have come to his compound on a regular basis is possible. Previously, scholars attempted to imagine the interior of a medical facility using textual descriptions and painted handscrolls. Goble, for example, refers to illustrations of medical implements from one scene in the humorous medieval handscroll *Scroll of Fukutomi* (*Fukutomi zōshi*), a helpful visual source for the study of ceramics and daily life as well as medical practices.[50] Yet the archaeological evidence from Ichijōdani shows us actual tools of the trade in their original context. For example, archaeologists unearthed a stone druggist's mortar (*yagen*) in nearly perfect condition. The mortar consists of an oblong stone dish, with a sturdy foot to keep it steady during use, and a thick disc-shaped wheel, also made of stone, that the doctor would hold by a wooden axle while grinding ingredients. Excavations also yielded ceramic examples of the same tool, as well as a variety of mortar and pestle sets made of both stone and ceramics (Figure 1.2). Metal ladles and spoons in various shapes and sizes survived as well. Most plentiful are ceramic dishes used to serve or

---

[48] Fukui, *Ichijōdani no ishi*, 5–20.

[49] The fragments are illustrated and transcribed in Fukui Kenritsu Ichijōdani Asakura Shi Iseki Shiryōkan, *Ichijōdani no ishi* (Fukui Kenritsu Ichijōdani Asakura Shi Iseki Shiryōkan, 2010), 6–19.

[50] Goble, *Confluences*, 49, and 137–138, n. 16.

Figure 1.2 Assorted and reconstructed ceramics excavated from the doctor's residence, Ichijōdani.
Used with permission of the Fukui Prefectural Ichijōdani Asakura Family History Museum.

administer medicine. Many of the wares are of Chinese manufacture, such as the spouted celadon bowls that may have been used both as mortars for crushing and mixing ingredients and as dispensers. Likewise, archaeologists found many sets of small porcelain and celadon dishes, likely used to hold ingredients during the preparation of concoctions. Many domestically produced ceramics were found as well, including Seto/Mino ware bowls and dishes and larger Echizen ware containers that were likely used for longer-term storage of medical ingredients. Also, as I will discuss in more detail in Chapter 4, more than half of the excavated materials in this site (as in many sites of the city) consisted of earthenware ceramics known as *kawarake*. These were usually used as disposable dishes for ritual offerings, drinking exchanges, and other ceremonial occasions, particularly those involving elite warriors (see Chapter 4). They also were used throughout medieval Japan to hold candles. In the case of the doctor's establishment, however, it is clear that these dishes were also used for the preparation and dispensing of medicine. One particularly unusual dish has two Chinese characters – *tsuki* (month) and *oni* (demon) – inscribed in an alternating pattern around the interior, which implies that it was used to administer medicine that would drive away a demon that was causing an illness.[51] All of these material remains help us to visualize the process by which the doctor(s) in Ichijōdani worked to prolong the lives of his customers.[52]

The doctor's compound was a large and well-provisioned professional property and residence that speaks to the significant role of the practitioner in the community. On the opposite end of the social spectrum are a range of residences that highlight the profoundly stratified society of late medieval Ichijōdani. Tucked amid the shops, townhouses, and warrior compounds of the Akabuchi neighborhood were a number of small homes clustered together out of sight, down back alleys that led to the middle of large blocks of properties. For example, excavations have revealed a cluster of eight small properties to the southwest of Saigōji that were served by two wells and a single toilet in a common courtyard area. This cluster of homes appears to have been a relatively recent development in the history of the city, probably built by a landlord in order to rent the spaces to low-status workers, a practice that was also seen in medieval Kyoto.[53] Such economic activities should not have been possible in a warlord's capital city, where the land was all occupied at the pleasure of the lord of the castle; yet archaeologists have found that warrior compounds were sometimes divided into smaller (though still large) residences, and merchant and artisan townhouses were likewise rearranged or divided over time. This implies that the Asakura did not have, or chose not to exercise, strict control over the redevelopment of properties in the town, and that some sense of private ownership of these urban plots of land may have emerged over time.

Conclusion

The power of the Asakura as rulers of the province of Echizen and as masters of the urban space of Ichijōdani was manifested in the layout of the city itself. The location of the urban agglomeration was determined by two factors: the defensibility of the mountain fortress above, and the

---

[51] Fukui, *Tokubetsu shiseki Ichijōdani Asakura shi iseki hakkutsu chōsa hōkoku X*, object 64, plate 17. Also, Fukui, *Ichijōdani no ishi*, 52.

[52] For a profile of a late sixteenth-century doctor's practice, see Andrew Edmund Goble, "Rhythms of Medicine and Community in Late Sixteenth Century Japan: Yamashina Tokitsune (1543–1611) and His Patients," *EASTM* 29 (2008): 13–61.

[53] Ono, *Sengoku jōkamachi*, 136–139.

position of the lord's residence, the Asakura palace, alongside the river below. The residence of the ruling family, with its three well-protected gates and two guard towers, projected and reinforced the authority of the lord over the population of urban residents and also served as the functional and literal center of the community. This complex was the stage for warrior gatherings, diverse social rituals, cultural performances, and other forms of politics and pageantry, but such practices and displays were not limited to the compound. Entering Ichijōdani through the lower or upper city gate was an opportunity to reify rank and social hierarchy. Processions through the city streets, and diversions to shops and temples, likewise helped to create social cohesion among warrior vassals of and visitors to the Asakura. As David Rollason noted about medieval urban centers in Europe, "the city was developed as a stage set for conveying messages of power."[54] And the power of the warlord who ruled the province was locally supreme, the center of gravity for all of the activities that unfolded inside the valley of Ichijōdani as well as those that spilled out into the surrounding terrains.

The diversity of neighborhoods, homes, and shops in this provincial capital also points, however, to the extent to which this community was more than simply a military settlement. In the large residences of Asakura family members and elite vassals we see the operation of power and privilege in the intertwined dimensions of space and architecture. In the streets of merchant and artisanal townhouses large and small we see functioning production and trade as well as the familial edifices that made such work possible. And in the geometry of urban space that subdivided these neighborhoods by street and road, large complex and small townhouse, major bridge and minor river crossing, we see the hierarchy of medieval society manifest in the material realm.

The discovery of extremely small, subdivided residences down back alleys, almost hidden away from the townhouses and public-facing gates of temples and large warrior residences of main streets, demonstrates that medieval cities were stratified, to be sure. We can also read these tiny residences as places where itinerants and discriminated-against populations might have lived, even if only temporarily, as a kind of refuge in their labors and travels. As Amino Yoshihiko has argued in multiple publications, peripatetic workers and wanderers in medieval Japan were productive and generative, if also often distrusted. For a provincial palace city, in particular, the benefits of sheltering diverse individuals who could offer services or goods that might not have been otherwise available were

[54] David Rollason, *The Power of Place: Rulers and Their Palaces, Landscapes, Cities, and Holy Places* (Princeton University Press, 2016), 169.

manifold. They might have included outcasts (who were not segregated
into distinct communities until the early modern period) who made and
sold particular kinds of goods, semi-religious performers such as blind
storytellers and female fortune tellers, or simply workers without any
connection to the land (*muen*), who may have served as valuable seasonal
laborers in a city like Ichijōdani.

Amino's work focuses on the first half of the medieval period, and he
seems less interested in the late medieval period, arguing that the rising
power of "secular authorities" like the Asakura severely limited the
freedom of diverse peoples who were outside the dominant (and perhaps
overemphasized in postwar historiography) system of agricultural production controlled through semi-feudal relations. Nonagriculturalist
itinerants, including semi-public (*kugai*) groups such as entertainers as
well as unconnected (*muen*) people from other places, were less able to
establish viable circuits and consistent social roles in the top-down world
of sixteenth-century power relations dominated by warlords and their
kin. Yet the case of Ichijōdani with its manifold small spaces, in-between
zones, and vibrant neighborhoods outside the city gates implies that even
the late medieval urban agglomeration of a warlord allowed "freedom" of
the sort identified by Amino.

One notable example is the existence of a significant Chinatown (*tōjin
no machi*) called Abaka at the conflux of the Ichijo and Suwa Rivers (see
Map 1.6). Abaka connected Ichijōdani to the maritime world, allowing
boats to travel along the Suwa to the Hino River, which then joined the
Kuzuryū River and flowed into the Sea of Japan at Mikuni harbor.
Similarly, Abaka was situated on the Mino Highway, which ran east-
west though Echizen and was a key route for the transportation of
goods.[55] According to the official demarcation of the border of the city –
the city gates that were guarded and controlled by the Asakura – it was
outside the proper urban agglomeration.[56] Yet, by Amino's measure of
what qualifies as urban space, Abaka and its adjacent commercial neighborhood of Abaka–Nakajima could be seen as the heart of the city, and
surely played a major role in the growth of the population, the success of
the mercantile and artisanal operations throughout the valley, and ultimately the prosperity of the warriors who lived, protected by city walls, in
their estates in the valley. Goods flowed in and out of Ichijōdani through

[55] Ono Masatoshi, "Hakkutsu sareta Sengoku jidai no machiya: Echizen no rei o chūshin
ni," in *Chūsei toshiba to shōnin shokunin: kōkogaku to chūsei shi kenkyū 2*, ed. Amino
Yoshihiko and Ishii Susumu (Meichō Shuppan, 1992), 115.
[56] For a discussion of power and status in the distribution of neighborhoods, see Iwata
Takashi, "Jōkamachi Ichijōdani no seiritsu to hen'yō," in *Toshi o tsukuru*, ed. Chūsei
Toshi Kenkyūkai (Shinjinbutsu Ōraisha, 1998), 58–60.

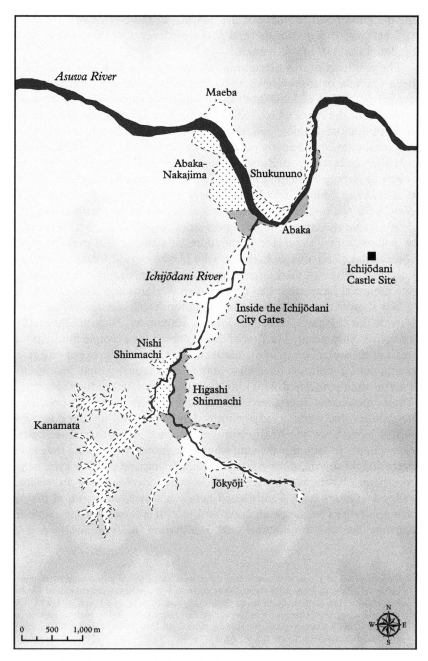

Map 1.6 Ichijōdani city and suburbs.
By Gabriel Moss.

this neighborhood throughout the century of the city's vibrant growth and activity, and in fact there is some evidence that Abaka may have predated the Asakura settlement.

The residents of this neighborhood, the majority of whom must have been Chinese or from elsewhere in East Asia, were key contributors to the urban quality of Ichijōdani; these outsiders participated in the construction of the space of Ichijōdani as much as the Asakura did. Similar communities of Chinese migrant merchants have been found in other medieval cities, particularly ports, such as the mercantile city of Hakata and the castle town of Bungo-Funai, both in Kyushu.[57] Kyoto, too, seems to have had neighborhoods of Chinese artisans and merchants in the sixteenth century and beyond, as I discussed in a previous book, *Handmade Culture*.[58] The implication of these various fragments of evidence is that the cities of Japan – port cities, capital cities, and provincial or palace cities – contained populations of Chinese and perhaps other continental merchants and artisans who played central roles in the economy and culture of their larger communities. There was much more to late medieval Japanese urban centers than warlords and their castles.

We should also note that other neighborhoods existed and thrived outside the city gates, including Jōkyōji, Kanamata, Higashi Shinmachi, and Nishi Shinmachi. The first of these, named for a temple found in the heart of the valley, south of the main city and outside the upper city gate, contained a population referred to at the time as townspeople (*machishū*), a term often associated with elite merchants in late medieval Kyoto.[59] These merchants specialized in the distribution of locally produced whetstones that were already being widely distributed up and down the Sea of Japan coast by the fifteenth century, according to archaeological excavations. In fact, this thriving whetstone industry and trade may have preceded the arrival of the Asakura in Ichijōdani, and perhaps even helps to explain why the warrior family chose what now looks like an isolated valley as a home base. Sandwiched between a merchant town at Jōkyōji that specialized in the production and sale of whetstones – valuable to warriors for the production and sharpening of weapons – and a

---

[57] Communities of Chinese artisans and merchants seem to have been found in many medieval cities, ranging from various port cities in Kyushu to the capital city of Kyoto. On Hakata, see Batten, *Gateway to Japan: Hakata in War and Peace*, 127–128. On Bungo-Funai, see Sakamoto Yoshihiro, "Bungo 'Funai' no Toshi kōzō to gaikokujin no kyojū," in *Chūsei no taiga kōryū: ba, hito, gijutsu*, ed. Ono Masatoshi, Gomi Fumihiko, and Hagihara Mitsuo (Kōshi Shoin, 2006), 36–39.

[58] Pitelka, *Handmade Culture*, 37–38.

[59] The poet Sōyō mentioned the "Jōkyōji machishū" in 1558. Cited in Ono, "Hakkutsu sareta Sengoku jidai no machiya," 117–118.

Chinatown at Abaka that was a regional hub for trade by land, river, and sea, the valley of Ichijōdani can be understood as a thriving commercial zone, ripe for the growth of a city rather than an isolated and empty territory chosen strictly for defensive reasons.

These documentary and material accretions encourage a somewhat radical reading of the balance of forces that made Ichijōdani a vibrant and significant urban site in medieval Japan. The remains of the city gates at either end of the valley, material manifestations of the limitations of the power of the Asakura, stand as markers of the official urban center but also as signs of the degree to which the urban agglomeration of Ichijōdani was much more than a warlord's city. This is also apparent in some of the few remaining documents related to the commercial activities of Abaka, found in the collection of Shinjuan, a subtemple of Daitokuji that claimed land holdings in the region. These documents mention the activities of a certain Tachibanaya, who was likely the head of the Chinese merchants' guild in Abaka. They also make reference to the existence of multiple units of measurement (*masu*) used by the Asakura and the Abaka temples and shrines, who would have represented the merchants' interests.[60] The ratio of the measurements was almost identical, with some variation between the two systems from document to document, which implies a high degree of cooperation but also a process of negotiation, revealing not just vertical ties between overlords and urban commoners, but horizontal or at least contested relations between different urban populations with evolving roles in the socio-economic landscape of the city. Amino's assertion that warrior authorities like the Asakura squelched all communal and mercantile forms of self-governance thus may have been something of an overstatement. It was rather in the dialectical relationship between diverse producers of the broad urban space of the neighborhoods in and around Ichijōdani – the tug and pull between elite warrior interests on one side and the mercantile, artisanal, and outsider residents of the city who serviced the lord yet also pursued their own private and personal interests on the other side – that a particular late medieval form of urban life is revealed.

---

[60] Ono introduces and analyzes these sources alongside archaeological materials in a brilliant, early think piece on Abaka and its meaning for Ichijōdani. He sees the correlation between the different units of measurement as a sign of Asakura dominance, of feudal "management" of Abaka, a reading with which I disagree. See Ono, "Hakkutsu sareta Sengoku jidai no machiya," 118.

> People make and use things for a vast array of reasons. Naming a few of
> those uses indicates the complexity: the need for warmth, to leave a
> physical mark of their presence, the desire for beauty, the urge to
> express pain, the need for a surface upon which to sleep or a
> receptacle in which to cook. Sometimes only an object will do –
> words, in whatever form, cannot keep the rain off one's head or
> hunger at bay.   —Leora Auslander, "Historians and the Study of
> Material Culture"

Archaeological sites yield many forms of historical evidence.[1] Post holes
and stone foundations allow us to visualize the size and scope of buildings. Layers of paving materials show us the layout and width of roads
and alleys. Metal and wooden tools and building materials sometimes
survive as well, though the natural degradation effected by time and the
elements tends to eliminate these forms of material evidence from all but
the most unusual archaeological sites. By far the most ubiquitous forms
found at urban and residential archaeological sites are ceramics, the most
important and useful genre of excavated material culture. Due to their
unique "temporal tenacity,"[2] ceramic objects represent a tangible record
of varied historical forces and events waiting to be read by scholars along
with documentary evidence. Compared with paper, wood, glass, and
metal, ceramics possess a greater durability. Once fired in the high temperatures of a kiln, the clay undergoes a chemical transformation that fixes
its form in a permanent signature. Even when no longer used, the resulting
ceramic objects are most often given away, broken into pieces (called
shards or sherds), or buried, where they are preserved until excavated
and documented by archaeologists, becoming an invaluable historical

---

[1] Some paragraphs in this chapter were previously published in Morgan Pitelka, "Chinese
Ceramics and Warrior Sociability in Sixteenth-Century Japan," in *Around Chigusa: Tea
and the Arts of Sixteenth-Century Japan*, ed. Dora C. Y. Ching, Louise Allison Cort, and
Andrew M. Watsky (Princeton University Press, 2017), 53–70.
[2] Thomas J. Schlereth, "Material Culture and Cultural Research," in *Material Culture:
A Research Guide*, ed. Thomas J. Schlereth (University Press of Kansas, 1985), 8.

record. Such records of the production, exchange, and consumption of ceramics represent a huge body of potential historical evidence, particularly valuable when used together with documentary sources.

As we shall see below, ceramics were abundant in Ichijōdani, both those produced domestically and those imported from China and Korea. Medieval Japan was awash in ceramics. Archaeologists have identified more than eighty kilns across the archipelago that were active between the late Heian and Muromachi periods, which produced a wide range of functional wares. These included sake flasks with narrow necks that were glazed and fired to a high temperature; large vats that were fired to a high temperature and decorated with natural ash glaze and used for storage; and unglazed, high-temperature mortars used in food preparation, among many other varieties.[3] Some of these domestically produced wares became fashionable in the late fifteenth century among tea practitioners, as seen in Murata Shukō's admonition in "Letter from the Heart" that all but the most experienced tea practitioners should avoid using domestic Shigaraki and Bizen wares.[4] Most common were low-temperature or earthenware vessels used for the rituals of daily life as well as shrine and altar offerings, though these were not high-status objects of the sort collected by elite warriors. Most of the ceramics produced domestically were used for storage and as tableware until the growing interest in tea ceramics in the sixteenth century spurred new production styles and centers.

Imported ceramics also circulated in large quantities throughout the medieval period and occupied most of the attention of elite warrior collectors looking for high-status objects. Large shipments of ceramics and other goods from China are known to have made their way to Japanese ports such as Hakata in the late Heian and early medieval periods.[5] The excavation of the Sinan medieval merchant shipwreck off the coast of South Korea, for example, yielded more than 20,000 pieces of ceramics (mostly Chinese), along with specie, precious wood, metal goods, and other objects, from a vessel that had set out with materials for temples in Japan in 1323.[6] The import of Chinese ceramics further increased during the time of the Ashikaga shogunate, when trade with

---

[3] Miho Museum ed., *Kotō no fu, chūsei no yakimono: Rokukoyō to sono shūhen* (Miho Museum, 2010).

[4] Dennis Hirota, *Wind in the Pines: Classic Writings of the Way of Tea as a Buddhist Path* (Asian Humanities Press, 1995), 198.

[5] Saeki Kōji, "Chinese Trade Ceramics in Medieval Japan," trans. Peter Shapinsky, in *Tools of Culture: Japan's Cultural, Intellectual, Medical, and Technological Contacts in East Asia, 1000s–1500s,* ed. Andrew Edmund Goble, Kenneth R. Robinson, and Haruko Wakabayashi (Association for Asian Studies, 2009), 163–182.

[6] Tōkyō Kokuritsu Hakubutsukan, *Shinan kaitei hikiage bunbutsu* (Chūnichi Shinbunm Shinbunsha, 1983). In English, see Wondong Kim, "Chinese Ceramics from the Wreck

China was officially licensed. This is seen in the excavation of extremely large quantities of Chinese (and, to a lesser extent, Korean and Southeast Asian) ceramics from consumer sites across Japan, ranging from Hakata in the south to Niigata in the north, and in particular urban sites in western Japan, such as Kyoto, Osaka, and Sakai.[7] Certainly, tea bowls, tea caddies, jars, vases, and flasks in a variety of shapes and styles were widely available to elite warrior collectors, as well as aristocrats, shrine and temple priests, and others with the means and interest in acquiring high-quality ceramics.

Collectively, ceramics and other forms of material culture excavated at Ichijōdani and similar sites illuminate the interconnected systems of production and circulation in late medieval Japan that linked regions within provinces, provinces within Japan, and Japan with neighboring cultures. But they also provide a window into the production and consumption of goods within Ichijōdani, a rare picture of daily life in provincial urban centers that is unmediated by the vagaries of the written record. Diary entries, letters, and other forms of documentary evidence often represent a highly edited or idealized version of daily practice: what the author should have been doing rather than what the author was doing. Materials excavated from trash pits, from wells, from ditches, and from moats reveal hints of the consumption patterns of urban inhabitants unvarnished by ambition or ideology.

In the case of Ichijōdani, as in most archaeological sites, archaeologists unearthed layers of evidence from each site. Layers of material usually correspond to different periods in the history of the site, and the analysis of this stratigraphy allows the materials to be roughly dated. Environmental changes and catastrophic environmental events can be used to date different layers, making the ash that is deposited after a major volcanic eruption, for example, useful in the delineation of layers in the stratigraphy. In Ichijōdani, of course, the major catastrophic event was the destruction of the city itself in 1573. Furthermore, most of the material evidence discussed in this chapter comes from the layers after 1510, when the Asakura seem to have adjusted the layout of the city in response to political shifts at home and outside the valley.[8] There were thus only sixty years or so in which the residents of the city occupied the basic layout of streets, shops, temples, and homes that we see represented

---

of a Yuan Ship in Sinan, Korea; with Particular Reference to Celadon Wares" (PhD dissertation, University of Kansas, 1986).
[7] Ono Masatoshi, *Nihon shutsudo no bōeki tōji*, 5 vols. (Kokuritsu Rekishi Minzoku Hakubutsukan, 1993–1994).
[8] Iwata Takashi, "Ichijōdani no shōhi to ryūtsū," in Mizuno and Satō, eds., *Sengoku daimyō Asakura shi to Ichijōdani*, 224–225.

in the excavations, with the preponderance of materials coming from the final years of the life of the town. Yet this limitation does not impair our ability to read the rhythms of daily life from the material remains of the valley. Ichijōdani in its final six decades was a thriving provincial palace city, with a population estimated at 10,000 people.[9] More than 100 commoner townhouses (*machiya*) have been excavated from within the city gates, and four times that number have been found outside these walls; these, in turn, are only a fraction of the residences and shops that once covered the valley and its environs.

Material Culture and the Rhythms of Daily Life

The majority of goods with which people surrounded themselves in the late medieval period have not survived to the present, yet it is possible to use the few excavated remnants to paint a picture of daily life in provincial cities like Ichijōdani. This is possible because of the scientific processes that archaeologists employ in the unearthing, preservation, and analysis of material evidence from late medieval sites, as well as the comparative analysis that occurs in the decades following excavation. Combined with creative examination of visual materials such as the seventeenth-century genre painting *Illustrated Handscroll of Types of Artisans* (*Shokunin fūzoku emaki*),[10] which illustrates a range of urban laborers from the sixteenth and seventeenth centuries, including the makers of bows, braided ropes, fans, sword wrapping, koto, arrows, umbrellas, and so on, and sellers of ceramics, noodles, tobacco, and other products, we can begin to picture the daily life of residents of urban spaces like Ichijōdani.

Unfortunately, no diary of any resident of the city of Ichijōdani is extant, but we can guess, based on our understanding of the daily

[9] The figure of "10,000 people" is ubiquitous in Japanese scholarship about Ichijōdani, and seems to be an estimate based on analysis of gravestones as well as the number and size of residences in the decades before the destruction of the city in 1573. It often strikes people as an optimistically large number. Yet William Wayne Farris reminds us that in the second half of the medieval period, Japan witnessed an explosion of urbanization, with hundreds of new cities appearing in the documentary record after Ōnin. See his *Japan's Medieval Population: Famine, Fertility, and Warfare in a Transformative Age* (University of Hawai'i Press, 2006), 245. Many of those urban centers were large enough to sustain populations greater than 5,000 people, and some, like Ichijōdani, had 10,000 or more. It is worth noting that this is similar to the estimated populations of other small medieval cities found throughout the world. Budapest, for example, is estimated to have had a population of around 10,000 people in roughly the same period.

[10] In the collection of Kokuritsu Rekishi Minzoku Hakubutsukan (Rekihaku), viewable online: www.rekihaku.ac.jp/education_research/gallery/webgallery/shokunin_f/shokunin_f.html (accessed May 5, 2020).

routines of elites, at a rough approximation of an average daily schedule. Warrior routines, for example, are described in the "Code of Conduct of the Odawara Hōjō," a text attributed to Hōjō Sōun (1432–1519):

Get up at the hour of the Tiger [3:00–5:00 a.m.], wash, worship, dress tidily, and give instructions to your wife, children, and retainers concerning the day's tasks; then begin attending to your duties before the sixth watch [i.e., before 6:00 a.m.]. Before you wash yourself in the morning, take a look from the toilet room and view the stables and gardens to the area in front of the gateway. First of all, tell those in charge which places should be cleaned up; next, use the washing water quickly; and, though water is a plentiful commodity, do not waste quantities of it for mere mouth-rinsing.[11]

Warriors then proceeded to their primary duty: attendance, or service, to the their superior; in Ichijōdani, this usually would have meant working at the Asakura residence or one of the Asakura family residences. At the end of the day, a warrior returned to his own property and ensured that it continued to operate effectively:

In the evening, at the sixth watch [i.e., at 6:00 p.m.], you should order the gateway to be closed. When people come in or go out, have it opened, but otherwise keep it shut .... In the evening, the fires in the kitchens and the living quarters should be inspected. You should issue strict orders to that effect and do the rounds in person. Further, inculcate the habit of watching out for spreading fire.

Sōun also notes that it goes without saying that warriors should dedicate themselves to religious practice as well as to the arts of war and culture, so we can assume that in the evening warriors engaged in religious rituals, study, letter writing, and so on. In the case of an artisan or shopkeeper who might not have servants, the basic routine of waking, washing, dressing, eating, inspecting one's residence and workplace, working, and then retiring for the day to religious ritual, pleasurable practices, another meal, and sleep is likely to apply. Even if we account for individual variation, this schedule probably fits most groups of urban residents, and provides a framework for us to examine the material culture from Ichijōdani and similar sites.

Let us begin with the first actions of the day: using the toilet and getting dressed. Archaeologists in Japan long struggled to definitively identify structures in sites as toilets, but in 1980 the first concrete discovery was made in Ichijōdani. A small structure with a roof and a large, subterranean, stone-lined tank for collecting waste was excavated,

---

[11] Translation from Carl Steenstrup, "Hojo Soun's Twenty-One Articles: The Code of Conduct of the Odawara Hojo," *Monumenta Nipponica* 29.3 (Autumn, 1974): 283–303.

and this seems to be one rare example of the remains of a communal toilet. Most residents may have used chamber pots or temporary toilet facilities outside, but the details are not known.[12] Over the course of decades of excavations in the valley, hundreds of toilets have been unearthed.

Residents next needed to decide on the clothes they would wear for the day, appropriate to their occupation and status. Material evidence here is rare; textiles are of course relatively fragile and are less likely to survive the depredations of war, fire, and burial than ceramics. Archaeologists were able to excavate a few fragments of cloth, such as cords used for tying garments and pieces of what appear to be indigo-dyed cotton. Although only a relatively recent transplant in Japan, having arrived in the fifteenth century via Korea,[13] cotton was popular among commoners alongside the preexisting ramie fiber because it was easier to wash, softer against the skin, and had multiple uses: as undergarments, as insulation in winter clothes in the form of cotton batting, and as comfortable, casual clothing.[14] Silk textiles were higher status but also higher maintenance, and were probably limited largely to elite warriors in provincial cities. The remarkable survival of cotton cloth in Ichijōdani's sites points to its widespread use by a majority of urban residents.

In another example, excavation of a commoner townhouse revealed a bundle of what appeared to be carbonized hemp, which promptly disintegrated when exposed to the atmosphere. Furthermore, in excavations of the Hirai neighborhood, archaeologists unearthed a fulling block (*kinuta*) from a warrior residence well, which was used for the preparation of hemp cloth. We thus have some evidence that both cotton and hemp cloth were commonly used in Ichijōdani. In addition, archaeologists found a range of tools and components associated with the production and maintenance of clothing, a reminder that in premodern Japan clothing was constantly patched, repaired, and reused. In excavations of commoner townhouses, archaeologists discovered three spindle bases, a spinning wheel, scissors, embroidery needles, and a diamond-shaped spool of thread.[15]

[12] Iwata Takashi, "Ichijōdani Asakura Shi iseki no benjo ikō ni tsuite," in *Kiyō 1999* (Fukui Kenritsu Ichijōdani Asakura Shi Iseki Shiryōkan, 2000). See also Iwamoto Shōji, *Kusado Sengen* (Kibito Shuppan, 2000), 79, for a discussion of toilet sites (and the general lack of archaeological evidence) in Kusado Sengen.

[13] Originally introduced in 799, cotton was not widely cultivated and employed until this second reintroduction from Korea. See Charlotte von Verschuer, *Rice, Agriculture, and the Food Supply in Premodern Japan* (Routledge, 2016), 26.

[14] Susan Hanley, *Everyday Things in Premodern Japan: The Hidden Legacy of Material Culture* (University of California Press, 1997), 94–95.

[15] Iwata, "Ichijōdani no shōhi to ryūtsū," 207–211.

Figure 2.1 Excavated Echizen jar, Ichijōdani.
Used with permission of the Fukui Prefectural Ichijōdani Asakura
Family History Museum.

Also significant for understanding the production and maintenance of clothing in Ichijōdani is the presence of multiple dyer townhouses, which combined the residence with the shop. Altogether ten potential sites have been discovered, marked by the presence of large Echizen ceramic jars (Figure 2.1) in a variety of patterns. Some of these sites revealed jars lined up in rows, while others were home to jars that had been partially buried, and archaeologists have speculated that the former represent layouts appropriate for dyeing while the latter may have been associated with the brewing and distillation of sake.

Thus, four of the ten townhouses with numerous large Echizen jars appear to have been dyers, making them one of the most common types of artisan shops in the city. Such shops played a key role in the multistage process of acquiring clothing such as a gown (*kosode*). Consumers would have purchased raw cloth from as yet unidentified textile shops in Ichijōdani, and then delivered the cloth to be colored at a dyer's shop. Then, this cloth would have been tailored at a separate shop, which included shaping the gown, lining it if padded, and preparing it to be worn. This process could take several weeks and could be quite expensive, depending on the materials of both the garment and its lining and/or padding.[16] Regardless, residents would have dressed in multiple layers in the cold of winter, including undergarments, a gown (such as a *kosode*), a jacket (*dōbuku*), and/or depending on gender and occupation, pants (*hakama*); and fewer layers, perhaps as little as pants and a loosely tied robe, in the summer.[17] The quality, detailing, styles, and durability of these garments would have varied greatly by occupation, status, and wealth. Samurai reporting for duty would have worn armor, as seen, for example, in fragments of a sleeve of armor excavated from a warrior residence located at the base of an observation tower in the city.[18] The remains include four rows of thirty-seven overlapping platelets (*kozane*) made of leather and hardened with black lacquer. The bottom row is additionally decorated with red lacquer.

According to genre paintings showing city life in the sixteenth century, while some people commuted and worked barefoot, many also wore straw sandals (*waraji*), thonged sandals (*zōri*), or indeed wooden clogs (*geta*). This final category of footwear is well represented in the excavated materials; archaeologists have discovered various examples of wooden clogs of a range of heights in excavations of sites in Ichijōdani, particularly former ditches and moats that originally had higher moisture content, which resulted in better preservation of fibrous materials. More than 100 examples have been found over the many years of excavations, made using a range of techniques. Some are carved from a single piece of wood, while others contain numerous wooden parts that are carefully joined together. Those with short "teeth" (the two wooden supporting blocks that extend from the flat base to the ground) were probably used for traversing the garden or going to the toilet, while those with longer teeth – as much as fifteen centimeters – were helpful for traversing town during periods of heavy snowfall, as was common each winter in Echizen, part of Japan's famed "snow country" (*yukiguni*).[19]

In addition to dressing, applying makeup was an important routine for many urban residents, not only elites but commoners as well. Excavations of Ichijōdani yielded a range of containers and tools associated with one of the best-known premodern Japanese makeup practices:

[16] Iwata, "Ichijōdani no shōhi to ryūtsū," 207–211.
[17] Izutsu Gafu, *Genshoku Nihon fukushoku-shi* (Kōrinsha Shuppan, 1989), 150–192, provides a helpful, illustrated overview of clothing styles in late medieval Japan.
[18] See object G008 in the collection of the Ichijōdani Asakura Family History Museum, found in excavation no. 104 in the Saitō residence. http://asakura-museum.pref.fukui.lg .jp/040_gallery/detail.php?id=8 (accessed May 2, 2021).
[19] Iwata Takashi, "Sengoku ki o aruita geta," in *Jitsuzō no Sengoku jōkamachi Echizen Ichijiodani*, ed. Ono Masatoshi (Heibonsha, 1990), 128–132.

the blackening of teeth (*ohaguro*).[20] Though originally an aristocratic practice limited primarily to adults, many warrior families adopted the blackening of the teeth of daughters, perhaps as a form of competitive grooming to prepare them for marriage. Archaeologists excavated some small Echizen-ware ceramic jars containing traces of iron indicating that they held the dissolved iron solution (*kanemizu*) used for tooth-blackening. Metal containers with a similar function and copper plates that were used for the application of the dyeing agents have been discovered as well. Chinese-manufactured porcelain plates and copper plates used in the application of makeup such as white powder (*oshiroi*), popular among elite women, some men, and aspirational commoners including successful artisans and merchants, were also found. Last, tools used for applying makeup as well as maintaining the proper hairstyle were abundant, including bronze mirrors, iron scissors and knives, hairpins, and tweezers.[21] We should not underestimate the significance accorded to this morning ritual, as one's exterior appearance played a major role in social negotiations and the maintenance of political standing in a status-conscious society like sixteenth-century Japan. The act of dressing and grooming was inherently understood to be political and powerful; it also was a way of distinguishing oneself in terms of status and economic means.

Next, most city residents probably turned to the preparation and consumption of the first meal of the day. In truth, we do not know what this meal consisted of. Food is by its very nature ephemeral, and the primary source of calories for most residents of Ichijōdani – cereals such as rice, millet, wheat, barley, and buckwheat, as well as a range of farmed and foraged vegetables, fruits, and tubers – rarely survive even in waste pit sites. The seeds of eggplants and melons and the pits of apricots and peaches are notable exceptions; these were found in great abundance in excavations of middens and toilet pits.[22] We can speculate that like other medieval Japanese, the residents of Ichijōdani foraged, cultivated, and ate fruits and nuts such as chestnuts, walnuts, pine nuts, pear, fig, and plum; as well as vegetables such as cucumber, turnip, lettuce, sorrel, chives, and mustard greens. They also made oil out of sesame, perilla, hemp, and Fagara.[23] But what about protein?

---

[20] See Sue Tomoko, "Girei sahō to shite no keshō," in Shiseidō, *Nihon no keshō bunka* (Shiseidō, 2007), 139–166, which examines the practice of tooth blackening.
[21] Mizuno, "Ichijōdani no kurashi," 236–237.
[22] Iwata, "Ichijōdani no shōhi to ryūtsū," 211.
[23] Verschuer, *Rice, Agriculture, and the Food Supply*, 197–199.

Archaeologists in Ichijōdani have found and analyzed the remains of a range of mammals, birds, fish, and shellfish in different excavation sites. Despite imperial decrees banning the consumption of meat in previous centuries, it is clear from late medieval sites such as Ichijōdani that meat continued to play an important role in the Japanese diet. Deer remains were the most plentiful among all mammal remains, and it appears that these common animals were widely hunted in the hills and mountains of Echizen and then brought into the city to provide meat. The skin and horn were used in the manufacture and repair of military garb as well as in other trades. About one-third as many dog remains were found as deer, but they were arranged in proper burial formations, which led archaeologists to posit that these were raised as pets rather than harvested as food. Medieval Japanese did sometimes consume dog meat, as excavations of the mercantile settlement Kusado Sengen have shown.[24] In Ichijōdani, however, it appears these animals were domesticated as companions and helpers.[25]

Archaeologists excavated a range of bird remains as well, with chicken being the most plentiful; surprisingly to modern readers, for whom chicken is a common part of the global diet, scholars speculate that in Ichijōdani these birds were raised for show or for cock-fighting rather than for food.[26] The other fowl remains, fewer in number, probably represented wild fowl that were hunted and eaten as an unusual and special delicacy: bean goose, wild goose, and duck are all examples found in the town. A single eagle carcass was recovered as well, perhaps the remains of a bird that a warrior raised for use in falconry. Certainly, the Asakura themselves practiced falconry, and they also famously took the hobby even further. Asakura Norikage (also known as Sōteki, 1477–1555) successfully bred and raised falcons rather than capturing them in the wild.[27] The poet Sōchō visited Norikage in 1524, writing (as I will discuss further in Chapter 3) that he successfully hatched falcon chicks, to the surprise of all.[28]

Fish remains were by far the most common form of food excavated from the sites in Ichijōdani, with sea bream alone accounting for

---

[24] Matsui Akira, "Sakan datta nikushoku," in Amino et al., *Yomigaeru chūsei*, vol. 8, 106–109.

[25] Iwata, "Ichijōdani no shōhi to ryūtsū," 212.

[26] This interpretation is supported by the lack of reference to chicken in medieval cookbooks and cutting manuals, as Eric Rath notes in *Food and Fantasy in Early Modern Japan* (University of California Press, 2010), 107.

[27] A monk recorded some details of the success of the Asakura in the text *Record of Cultivating Falcons (Yōyōki)*, which is transcribed in Hanawa Hokinoichi, ed., *Gunsho ruijū*, vol. 12 (Keizai Zashisha, 1905), 476–478.

[28] H. Mack Horton, *The Journal of Sōchō* (Stanford University Press, 2002), 45.

71 percent of recovered fish remains and 55 percent of all seafood remains. Sea bream was plentiful in the Sea of Japan off the Echizen coast and was likely imported to Ichijōdani in various formats depending on the season. This also tells us that the trading route from the Mikuni harbor was open, efficient, and commonly used. The next most common (though in far lower quantities) was the red gurnard, a bony, bottom-feeding fish popular today for sushi, sashimi, and in stews. Yellowtail, another widely consumed fish today, was also relatively common in the excavations. Also found, though often in very small quantities, were salmon, carp (the sole freshwater fish), cod, sea perch, fugu, flounder, striped mullet, and grouper. It is likely that more freshwater fish and common Sea of Japan fish (such as mackerel) were consumed in Ichijōdani, but their remains have not been found. This again speaks to the profoundly imperfect and contingent nature of archaeological evidence, particularly for an ephemeral form of material culture such as food.[29]

Last, shellfish remains were excavated, but not in the large quantities one might expect considering the quantity of fish that was consumed and the town's proximity to the coast. Abalone, for example, a popular delicacy in modern Japanese cuisine, was apparently considered sacred by the Asakura and thus was officially banned in Ichijōdani. Despite this ban, and perhaps pointing to the taste for the shellfish even in the sixteenth century, some abalone remains were excavated. Also, turban shell (*sazae*) was excavated in medium quantities, but this may be a result of the size and relative durability of the shell itself. Other shellfish – veined rapa whelk (*akanishi*), various types of clam, oyster, crab, and mussel – were discovered only in small quantities. We can speculate that residents did eat shellfish in abundance, but that the shells were used after the shellfish was consumed. It is also feasible that the merchants who supplied Ichijōdani with fish did not specialize in shellfish, but we lack the evidence to reach a solid conclusion.

A problem that is easier to address is how the residents of Ichijōdani prepared and served their food, largely because of the aforementioned durability of ceramics in the archaeological record and the survival of stone-constructed or, in some cases, wooden kitchen elements. At the beginning of the day, most residents would have started a fire in order to boil water for tea and food preparation. Furnaces (*kamado*) were not used in Ichijōdani as were sometimes found in other parts of medieval Japan; instead, sunken hearths and sunken fireplaces were common and have been excavated in great variety in residences across the status and

---

[29] Iwata, "Ichijōdani no shōhi to ryūtsū," 211–213.

economic spectrum. These stone-lined facilities provided both heat and a place to cook. From the huge dual hearths found in the Asakura kitchen, which measured two meters by one and a half meters each, to the tiny individual hearths found in the homes of most commoners, this basic structure was ubiquitous in the city. Likewise, for cooking and boiling water, residents exclusively used an iron pot with a handle. In other parts of Japan earthenware rice cookers and earthenware pots were common, but these are mostly not found in Ichijōdani.[30] In truth, even iron pots have rarely been found in the town's excavations, but this is because with use, pots developed holes that made them nonfunctional, and they were then recycled by returning them to a metal caster who would give a discount on the purchase of a new pot.[31]

Residents drew water from wells that were usually located inside the home or in a nearby garden. Most wells would have been framed by horizontal timber beams, interlocked to create a wall and ridge around the opening, or by vertical boards strapped together like a barrel. Alternatively, because high-quality stone was plentiful in Echizen, a stone well frame (also known as a well curb) was sometimes constructed for a more durable and rustic facility.[32] A post above the well, perhaps with a small roof, would have held a bucket on a rope or a bamboo pole for retrieving water from the depths. Such water was vital to the daily routine of households big and small, as Edward S. Morse describes in his *Japanese Homes and Their Surroundings* from 1886:

An enormous quantity of water is used in the kitchen of a Japanese house; and if the well is outside, then a trough is arranged beside the well, into which the water is poured, and from this trough a bamboo spout conveys the water into a big water-tank within the kitchen. In the vicinity of the well it is always wet and very sloppy; the vegetables, rice, dishes, and nearly every utensil and article of food seems to come under this deluge of water.

Morse's description of provincial homes and their kitchens, though written several centuries later, captures the style and rhythms of daily life from centuries earlier. He provides a sketch of a rural kitchen from Kabutoyama in Musashi Province that shows a handsome well, curbed by vertical boards in the style of a barrel, with a pulley system allowing easy access to the water beneath. A housewife wearing wooden clogs

[30] Ono Masatoshi, "Hibi no kurashi," in *Jitsuzō no Sengoku jōkamachi Echizen Ichijiodani*, ed. Ono Masatoshi (Heibonsha, 1990), 103–104.
[31] Iwata, "Ichijōdani no shōhi to ryūtsū," 221–222.
[32] See examples of excavated well frames from other sites in medieval Japan, as well as illustrated artists' renditions, in Kokuritsu Rekishi Minzoku Hakubutsukan, *Jidai o tsukutta waza: Chūsei no seisan kakumei* (Kokuritsu Rekishi Minzoku Hakubutsukan, 2013), 32–33.

Figure 2.2 Excavated mortar bowl, part of a mortar and
pestle set, Ichijōdani.
Used with permission of the Fukui Prefectural Ichijōdani Asakura
Family History Museum.

while on the dirt floor of the kitchen bends over the well to fetch water for
meal preparation.[33] Morse notes that "the kitchen is nearly three hundred years old," putting it squarely in the style of provincial homes of the
sixteenth century.[34]

Another food preparation tool that many would have used in the
morning, or when preparing meals later in the day, was the mortar
(*suribachi*), which archaeologists have found in huge numbers and in a
wide range of shapes and sizes (Figure 2.2). These ceramic bowls had
grooved patterns impressed into the interior, which the user would
scrape with a pestle (*surikogi*) – typically, a stout wooden rod – to make
miso paste, to mix sauces, to grind fish or meat into the correct consistency for dumplings, and so on. The quantity of mortar sherds, 130,000
pieces from inside the town gates, indicates that these tools were ubiqui-
tously deployed in every home in the town, and probably lasted just a
year or two because of regular and intense usage.[35] Archaeologists know
that Ichijōdani residents ate eggplants from the presence of their seeds in
excavations, so perhaps some townspeople started their day with a morning meal of freshly ground miso on cooked eggplant (*nasu dengaku*), a
food that we know was popular in the late sixteenth century.[36]

[33] The original sketch is at www.gutenberg.org/cache/epub/52868/images/fig167.jpg.
[34] Edward Sylvester Morse, *Japanese Homes and Their Surroundings* (Ticknor and
    Company, 1886), 186–188.
[35] Iwata breaks down the numbers in "Ichijōdani no shōhi to ryūtsū," 222.
[36] Okada Tetsu, *Nabemono kigen jiten* (Chikuma Shobō, 2013), 305.

Evidence for how food was served and contained is of course voluminous. The primary types of dishes excavated from warrior residences,
commoner townhouses, and temple sites were celadon ceramics, iron-
glazed ceramics, ash-glazed ceramics, white porcelains, blue and white
porcelains, and lacquerware. Let us begin with celadons, a category of
ceramics that in medieval Japan implied luxury. Technically, the term
"celadon" refers to a lime-glazed ware ranging in color from green to
blue, with a clay body that can vary from an iron-bearing stoneware to a
pure-white porcelain. The designation thus signifies a particular genre of
glazed ceramics rather than a particular kiln or even a strictly defined clay
body. Potters developed celadons in China over the course of centuries
of experimentation with ash glazes. Gradually, the distinctive blue-green
coloration and subtle translucence of a particular range of ash glazes
became recognized in China and were produced for consumption by
the imperial court. The Song dynasty (960–1279) was a high point for the
production of these diverse courtly wares, with multiple kiln complexes –
the Ru kilns, the Guan kilns, the Yaozhou kilns, the Yuezhou kilns, and
the Longquan kilns – manufacturing celadons for widespread elite and
limited mass consumption.[37] Korea, too, produced remarkable celadons
throughout the Goryeo Dynasty (918–1392) that were widely appreciated not only by Korean elites but in China and Japan as well. The
Goryeo celadons were said to contain a "secret color" that was virtually
indescribable and carving that was "the most extraordinary among the
various ceramics vessels," according to one Chinese observer.[38]

In sixteenth-century Japan, celadons were associated with luxury and
sophistication. A famous picture scroll from the fifteenth century, the
aforementioned *Fukutomi zōshi*, tells the amusing story of a commoner
couple who developed surprising and sudden wealth because of the
husband's virtuosic flatulence. The artists who produced the scroll represented the couple's rapid ascent into the ranks of the newly rich by
placing celadon ceramics around them in their home, indicating that
these imported, Chinese-manufactured objects symbolized social status
and prestige in an idiom that commoners (and the various elite readers of
the scroll) would have recognized.[39] Likewise, early tea diaries from the

[37] See Rose Kerr, *Song Dynasty Ceramics* (V & A Publications, 2004), for a broad overview,
   and in Chinese, see Zhu Boqian, *Longquanyao Qingci* (Yishujia Chubanshe, 1998), for an
   example of modern scholarship on a particular style of celadon.
[38] Itoh Ikutaro, "Korean Ceramics of the Koryo and Choson Dynasties," trans. Morgan
   Pitelka, in Itoh Ikutaro, *Korean Ceramics from the Museum of Oriental Ceramics, Osaka*
   (Metropolitan Museum of Art, 2000), 10.
[39] Kokuritsu Rekishi Minzoku Hakubutsukan, *Tōjiki no bunkashi* (Kokuritsu Rekishi
   Minzoku Hakubutsukan, 1998), 138.

Figure 2.3 Excavated celadon incense burner (Chinese), Ichijōdani.
Used with permission of the Fukui Prefectural Ichijōdani Asakura
Family History Museum.

sixteenth century indicate that celadons were among the most desirable
form of imported ceramics for use in tea gatherings and similar high-
status social events, which often included warriors, elite commoners, and
Buddhist priests. The early tea innovator Murata Jukō (1423–1502), the
so-called father of rustic (*wabi*) tea practice, for example, was known to
use celadon tea bowls in his tea practice; in fact, today, dozens of extant
celadon bowls known as "Jukō celadon bowls" can be found in museum
collections in Japan, and twenty-three references to these or similar
works can be found in tea diaries between 1542 and 1575.[40] In short,
we should expect to find plentiful examples of celadon ceramics in
Ichijōdani, particularly in the locations where tea culture was likely
practiced, such as the residence of the Asakura.

It is interesting to note, therefore, that in Ichijōdani, archaeologists
found celadon ceramics primarily in commoner townhouses, as well as in
Buddhist temple complexes, more than in warrior residences. A celadon
incense burner (Figure 2.3) excavated from a temple site near the Asuwa
River is an excellent example of just such a high-quality Chinese product.
In fact, the distribution of ceramics across the different groups of sites in
Ichijōdani is surprising in many ways and shows that consumption patterns differed greatly not only by status but also by region. Each medieval
city was unique. Despite the association of imported celadon with luxury,
only 805 pieces were excavated form the Asakura residence and

---

[40] Koyama Masato, "Jukō chawan no kyomō," in *Kyoto-fu Maizō Bunkazai Ronshū*, vol. 6
(Kyoto-fu Maizō Bunkazai Chōsa Kenkyū Sentaa, 2010), 365.

Figure 2.4 Excavated celadon platter (Chinese), Ichijōdani.
Used with permission of the Fukui Prefectural Ichijōdani Asakura
Family History Museum.

surrounding family residences and structures. By contrast, 1,411 celadon
pieces were excavated from commoner townhouses and 1,039 from the
main temple complex and the residences around it. We can thus speculate that it was not uncommon for a family of merchants or artisans, or a
group of Buddhist priests, to serve food on an attractive, incised platter
decorated with a luscious green celadon glaze (Figure 2.4) as a kind of
daily ritual. Perhaps the relative durability of celadon wares made them
more attractive for the working commoner elites who occupied the townhouses of the city. Or perhaps trends in ceramic consumption in the mid
to late sixteenth century simply led the warrior rulers of the city to
purchase less of this particular style.[41]

Even more voluminous than celadons were porcelains, which were
imported primarily from China until the beginning of domestic
Japanese manufacture of this style in the seventeenth century, long after
the destruction of Ichijōdani. Porcelain is defined as a ceramic with a
pure white clay body, covered with a clear glaze and fired to more than
1,200°C, making it more vitrified (converted into glass) than any other
form of ceramic. Porcelains first appeared in China in the sixth century
and were consistently developed and improved over the centuries. They
became widely distributed in China and were exported across Asia and
even as far as the Middle East as a key commodity that flowed along the

---

[41] Iwata, "Ichijōdani no shōhi to ryūtsū," 214.

many routes of the Silk Road and its maritime counterparts. Japanese archaeologists divide porcelains into two broad categories in the analysis of excavated materials: white porcelain (*hakuji*), which refers to wares such as Ding or Xing, and blue and white porcelain (*seika* or *sometsuke*), which refers primarily to porcelains produced in the imperial Jingdezhen kilns, decorated with underglazed cobalt-blue designs and motifs as well as more complicated markings such as imperial reign marks.

Porcelain dishes and plates were found in large quantities in the various types of warrior sites in Ichijōdani, with the largest concentration being white porcelain plates. In the Asakura residence, for example, archaeologists excavated 264 celadon plate fragments, 366 blue and white porcelain plate fragments, and 1,208 white porcelain plate fragments. As a portion of all of the ceramic tableware found in warrior residences, porcelain was the greatest in number. Porcelain dishes were also found in extremely large numbers in commoner townhouses and temple sites, meaning that the distribution of this form of Chinese ceramics was consistent across status groups, unlike celadon, which despite its luxurious connotations, was more popular in commoner sites. For scholars of regional trade, this evidence is helpful to understand the flow of Chinese commodities around Asia, but for the purpose of imagining daily life in a late medieval provincial palace city, it also paints a powerful image. Based on the archaeological evidence, we can confidently visualize members of the Asakura family eating meals off imported Chinese porcelains, such as a low blue and white porcelain dish (Figure 2.5) that might have been used to hold steamed vegetables or pickles, on a daily basis. Likewise, in the shops and residences of commoner artisans and merchants throughout the city, we can envision a more eclectic assemblage of tableware, with celadon dishes and porcelain plates holding different food items at mealtime, not unlike the plethora of ceramic dishes we are likely to encounter in a restaurant in Japan today.[42]

Two other types of ceramics merit our attention. The first is another category of imported Chinese pottery, known as iron-black or Jian ware, produced in the Fujian and Jiangxi regions of China.[43] The color of these stonewares in fact ranged from light brown to black depending on the content of iron in the glaze and clay, as well as the atmospheric conditions during the firing of the kiln. It was the range of colors and decorative effects in the glazes that seems to have made these ceramics popular in Japan, particularly for tea drinking. Jian tea bowls (known as *kensan* in

[42] Iwata, "Ichijōdani no shōhi to ryūtsū," 214.
[43] See Hasebe Gakuji, "An Introduction to Song Ceramics" (trans. Maiko Behr), in *Sōjiten* (Asahi Shinbunsha, 1999), 30–35.

Figure 2.5 Excavated blue and white (*somestsuke*) bowl
(Chinese), Ichijōdani.
Used with permission of the Fukui Prefectural Ichijōdani Asakura
Family History Museum.

early medieval documentation and as *tenmoku* in most later tea records)
were highly valued for their black and brown glazes that showed iridescent patterns, lustrous silver threads, oil-spot patterns, and in some cases
elaborate crystallization, all of which resulted from the contingent chemical processes of the firing; as a result certain patterns were rare and thus
became highly sought after by tea practitioner collectors in Japan. These
ceramics were imported to Japan as early as the Kamakura period,
around the twelfth century, are found in various medieval sites, and are
also mentioned in documentation associated with tea drinking.[44] Part of
the appeal of an iron-black glazed tea bowl, we must remember, was that
the lustrous green of the frothy, powdered tea (*matcha*) was even more
beautiful when contrasted against the variegated brown and black glaze
of the bowl (Figure 2.6). In Ichijōdani, a range of iron-black glazed wares
has been excavated, though not in quantities that are comparable to
porcelain tableware. In the Asakura residence, for example, 444 pieces
of iron-black glazed bowls were unearthed, while in townhouse sites
615 pieces were found, and in the main temple complex site, 777 pieces
were excavated.[45] The implication of this discovery is that tea drinking
was ubiquitous across status groups, but was practiced most regularly or
by the largest number of people around the Buddhist temples of the city.
This should come as no surprise when we consider the entangled history

[44] See Nishida Hiroko, "Tenmoku: The World of Iron-Black Glazed Ceramics Preserved
in Japan" (trans. Martha J. McClintock), in *Sōjiten* (Asahi Shinbunsha, 1999).
[45] Iwata, "Ichijōdani no shōhi to ryūtsū," 214–215.

Figure 2.6 Excavated shard of an iron-black glazed stoneware
bowl (Chinese, Jian ware), Ichijōdani.
Used with permission of the Fukui Prefectural Ichijōdani Asakura
Family History Museum.

of tea culture and Buddhism or the close linkage of Buddhist material
culture and the art of the world of tea.

The final type of ceramics used at the table was ash-glazed wares, a
rather broad description of utilitarian ceramics made in Japan and fired
to allow natural ash from the wood that fueled the kiln to decorate and
seal the pots, producing naturalistic effects. Styles varied widely, ranging
from ceramics with very little ash glaze to those with heavy deposits.
Ceramics in this tradition were increasingly being appropriated by tea
practitioners for innovative uses in tea gatherings, but the ash-glazed
wares that I am referring to here are simple, inexpensive plates and dishes
used at the table, not those mixed and matched by tea practitioners.
These wares were most common in the townhouses found outside the
city gates, the less central communities of merchants and shopkeepers
who were perhaps less wealthy than those able to live in the main
neighborhoods of the city. For example, 267 sherds of ash-glazed plates
were excavated from townhouses outside the city gates, compared with
just 59 celadon plate remains, 215 white porcelain plate remains, and
142 blue and white plate sherds.[46] As a ratio of the total, the cheaper,
more utilitarian ash-glazed wares thus seem to have been more important
to the daily habits of Ichijōdani residents with less economic means.

In addition to ceramic tableware, archaeologists have discovered
lacquered wooden dish remains in quantities that indicate that these
forms of bowls and plates may have been as common in the homes of

---

[46] Iwata, "Ichijōdani no shōhi to ryūtsū," 214–215.

Figure 2.7 Excavated lacquerware (Japanese), Ichijōdani.
Used with permission of the Fukui Prefectural Ichijōdani Asakura
Family History Museum.

Ichijōdani as the pottery styles discussed above. This is not to suggest that lacquerware – which is made by applying a treated sap coating to wooden vessels in multiple layers – is as durable as ceramics. In fact, it is only in damp excavation sites that lacquered objects have any hope of surviving the vicissitudes of time and decay. Yet such sites (like the area around the Asakura residence, which had both moats and a wet kitchen that used a large amount of water) are not uncommon in Ichijōdani, and as a result it appears that lacquerware made up as much as 25 percent of the tableware in some sites. If we remove the iron-black glazed bowls that were so popular for tea drinking from this group, we find that lacquerware bowls made up 36 percent of the tableware used for consuming food. Lacquerware was somewhat expensive, and thus is excavated less frequently from commoner sites, but in the Asakura residence and the complexes of high-ranking warriors, it seems these wares may have outnumbered ceramics at the table (Figure 2.7). The highest quality pieces used Japanese zelkova for the wooden interior, while more common pieces use Japanese horse chestnut or Japanese beech. Archaeologists have speculated that the higher-quality pieces were imported from Kyoto, while the more numerous and more popular pieces were produced elsewhere in Echizen.[47]

---

[47] Iwata, "Ichijōdani no shōhi to ryūtsū," 217–218.

After the morning meal, the residents of Ichijōdani next would have embarked on the work that would occupy them for most of the day, and this of course varied by status and occupation. Archaeologists have excavated a range of tools that point to some of the labor that occurred in the city, including occupations that involved production as well as fundamental work such as the maintenance of the household. One of the most common examples is the Echizen-ware large jar (Figure 2.1). Archaeologists discovered remains of these pots in many sites across Ichijōdani, sometimes clustered together in groups as mentioned above. Elite warrior residences often had five or six jars, which they probably used for storing foodstuffs such as miso and sake.[48] Commoner artisans such as dyers likewise had numerous Echizen jars in their townhouses. In addition, broken jars were found in lower layers of many sites, pointing to the fact that these vessels, despite their remarkable durability, had a limited lifespan, estimated to be twenty to fifty years. If vessels cracked because of accidents or cold weather, their owners repaired them with cloth and lacquer, but eventually they ceased to function and had to be discarded. This explains the discovery of as many as thirty jars in certain locations, not arranged for daily use but rather heaped together in a trash pit, a kind of resting place for these vital ceramic tools that played a major role in the lives of the town's residents.

Large Echizen jars have been excavated in many sites throughout the valley, and often help us to identify the occupation of the inhabitants. But in addition to dyers and the doctor and Buddhist bead maker discussed earlier, archaeologists have also discovered signs of artisans such as tailors, lacquerers, carpenters, and earthenware potters. Looking more broadly at urban sites throughout Japan, archaeologists have excavated tools of a startling variety: metal, bone, and stone dishes used in food preparation alongside the more common ceramic vessels I discussed above.[49] Rare examples of the tools of a lacquermaker were excavated from the trading town of Kusado Sengen, including a lacquered paper bucket that would have held the liquid lacquer, and a brush for repeatedly applying it to a wooden base in thin layers.[50] Various examples of the finished lacquerware product were of course excavated from sites in Ichijōdani, including a fine lobed red container in the shape of a chrysanthemum and a luxurious black lacquered comb produced using the *maki-e* technique, in which gold powder was sprinkled into the layers of lacquer.[51] Lacquer-makers often used wooden vessels that were turned

---

[48] Iwata, "Ichijōdani no shōhi to ryūtsū," 223.
[49] Kokuritsu, *Jidai o tsukutta waza*, 20–21.   [50] Kokuritsu, *Jidai o tsukutta waza*, 36.
[51] Kokuritsu, *Jidai o tsukutta waza*, 38.

by specialist woodworkers, who used a hand-powered lathe to spin a piece of wood and carve it into a round and hollowed form. Metal tools for cutting wood into boards and other forms likewise have been excavated from Kusado Sengen, including toothed blades with sharp points, a flat back, and a machete-like shape.[52] Hatchets, sickles, hoes, and other daily tools have also been recovered. In the snowy winter, Ichijōdani's residents must have spent a great deal of time using such tools to remove snow from the roof, to prevent damage to their homes.

Ichijōdani residents also found time for relaxing activities that ranged from games to study of the arts. Archaeologists have excavated a huge sampling of examples, but the most abundant is perhaps again the category of ceramics that points to the central role of tea ritual, or *chanoyu*, in the lives of many elite residents. The palace of the Asakura under Yoshikage, the last head of the family, included decorative features in the *shoin-zukuri* style that incorporated the built-in innovations of Ashikaga palaces, such as the decorative alcove and staggered shelves. These rooms could be used for tea gatherings, and faced a strolling garden with a pond. Excavations yielded substantial quantities of high-quality tea utensils, particularly ceramics, which in some cases exceeded those noted in the documentary record. The range and depth of the collection are notable. Excavated wares include Ding porcelains, Longquan celadons, Jingdezhen porcelains, Jian-ware tea bowls, and many other varieties of ceramics from China. Additionally, archaeologists found inlaid Goryeo celadon from Korea. Among the excavated imported wares, some of the pieces recovered were already antiques at the time of their usage in the sixteenth century, having been imported to Japan hundreds of years earlier.[53]

One particularly abundant site is a former elite warrior residence (site 57) not far from the Asakura palace, probably the home of a retainer of the warlord. Archaeologists unearthed a range of Chinese tea wares from this site, including iron-black glazed tea bowls and two large and one medium-sized tea-leaf storage jars.[54] These materials indicate that not only the Asakura themselves but also their elite retainers collected a range

---

[52] Kokuritsu, *Jidai o tsukutta waza*, 47.

[53] For a summary of excavated tea ceramics, see Ono Masatoshi, *Jitsuzō no Sengoku jōkamachi Echizen Ichijiodani* (Heibonsha, 1990), 111–113 for a summary of excavated tea ceramics, and 182 for a brief discussion of the Asakura tea house. For more detail, see Ono Masatoshi, *Sengoku jōkamachi no kōkogaku: Ichijōdani kara no messeiji* (Tankōsha, 1997). Color images of some of the best examples of excavated ceramics can be found in Fukui, *Hana saku jōkamachi Ichijōdani*.

[54] Fukui Kenritsu Asakura Shi Iseki Shiryōkan, *Tokubetsu shiseki Ichijōdani Asakura shi iseki hakkutsu chōsa hōkoku VI* (Fukui Kenritsu Asakura Shi Iseki Shiryōkan, 1988), 35–50, as well as accompanying plates and diagrams.

of high-quality Chinese ceramics. This implies that the distribution of such wares was widespread among aspirational samurai, which is perhaps an indication that owning such objects was necessary in order to participate in the social activities of their masters.

Another site that has yielded Chinese ceramics, including tea wares, is the former location of Saigōji, a Nichiren temple located in a neighborhood of warrior residences and religious structures on the west bank of the river, across from the Asakura residence. A notable piece (reconstructed from shards) is a large tea jar comparable in size and decoration to famous Chinese manufactured jars such as the piece owned by the Freer Gallery of Art and Arthur M. Sackler Gallery at the Smithsonian, named Chigusa, or the piece owned by the Tokugawa Art Museum in Nagoya, named Shōka, and other famous objects in circulation during this period.[55] In Kyoto, warriors often organized tea gatherings, poetry gatherings, and other social occasions at Buddhist temples, which frequently included purpose-built tea rooms and gardens. The excavation of Saigōji in Ichijōdani points to similar use of temple spaces for the display of Chinese ceramics in the provinces as well.

Most residents did not, of course, engage in the tea ceremony, which even in urban centers remained an elite practice until the spread of the tea schools in the early modern period. But many pleasurable past times can still be read through the archaeological record. It is clear that many Ichijōdani residents were literate based on the plethora of excavated objects associated with writing[56] as well as evidence of scholarship and cultural study (examined more in Chapter 5), and composing letters, practicing calligraphy, and reading and otherwise enjoying poetry were common. Storytelling, singing, and dancing are also common in the visual representations of late medieval urban life, seen in the "In and around the capital" (Rakuchū rakugai) genre screens, in particular.[57] These practices rarely leave behind concrete remains. Instead, we find voluminous evidence of games of various sorts in the excavations of the city. Archaeologists have found stone pieces from Go (sometimes called Igo) sets, the ancient Chinese strategy game that had long been popular in Japan by the sixteenth century. Sugoroku pieces have also been found, parts of a game that is similar to backgammon. Other excavated game pieces include dice, chess (*shogi*) pieces (Figure 2.8), wooden and metal

---

[55] See the color photo in Ono, *Jitsuzō no Sengoku jōkamachi*, 13. A fine Jian-ware tea bowl and tea caddy were excavated as well. Fukui Kenritsu Asakura Shi Iseki Shiryōkan, *Ichijōdani no shūkyō to shinkō* (Fukui Kenritsu Asakura Shi Iseki Shiryōkan, 1999), 25.
[56] Mizuno, "Ichijōdani no kurashi," 248–249.   [57] McKelway, *Capitalscapes*, 188–189.

Figure 2.8 Excavated chess (*shogi*) pieces (Japanese), Ichijōdani. Ink brushed on wood.
Used with permission of the Fukui Prefectural Ichijōdani Asakura Family History Museum.

dolls, miniature boats, and wooden swords.[58] Also found are stone tops (*koma*) and wooden paddles (*hagoita*). The tradition of playing with tops goes back at least to the Asuka period (538–710), and archaeologists have unearthed examples from the then capital city of Fujiwara (present-day Kashihara), from Heian-era Kyoto, from the first warrior capital of Kamakura, and from the merchant city of Kusado Sengen.[59]

---

[58] Mizuno Kazuo, "Kodomo no asobi: koma to hagoita to," in *Jitsuzō no Sengoku jōkamachi*, 116.
[59] Mizuno, "Kodomo no asobi," 116–117.

Illustrations of the practice of playing with tops, seen in paintings such as the fourteenth-century handscroll *Illustrated Biography of the Buddhist Priest Kakunyo* (*Bokiekotoba*), show children enthusiastically crouching next to two spinning tops, competing for the longest spin, while adults smile and look on. Similarly, several wooden paddles were excavated from Ichijōdani, used to play a game called *hanetsuki* that is superficially similar to badminton, though it may have originated in religious ritual. Our image of the daily life of Ichijōdani thus must include not only morning preparation, meals, and labor, but the visceral pleasure of watching children play with toys alongside the road or in the interior garden.[60]

At the end of the day, residents would of course return to their kitchens for more food and perhaps some drink; ample evidence for a culture of consuming alcohol can be found in the excavated ceramics, ranging from the large Echizen-ware jars that may have been used to ferment and contain sake to the wine cups and bottles that were surely used to serve it. Small earthenware plates (a style of ceramics named *kawarake* discussed in Chapter 4) held flammable oil or a kind of candle that provided faint light in the darkness of evening and night; alternatively, pine torches or lamps may have been used if candles were not available. Small charcoal braziers (*hibachi*) provided heat.[61] In the Asakura residence, a structure that appears to have functioned as a bathhouse has been excavated, and it seems likely some sort of public bathing facilities may also have been available for residents of the town in general.[62]

Warmed by a bath, Ichijōdani residents tucked into bed and snuffed out their candles or lamps, though the soft and comfortable futon bedding of modern Japan was not known in late medieval cities. Instead, it is believed that residents slept on raised boards or straw mats. We do know that winter nights in the town were harshly cold (in January the average low temperature in Fukui is −4°C) and residents seem to have attempted to counter the chill by employing stone warmers (*bandoko*) near their beds at night (Figure 2.9). Large numbers of these in various shapes, carved out of local volcanic stone, have been excavated from sites across the community. Most were shaped like boxes, allowing warm charcoals inside to continue providing heat throughout the night.[63]

---

[60] See also the discussion of play in Mizuno, "Ichijōdani no kurashi," 250–251.
[61] Ono, "Hibi no Karashi," 113–114.   [62] Mizuno, "Ichijōdani no kurashi," 252.
[63] Kakiuchi Kōjirō, "Seki no anka," in *Jitsuzō no Sengoku jōkamachi*, 137–138.

Figure 2.9 Excavated stone warmer (Japanese), Ichijōdani.
Used with permission of the Fukui Prefectural Ichijōdani Asakura Family
History Museum.

Conclusion: Local Ceramics and Economic Integration

One of the most commonly excavated materials in Ichijōdani, as mentioned above, was the Echizen ceramic jar (Figure 2.1), used for a variety of purposes in residences across the status spectrum. These ceramic vessels were not produced in the town, however, but shipped here from another site in the province. How were they made and distributed, and what do the answers tell us about Ichijōdani's integration into larger economic networks? And what other kinds of evidence do we find in the city's sites that help us to understand its position in provincial, regional, national, and international trade?

First, we must ask where all this pottery came from. Echizen ware has long been understood as one of the primary ceramic traditions of medieval Japan, a categorization known as the "six old kilns" from the early postwar era until the 1970s. Early ceramic historians identified what they thought were six primary kiln clusters that produced all of the major domestic ceramics of the medieval age in the archipelago: the Seto kilns in the Seto and Mino region, famous for their later tea ceramic production but active in the medieval age in the production of utilitarian vessels; Shigaraki in what is now Shiga prefecture, a natural-ash glaze tradition;

Bizen in present-day Okayama prefecture, another natural ash-glaze tradition; Tanba near Kyoto in modern Hyogo prefecture, which also made ash-glaze wares; and Tokoname in present-day Aichi prefecture, a huge cluster of kilns that produced a range of unglazed utilitarian vessels including jars and vats. Echizen, the last of these six kiln groups to be discovered, sealed the Japanese term "six old kilns" (rokkoyō), which became a popular and easy to understand way of identifying medieval ceramics for Japanese tea ceremony practitioners and pottery collectors.[64]

Unfortunately, this accessible and attractive schematic proved to be entirely false and fundamentally misleading, and has continued to this day to be disseminated in tourist brochures, online explanations of Japanese ceramic history, and other nonscholarly forums. Archaeologists have unearthed, and widely disseminated in Japanese, a nuanced and complex model for the spread of medieval ceramic production that is both more accurate and useful for contextualizing the production and distribution of Echizen ceramics. According to this genealogical model, medieval ceramic production can be divided into three large families and subdivided into numerous smaller groupings. The first group, the Haji-tradition kilns, engaged in earthenware ceramic production, which I will discuss further in Chapter 4. The second type, the Sue-tradition kilns, fired ceramics to a high temperature (more than 1,000°C) in a reduction atmosphere, which produced a charcoal gray surface on the wares, which were otherwise undecorated. One of the most famous medieval ceramic traditions in Japan, Bizen ware, is today associated with red firing effects and is often grouped together with natural-ash glazed ceramics, but the style actually evolved from this gray Sue-tradition technique, as is visible in medieval shards that can still be found today in the hills around Inbe in the Bizen region. The third type, the Shiki-tradition kilns, produced high-fire ceramics using natural ash-glazing techniques. The Echizen kilns fall into this third and final category.

Postwar research into ceramic production thus revealed a diversity of sites that did not fit into the six old kilns theory, including a range of kilns in the region around Echizen: the Kyogamine kiln in present-day Toyama and the Shikaura kiln in present-day Shikamachi, Ishikawa Prefecture, for example, both operated during the medieval period and are considered Shiki-tradition kilns, yet cannot be included in the grouping of ceramics known now as Echizen ware.[65] Looking at the entire Sea of Japan coast, which in the original theory was ostensibly

---

[64] Inoue Kikuo, "Medieval Japanese Ceramics: The Six Old Kilns and Their Contexts," in Kotō no fu, chūsei no yakimono: Rokukoyō to sono shūhen, ed. Miho Museum (Miho Museum, 2010), 456–457.

[65] Inoue, "Medieval Japanese Ceramics," 458–459.

home to only one medieval production tradition, Echizen ware, we instead find a lively landscape of potters and kilns operating in a range of traditions, an example of the impressive economic integration of the region. The Noto Peninsula was home to Suzu ware, a Sue-tradition grouping of kilns with wide distribution. Kaga was home to the Kaga kilns as well as the aforementioned Shikaura kilns, both in the Shiki tradition. Etchu Province was home to the Kyogamine kilns and Echigo was home to the Gozu-sanroku kilns.[66] Among all of these traditions, Echizen still appears to have been the largest and most influential medieval ceramic production site, but it was hardly the sole operator in the busy field of making pottery for daily use.

How did Echizen ware make its way to Ichijōdani? As the capital of the province, the city was quite well integrated with the networks of exchange surrounding it, and in the case of Echizen ceramics, it seems likely that pots were shipped overland to supply the largest urban center in the region. We can thus read the abundance of Echizen ceramics in the town as a story about the urban life of Ichijōdani as well as the centripetal force of its consumers' demand for goods. We can also, however, read this same evidence as a story not about Ichijōdani as an urban center that drove demand but about Echizen ceramics as a vital regional product. Archaeologists have located more than 200 kiln sites in Echizen, some of which date back to the twelfth century, and these produced jars with narrow necks, which could be sealed and used for shipping and storage; large vats useful for dyeing, brewing, and other tasks; spouted bowls and jars; water containers; cups; and many other forms. Potters in these kilns used local clay, which was white to light gray in color and could withstand the high temperatures of firings that would allow the production of high-quality stonewares. Potters employed coil-building techniques to produce vessels, which involved rolling the clay out into a long, thin, and regular cylinder, and then stacking and joining these coils to form a cylindrical shape. Next, potters used their hands or wooden scrapers and paddles to rub, file, and smooth the rows of coils into a thin and flat wall. The production process was slow, requiring time to carefully place each coil, followed by a rest of up to several hours to allow the newly added layer of clay to partially dry and thus develop the strength to support the next coil. Only when the coils had all been stacked, joined, and allowed to sufficiently harden could the flattening and thinning of the walls occur, a delicate procedure that largely determined the quality of the final piece.[67]

---

[66] Inoue, "Medieval Japanese Ceramics," 459–460.

[67] For a summary of contemporary Echizen ceramic production, see Birmingham Museum of Art, *Echizen: Eight Hundred Years of Japanese Stoneware* (University of Washington Press, 1994), 18–19. For a more detailed discussion in Japanese, with illustrations, see

The potters allowed the resulting pots to dry and continued production to accumulate a sufficient quantity and volume to fill a kiln. Echizen kilns were partially dug into the earth on a slope, and consisted of a large, single chamber of fired clay in the shape of a tunnel. In Japanese this style of kiln is called a tunnel kiln or, literally, a "hole kiln" (*anagama*). Based on excavated Echizen kilns, it seems that as many as 64 large jars, 64 normal jars, and up to 1,170 mortars could be fired at once, requiring 50 tons of wood to fuel the flames over a period of a week or more.[68]

The production of Echizen ceramics seems to have steadily increased over the course of the medieval period, and by the late fifteenth century this ware had supplanted the neighboring tradition of Suzu ceramics and was distributed as far north as Hokkaidō and as far south as southwest Honshū.[69] Such a massive expansion required not just increased production, however, but efficient and reliable distribution networks. One method for the dissemination of Echizen ceramics was transportation by ship, an oft-overlooked structure of sixteenth-century trade and the circulation of goods. Wholesale merchants (*toimaru*) based in Tsuruga played a major role in this distribution, according to the research of Yoshioka Yasunobu.[70] From the site of production, Echizen wares were transported along roads over the mountains that surround the valley. Echizen city was located approximately twelve kilometers to the east of the kilns. A variety of roads leading out of Echizen made possible the transport of the ceramics overland, such as to Ichijōdani, ten kilometers east of Echizen. Most significantly, the Kuzuryu River allowed easy transport to the port near Fuchū on the coast to the north, which in turn allowed distribution via the Sea of Japan to the entire northern and western coastal regions of Japan.[71] As Takagi Hisashi notes, they were then sold in marketplaces in towns and other urban centers.[72] Even in this period of ostensible social and political fragmentation and insecurity, economic integration that extended from the northernmost region to

Idemitsu Bijutsukan, *Echizen kotō to sono saigen: Kuemongama no kiroku* (Idemitsu Bijutsukan, 1994), 13.

[68] Idemitsu Bijutsukan, *Echizen kotō to sono saigen*, 19.

[69] Inoue, "Medieval Japanese Ceramics," 461.

[70] Yoshioka Yasunobu, "Tōhoku Nihon kaiiki ni okeru chūsei tōki no seisan to ryūtsū," in *Chūsei Sueki no kenkyū* (Yoshikawa Kōbunkan, 1994), and *Nihon kaiiki no doki/tōji, chūsei hen* (Rokkō Shuppan, 1989), particularly chapter 3, section 3.

[71] Takagi Hisashi, "Chūsei ni okeru Echizenyaki no seisan to ryūtsū," *Tōsetsu* (2002–2008): 25–30.

[72] For a thorough account of how medieval merchants pursued their economic interests, see Hitomi Tonomura, *Community and Commerce in Late Medieval Japan: The Corporate Villages of Tokuchin-ho* (Stanford University Press, 1992), particularly chapter 5, "The Assertion of Commercial Interests."

western Japan is legible in excavations of large, domestically produced Echizen ceramic jars.[73]

How does Ichijōdani's economic integration compare with other provincial urban centers in the sixteenth century? Contrasting the Asakura's capital with port towns such as Tosa Minato, Hakata, Bungo Funai, and Kusado Sengen highlights that Ichijōdani had comparatively less direct access to overseas markets and major regional trade routes, which makes the abundance of imported material culture all the more significant. Tosa Minato, for example, was perhaps the primary port city at the northernmost tip of Honshū, and with its well-protected harbor and easy access to both the Sea of Japan coast and the Pacific coast, was ideally situated for local, regional, and international trade. It also served as the headquarters of the Ando family of Japanese warlords, who dominated the region and engaged in trading with northern populations of indigenous peoples. Ceramics excavated from Tosa Minato demonstrate its connections to various trading networks, with an abundance of locally produced earthenware ritual vessels, glazed stonewares imported from the Seto and Mino kilns, as well as unglazed, high-fire wares from Tokoname, Suzu, Echizen, and Bizen, representing an extremely broad swath of territory across Japan. Similar diversity is seen among the excavated imported ceramics, which include Chinese porcelains, celadons, and iron-glazed brown and black wares, as well as surprisingly large quantities of Korean celadons.[74]

Ichijōdani is thus not unusually well integrated into the thriving late medieval networks of trade. In fact, compared with port towns that had direct access to maritime trading routes, it shows less evidence of imported ceramics and other markers of international trade. For understanding the tremendous growth that occurred over the course of the late fifteenth and sixteenth centuries in artisanal production, local and regional trade, and some international exchange, however, Ichijōdani presents perhaps our best and most compelling evidence. Kyoto, as the national capital, is exceptional in every way, and does not represent the diversity of experiences despite the fact that it usually stands in for "Japan" in most narratives of historical and cultural change in this period. Ichijōdani, by contrast, is a balanced and representative example

---

[73] Takagi, "Chūsei ni okeru Echizenyaki," 25–30.

[74] On Tosa Minato, see Kokuritsu Rekishi Minzoku Hakubutsukan, ed., *Chusei toshi Tosaminato to Ando shi* (Kokuritsu Rekishi Minzoku Hakubutsukan, 1994); Kikuchi Tetsuo and Fukuda Toyohiko, eds., *Yomigaeru chūsei, vol. 4: Kita no chūsei: Tsugaru, Hokkaidō* (Heibonsha, 1989), 51–99; and Hiroshima Kenritsu Rekishi Hakubutsukan, *Umi kara chūsei o miru: chūsei no minatomachi* (Hiroshima Kenritsu Rekishi Hakubutsukan, 1996), 27–36.

of the provincial urban experience: not a port city, with unusually easy access to the coast, but also not in an isolated, remote location, making access to trade difficult. The town's location allowed its residents to purchase goods like ceramics with relative ease: locally manufactured earthenware vessels for ritual and daily use, regionally produced Echizen-ware ceramics for longer-term use, and imported Chinese ceramics for higher-end tableware and tea ceremony use. Ichijōdani also demonstrates that the production and circulation of material culture that was vital for daily life in medieval Japan unfolded regionally, driven by provincial forces rather than by the engine of the consumption needs of the capital city.[75] The archaeological assemblage at Ichijōdani thus presents us with a clear picture of daily life in a late medieval provincial urban center.

---

[75] Japanese historians have long debated the networks of production and distribution in the medieval period, and whether these spheres were primarily centered on the capital city and its urban neighbors of Nara and Sakai, or whether multiple overlapping spheres coexisted. See, for example, Wakita Haruko, "Muromachi ki no keizai hatten," in *Iwanami Kōza Nihon rekishi, vol. 7: Chūsei 3* (Iwanami Kōza, 1976), 51–98, and Miura Keiichi, *Nihon chūsei no chiiki to shakai* (Shibunkaku Shuppan, 1993).

3   Late Medieval Warlords
and the Agglomeration of Power

> For the site of his own mansion he selected Tsukama and there set up
> his household. Regardless of social standing, everyone obeyed him; his
> domain was governed in peace and tranquility under the protection of
> the gods and buddhas. He lived for 120 years, produced many
> descendants, and his family overflowed with the seven treasures and
> abundant wealth.   —*Lazy Tarō (Monogusa Tarō)*, late medieval period[1]

In the fourth month of 1573, the last ruler of Ichijōdani, Asakura
Yoshikage, wrote to one of his vassals that he was unable to respond to
Shogun Ashikaga Yoshiaki's request for troops. The shogun had recently
decided to turn on his erstwhile benefactor Oda Nobunaga and was
ensconced in Nijō Castle in Kyoto, where he needed reinforcements.
Yoshikage, however, had been summoned by his ally Azai Nagamasa to
Odani Castle, recently threatened by Nobunaga, where he and his troops
were helping to reinforce the fortifications. Yoshikage thus instructed his
vassal to continue strengthening Echizen in preparation for further
attacks instead of responding to the plea of the shogun.[2] Nobunaga, both
Yoshikage and Yoshiaki must have hoped, faced too many enemies to
further his campaign to unify the realm. The old warlord Takeda
Shingen had enjoyed a string of victories over Nobunaga's ally
Tokugawa Ieyasu in Tōtōmi Province. The Asakura and the Azai continued to resist Nobunaga in central Japan. The various Single-Mind
religious leagues (*ikkō ikki*) were attacking Nobunaga at every turn, and
the fortified Honganji temple complex in Osaka was similarly determined
to maintain its autonomy. Perhaps the shared determination of this
heterogeneous lineup of adversaries would be successful. Instead, within
a few months Takeda Shingen had died of natural causes and Nobunaga
had banished Ashikaga Yoshiaki and ended the Ashikaga shogunate.

---

[1] Virginia Skord, "Monogusa Tarō: From Rags to Riches and Beyond," *Monumenta Nipponica* 44.2 (Summer, 1989): 171–198.
[2] Fukui Kenritsu Ichijōdani Asakura Shi Iseki Shiryōkan, *Asakura shi godai no hakkyū monjo* (Fukui Kenritsu Ichijōdani Asakura Shi Iseki Shiryōkan, 2004), letter no. 259, p. 231.

He had also comprehensively defeated and eliminated the Asakura and the Azai.

This narrative seems to tell us about a key moment in the story of the rise of the first of the three unifiers, the hegemon Nobunaga, over an array of adverse circumstances. His triumph over this diverse lineup of opposing forces, which continued until his death in 1582, seems providential rather than contingent. This "fated" quality is seen both in early modern accounts of his rise – such as Ōta Gyūichi's *Chronicle of Lord Nobunaga*, in which the unifier is referred to as "His Gracious Majesty, the Master of All the World and Lord of Ten Thousand Chariots"[3] – as well as in modern historiography, which relentlessly emphasizes the individual accomplishments of Nobunaga in the heroic mode.

A different reading of this story, however, might highlight the distribution of power across a wide geographical range, enabling manifold actors to assert their authority and determination to resist the hegemony of a single ruler. Without romanticizing in any way the independence and authority of the warlords of this period, we can interpret the conflict between Nobunaga, the Asakura, the Azai, the Takeda, and others in 1573 as a lesson in the evolution of the warlords of the Age of Warring States. Perhaps this is a story about not the accomplishments of one individual but the culmination of the development of warlords as a new and distinctive type of regional ruler, men whose authority was strongly rooted in direct control over vassals, land, trade, and culture.[4] The local control of the warlord manifested most clearly in the emergence of urban centers that functioned as military bases, residential headquarters, and cultural capitals. These power agglomerations provided benefits over time to the ruling warlord and the residents of the city, as a result of the clustering of different activities and populations. This regional concentration of power and population in the form of provincial and palace cities represents a counter narrative to the tale of unification because these centers as constituted during the Age of Warring States were politically independent.

---

[3] In English translation, see Ōta Gyūichi, *The Chronicle of Lord Nobunaga*, ed. Jurgis S. A. Elisonas and Jeroen P. Lamers (Brill, 2011), 422. In Japanese, see Ōta Gyūichi, *Shinchō kōki*, ed. Okuno Takahiro and Iwasawa Yoshihiko (Kadokawa Shoten, 1969), 374.

[4] Some historians of the sixteenth century writing in Japanese have questioned the mythohistorical treatment of Nobunaga, including Asao Naohiro and Wakita Osamu. Yet their narratives of historical change in this period are still relentlessly unifier-focused, and frequently refer to the "genius" of the Oda lord as a tactician. See, for example, their respective chapters (in translation) in *Cambridge History of Japan, vol. 4: Early Modern Japan*, ed. John Whitney Hall (Cambridge University Press, 1991).

This chapter examines the rise of the Asakura family from the position of deputy governors (*shugodai*) under the Shiba, who were the officially appointed governors (*shugo*) of Echizen province, to warlords (*daimyō*) who ruled and controlled Echizen for a century until their destruction in 1573. Like "Lazy Tarō," the fictional character from the eponymous medieval tale cited in the epigraph, who transforms from an indolent villager into a member of the landed gentry, the Asakura became prosperous and effective rulers. They seem to embody the spirit of the late medieval period, combining independence and self-interest to achieve impressive local success. In a sense, they represent the aspiration of the late medieval elite, who sought to at least attain regional stability despite the weakness of traditional institutional structures around them. How, then, did the Asakura come to occupy the position of warlord? What role did the urban agglomeration of Ichijōdani play in the establishment and maintenance of their authority over time? And what does the history of the Asakura and the urban space of Ichijōdani reveal about late medieval history in Japan? As we will see below, the emergence of the Asakura as a regional power is contemporaneous to the growth of Ichijōdani as a multifunctional palace city. This story is less explicitly focused on the archaeology of Ichijōdani and the material heritage that allowed us, in the previous chapters, to consider the spatial history of the city and the materiality of daily life. Instead, it examines the rise of the Asakura and highlights moments in their rule of Echizen province to clarify the political context for the growth (and destruction) of Ichijōdani as the regional capital.

Power and Violence: "Those Below Overthrow Those Above"

In this book I use "warlord" as a rough translation for the Japanese term *daimyō*, which originally referred to rice field proprietors in the imperial Ritsuryō legal and administrative system instituted in the late seventh to early eighth century. In many ways the Japanese and English terms here do not match. The term *daimyō*, literally "great name," indicated status in the hierarchical society of premodern Japan, with no reference to military activity, while "warlord" is a relatively new word in English (dating to the mid-nineteenth century according to the *OED*) that indicates a military commander. Yet this translation is helpful because it references both the high rank of the holder as a "lord" while also reminding us of the samurai, or warrior, occupation of the individual or family being named. Indeed, in the usage of modern historians of late medieval Japan, the term has come to refer exclusively to warrior leaders who either inherited bureaucratic positions as regional powerholders (governor warlords, or *shugo daimyō*) or overthrew those who were responsible for ruling variously sized territories (*Sengoku daimyō*, or Age of Warring States warlords). This contrast captures one of the primary tensions of the period, between older bureaucratic structures of administration that the warrior class originally appropriated from the courtly society of Kyoto and the newer networks of military service that allowed lower-ranked warriors, such as provincial rulers (*kokujin*), to overthrow the governors appointed by the shogunate. This phenomenon, referred to by the phrase "those below overthrow those above" (*gekokujō*) is emblematic of this period, though the concept is perhaps overly reductive.[5]

The case of the Asakura is instructional. The early history of the family was not well known until recent research began to piece together the genealogy before the house moved into Echizen Province. Briefly, the Asakura lineage appears to have originated in the town of Asago in Tajima Province (present-day Hyōgō Prefecture), as a branch of the Kusakabe family.[6] The Kusakabe held Akabuchi Shrine in Asago as its family shrine, and the Asakura continued the worship of Akabuchi throughout their history. In addition to the shrine connection, an estate in Tajima was known as Asakura, and this is probably the direct origin of the family name. The early Asakura appear to have taken part in the Genpei War that marked the transition from the Heian to the Kamakura Period. A certain Asakura Takakiyo is mentioned in *The Tale of the Heike* as a direct retainer (*gokenin*) of the Minamoto family, founders of the first warrior government.[7] The fate of Takakiyo and his lineage is unknown, though there are hints that he may have moved east to Kamakura.[8]

The founder of the Echizen Asakura (see Table 3.1), the lineage with which we are concerned here, was Asakura Hirokage (1255–1352), who

[5] David Spafford deconstructs the notion of *gekokujō* in "An Apology of Betrayal: Political and Narrative Strategies in a Late Medieval Memoir," *Journal of Japanese Studies* 35.2 (2009). Some of the language in this paragraph also appears in Morgan Pitelka, "A Melodramatic Age," in *Letters from Japan's Sixteenth and Seventeenth Centuries: Correspondence of Warlords, Tea Masters, Zen Priests, and Aristocrats*, ed. Morgan Pitelka, Reiko Tanimura, and Takashi Masuda (Institute of East Asian Studies, 2021).

[6] For a detailed treatment of the origins of the Asakura lineage in Tajima, see Satō Kei, *Asakura Takakage: Sengoku daimyō Asakura shi no ishizue kizuita mōshō* (Ebisu Kōshō, 2014), 10–30.

[7] Royall Tyler, trans., *The Tale of the Heikei* (Penguin, 2012), 682–683. On the early history of the Asakura, see Fukui Kenritsu Ichijōdani Asakura Shi Iseki Shiryōkan, *Asakura shi no kakun* (Fukui Kenritsu Ichijōdani Asakura Shi Iseki Shiryōkan, 2008), 1–3; and Satō Kei, "Asakura shi no seisui to Ichijōdani," in Mizuno and Satō, eds., *Sengoku daimyo Asakura shi to Ichijōdani*, 11–13.

[8] Satō, *Asakura Takakage*, 20.

Table 3.1. *Asakura family heads*

Early heads of the Asakura house
Asakura Hirokage (広景), 1255–1352
Asakura Takakage (高景), 1314–1372
Asakura Ujikage (氏景), 1339–1405
Asakura Sadakage (貞景), 1358–1436
Asakura Norikage (教景), 1380–1463
Asakura Iekage (家景), 1402–1451

Asakura warlords
Asakura Eirin (英林), 1428–1481
　　(also Takakage 孝景 and Toshikage 敏景)
Asakura Ujikage (氏景), 1449–1486
Asakura Sadakage (貞景), 1473–1512
Asakura Takakage (孝景), 1493–1548
Asakura Yoshikage (義景), 1533–1573

likely served the military leader Shiba Takatsune (1305–1367). Takatsune was a relative and a key ally of the founder of the Ashikaga shogunate, Takauji (1305–1358), and was appointed to be the governor of Echizen and Wakasa Provinces after the Ashikaga seized power. Asakura Hirokage probably accompanied Takatsune into Echizen as a result of the shifts that followed the establishment of the new military government.[9] Hirokage reportedly built a family temple, Kōshōji, that was part of the Zen Buddhist monastery system known as the Ten Temples (*Jissetsu*), second in rank after the Five Mountain (*Gozan*) temple system in Kyoto.[10] He also wrote a letter to his heir instructing him to complete the construction of the temple complex, representing at the least the intention of Hirokage to establish a family legacy and sense of continuity.[11] That heir was Hirokage's second son, Takakage (1314–1372, not to be confused with the penultimate head of the family, with the homophonic name Takakage), who reportedly fought

---

[9] The *Asakura-ke denki* claims that Hirokage moved to Echizen in response to a dream that instructed him to migrate for religious reasons. Likewise, *Asakura shimatsuki* claims that Hirokage took part in Takatsune's military actions under the command of Takauji when he was supporting Emperor Godaigo in 1333. See the discussion in Fukui, *Asakura shi no kakun*, 3. Also, Fukui Shi, "Asakura shimatsuki," transcribed in *Shiryō hen 2: kodai, chūsei*, in *Fukui shishi* (Fukui Shi, 1983–2008), 816–817.
[10] Satō, *Asakura Takakage*, 50–54.
[11] In addition, some have pointed to the document *Hirokage ikun*, or "Dying Instructions of Hirokage," which is attributed to Asakura Hirokage, but appears to be an early modern pastiche of texts and anecdotes from other warrior families and precepts. See Fukui, *Asakura shi no kakun*, 4.

meritoriously for the Ashikaga on several occasions, winning recognition directly from at least one shogun. Little is known of the four generations of the Asakura family after this point. Unfortunately, included in the long list of Asakura-related unknowns is the exact time of their adoption of Ichijōdani as the family's headquarters. The historian Satō Kei, who rigorously reviewed all the extant documentary evidence, is able to conclude only the following: "The Asakura family in all likelihood established Ichijōdani, located in the southeastern tip of the Fukui plain, as their principal base early [after their arrival in Echizen]."[12]

Functionally, the more central founder of the Asakura family as major regional political leaders and powerful players in the conflicts of the Age of Warring States was Asakura Eirin (1428–1481), technically the seventh generation of the Echizen Asakura lineage (Figure 3.1). Eirin's life and career are better documented than any previous member of the Asakura family. Forty-three letters that he or his scribes wrote are extant in one form or another.[13] More significantly, his actions appear in many contemporaneous documents and chronicles because of the central role he played in one of the most transformative conflicts in medieval Japanese history: the Ōnin War of 1467–1477, which destroyed Kyoto, delegitimized the Ashikaga Shogunate, and opened a century of internecine conflict that wracked every region of Japan. In short, Eirin's involvement in the strife that came to define the Age of Warring States also elevated him and his family from the post of "vassal to the Shiba" to the position of warlord and ruler over a province.

The Ōnin War resulted from the collision of several unrelated but similar conflicts over warrior house succession in and around Kyoto, the details of which can be found in *The Chronicle of Ōnin*.[14] One of the key conflicts occurred within the Shiba family, where two rival claimants to the position of head of the house as well as governor engaged in both legal and military actions against each other, which created opportunities for three of their primary vassals – the Asakura, the Kai, and the Oda – to reposition themselves in relation to their lords and each other. Conflict in the Shiba family had far-reaching implications for Ashikaga governance, because the lineage had traditionally been one of three to hold the office of shogunal deputy (*kanrei*). Asakura Eirin was in his late twenties when tension over the Shiba family headship began to surface in Kyoto politics in 1456. His father, Iekage, had died five years previously, but his

---

[12] Satō, *Asakura Takakage*, 76.   [13] Fukui, *Asakura shi godai no hakkyū monjo*.
[14] See the translation in H. Paul Varley, *The Onin War: History of Its Origins and Background* (Columbia University Press, 1966); and discussion in Berry, *The Culture of Civil War in Kyoto*, 11–13.

Figure 3.1 Posthumous portrait of Asakura Eirin (Japanese).
Used with permission of Shingetsuji.

grandfather, Norikage, was still alive and active as head of the clan. The contingent timing for the Asakura was thus beneficial in terms of the opportunity for Eirin to grow as a leader.

Like many of the key actors in this story, Eirin spent much of the period leading up to the Ōnin War in Kyoto, where he enjoyed the courtly pleasures of the imperial capital, but also became enmeshed in the conflicts that ultimately undermined the authority of the shogunate. In fact, he and his men were somewhat unruly, taking part in 1457 with the leader of the Kai as well as members of the Oda and Yamana clans in an attack on some Shiba family samurai, killing as many as forty, in the Nijō neighborhood of the capital.[15] Clearly, the shogunate lacked the control to maintain peace in the city that was ostensibly the headquarters of Ashikaga power.

The Kai, Asakura, and Oda were relatively united in their opposition to the Shiba, and in 1458–1459, this erupted into open conflict back in Echizen.[16] They fought the Shiba in a series of battles in northern Echizen, and successfully defeated the forces of Shiba Yoshitoshi. Eirin was rewarded by the shogunate with new allotments of land in Etchū and Echizen; when Asakura Norikage, the patriarch, died in 1463, it was with the confidence that the Asakura were better positioned than ever before. However, in just a few years, much of their progress was undone. Shiba Yoshitoshi was pardoned and allowed to return to Kyoto, and was again made governor of Echizen, Owari, and Tōtōmi. This, along with conflicts over the headship of the Hatakeyama house, was one of the sparks that ignited the outbreak of the Ōnin War in early 1467 in the capital. The violence was widespread, and the results devastating.

In the early days of the Ōnin War, Asakura Eirin fought on the side of the Western Army in support of Shiba Yoshikado, the rival claimant for the headship of the Shiba family.[17] Eirin joined, for example, Hatakeyama Yoshinari in the famous and devastating attack on Eastern Army forces encamped at Shōkokuji, a Zen temple complex that had been patronized by the Ashikaga. However, after several months of fighting in Kyoto, Eirin was convinced by the wily and, according to *The Chronicle of Ōnin*, corrupt politician Ise Sadachika to change sides.[18] Sadachika was advisor to the Shogun, and much of the political flip-flopping of Ashikaga Yoshimasa in these years, as well as the resulting chaos, seems to have been of his making. On Sadachika's advice, Eirin returned to Echizen and extended the olive branch to Shiba Yoshitoshi; his real intention was to extinguish Shiba Yoshikado, to gain the support of the mid-level samurai leaders of the province, and to multiply his own power and authority. He may have had assurances from Sadachika that the shogunate would support him in these endeavors. Certainly, in early 1469, the Shogun sent letters to key samurai leaders (*kokujin*) indicating that he had commanded Eirin to exterminate Shiba Yoshikado, whom he

---

[15] Fukui, *Asakura shi no kakun*, 6, claims forty victims. *Daijōin jisha zōjiki*, the diary of Jinson (1430–1508), cited in Fukui, *Echizen/Asakura shi kenkei nenpyō*, 41, claims the number killed was twenty-seven.

[16] Satō, *Asakura Takakage*, 89–92.

[17] The most recent examination of the involvement of Eirin (Takakage, also sometimes called Toshikage) in the Ōnin War is Satō, *Asakura Takakage*, 141–175.

[18] See Varley, *The Onin War*, 111–112, for comments on Sadachika.

Table 3.2. *Conquering Echizen*

1472/8/2: The Asakura defeat the Kai in Echizen, though Kai Hachirō escapes to Kaga Province.

1473/8/8: Kai forces invade Echizen from Kaga, soon withdraw.

1474/1/18: Kai forces invade Echizen from Kaga, are repelled.

1474/5: The Kai mount a major invasion and attempt to push through to Ichijōdani over the course of more than a month, but are rebuffed.

1475: The Shiba are finally driven out of Echizen.

1479/i9: The Shiba and the Kai attempt to invade Echizen but the Asakura block roads; the following month the Kai get through; the Shiba and the Kai "wage a war of attrition" amid harsh winter weather.

1480: The Kai take more of northern Echizen.

1481: News that Asakura Eirin is ill reaches the capital region; the Kai launch another offensive, are defeated, and withdraw.

1481/7/26: Eirin dies and Ujikage, his son, takes over as head of the Asakura family.

---

called a "ronin," and that these men should join Eirin to enjoy the glory of victory in battle. Within months, many had joined Eirin as vassals.

The shift (or betrayal) by the Asakura was soon officially rewarded, when the shogunate announced that Eirin was appointed to the post of governor of Echizen in 1471.[19] The deal was sealed by Eirin's son Ujikage, who had stayed behind in Kyoto to attend a banquet with Yamana Sōzen before declaring his allegiance to the Eastern army. In an official audience with Shogun Yoshimasa on 1471/6/10, Ujikage presented a sword from the collection of the Asakura family.[20] This ritual marked, it seemed, the official approval of a fading central authority for an act that actively undermined its own claim to legitimacy. This is how the Ashikaga Shogunate became irrelevant, and new regional powers like the Asakura achieved some prominence as warlords.[21]

The Asakura were by no means secure in their new rule of Echizen, and had to wage defensive wars against the Kai and the Shiba, among other hostile powers in the region. The details are complicated, but in broad strokes, the conflict unfolded as shown in Table 3.2 during the lifetime of Eirin, after he became the ruler of Echizen Province.

All of the discussion of Asakura activities and the lively urban life of Ichijōdani elsewhere in this book was contingent, in a sense, on the successful navigation of these conflicts by Eirin and his successors. The

---

[19] See Fukui Ken, *Shiryō hen: chūsei, vol. 2: Fukui kenshi* (Fukui, 1986), 623. Also, Sato, *Asakura Takakage*, 180–182.

[20] Fukui, *Asakura shi no kakun*, 8.   [21] Satō, *Asakura Takakage*, 182–185.

Table 3.3. *Asakura timeline*

1337: The Asakura enter Echizen from Tajima Province.
1342: The Asakura establish a family temple (*ujidera*), Kōshōji, in what is now the Kanaya neighborhood of Fukui.
1429: By this point, the Asakura are vassals of the Shiba, along with the Kai and the Oda.
1450: Ichijōjō (一乗城) – meaning either a castle located in Ichijō or a fortified settlement in Ichijō – is completed around this time.
1467: The Ōnin War begins, and Asakura Eirin fights for the side of the Western Army.
1471: Eirin switches to the side of the Eastern Army, and is appointed to the position of governor (*shugo*) of Echizen.
1487: Asakura forces take part in an attack on the Rokkaku clan of Omi. The attacking side is led by the ninth shogun, Ashikaga Yoshihisa.
1506: The Asakura, led by Asakura Sōteki, suppress the Single-Mind league (*ikkō ikki*) in Echizen.
1527: At the request of shogun Ashikaga Yoshiharu, Asakura Sōteki leads an army into Kyoto and fights against the forces of the Hatakeyama and Miyoshi, ending in a deadlock.
1531: Asakura Sōteki leads an attack on Single-Mind league forces in Kaga Province.
1544: Asakura Sōteki leads an attack on Inabayama Castle in Mino.
1555: Asakura Sōteki leads an attack on Single-Mind league forces in Kaga Province.
1556: Asakura Sōteki dies.
1559: After mediation by shogun Ashikaga Yoshiteru, Asakura forces withdraw from Kaga Province.
1564: Asakura Yoshikage leads an invasion of Kaga Province.
1565: Shogun Ashikaga Yoshiteru is attacked in his Kyoto Palace, and dies.
1566: The shogun's younger brother, Ashikaga Yoshiaki, takes refuge in Echizen.
1567: Ashikaga Yoshiaki moves into An'yōji, a temple in Ichijōdani.
1568: Ashikaga Yoshiaki joins forces with Oda Nobunaga and is appointed Shogun in Kyoto.
1570: Battle of Anegawa, in which the armies of the Asakura and Azai are driven back by the armies of Oda Nobunaga and Tokugawa Ieyasu.
1573: Oda Nobunaga's armies defeat the Azai and the Asakura, invade Echizen, and destroy Ichijôdani.

Asakura could easily have been unseated and eventually, of course, would be destroyed entirely. But for five generations and exactly one century after Eirin became the lord of the province and then proceeding under the rule of his four successors (Ujikage, Sadakage, Takakage, and the final generation, Yoshikage), the Asakura secured their home base of Ichijōdani and maintained a relatively stable rule in this Age of Warring States (see Table 3.3). This is not to glorify their military activities as warlords, the top-down nature of their warrior rule, or the intentions of their leadership. Rather, my intention here is to mark what I see as a meaningful distinction between warlords who focused their governing on provincial problems and interactions with neighbors (the Asakura, and indeed the majority of their peers) rather than the grandiloquent and ultimately massively more destructive goal of "pacifying the realm."

The Asakura rose to power by engaging in the politics of betrayal and through the judicious deployment of violence, but it is also worth noting that there was hardly a simple binary between "those below" and "those above" in the late fifteenth century. The Asakura were certainly vassals of the Shiba, but so were the Kai, who became their primary adversaries. The Shiba undermined their own position and authority, as did the Ashikaga, through inept family leadership and poor governance. The Asakura and the Kai both recognized the opportunity for advancement and seized it. "Those above" – the Shiba – self-combusted, aided by the political machinations of politicians in the capital city, and "those below" avoided a similar fate by taking advantage of the weakness of their recent masters to seek self-empowerment and independence. The intentionality implied in the phrase *gekokujō* belies the contingency of the social and political fragmentation that actually caused the conflicts that opened up spaces for new leaders to emerge.

How did the Asakura's rise to the position of warlord compare with other warrior families? One useful juxtaposition is with the Ōtomo family, based in Kyushu. They too traced their lineage to a meritorious ancestor who was ostensibly involved in the first generation of warrior government. Their founder, Ōtomo Yoshinao (1147–1199), was one of the "most influential vassals" of the Kamakura shogunate, according to Jeffrey Mass, and in the (unlikely) claims of the Ōtomo family genealogical documents, was also an illegitimate child of Minamoto Yoritomo, the founder of that first warrior government.[22] However, unlike the Asakura, who did not have a continuous lineage as major players in the medieval political system but instead enjoyed a relatively rapid rise to national prominence during the Ōnin War, the Ōtomo were continuously established as one of the key warrior families of Kyushu, and held the shogunal positions of governor of Bungo, Buzen, Chikugo, and Higo Provinces at various points during and after the Kamakura period (with considerable fluctuation in exact responsibilities and territory over time). They were actively involved in shogunal and court politics, and did maintain a residence in Kyoto, but the peripheral location of their lands and headquarters insulated them from the titanic shifts that caused the downfall of so many of their peers.

---

[22] Jeffrey P. Mass, *Lordship and Inheritance in Early Medieval Japan: A Study of the Kamakura Soryō System* (Stanford University Press, 1989), 65. See also Christopher Michael Mayo, "Mobilizing Deities: Deus, Gods, Buddhas, and the Warrior Band in Sixteenth-Century Japan" (PhD dissertation, Princeton University Press, 2013), 46.

Regional rivalries and internal squabbles did wrack the family at times, as during the fifteenth century, when two sons of the Ōtomo lord squabbled over the line of succession. The Ōtomo clan was also rent asunder by disagreements over the two sides in the Ōnin War, with one family leader assassinating another, fleeing to a neighboring province, and eventually committing suicide.[23] In the fallout from this conflict, and in the new post-Ōnin landscape in which political authority became increasingly decentralized, the Ōtomo evolved from "governor warlords" (*shugo daimyō*) into "warring-states warlords" (*Sengoku daimyō*). They were victorious in a series of regional battles, and successfully recruited more soldiers from their territories to strengthen their military capacity. When the Ōtomo issued a set of provincial laws in 1515 under the leadership of the nineteenth lord Yoshinaga, this transformation was complete.[24]

Another family worth considering is the Oda, ironically the warrior lineage that would ultimately destroy the Asakura. Like the Asakura and the similarly prominent Takeda, the Oda were vassals of the Shiba who worked at the provincial level, while the Shiba were primarily active in the capital. The Oda successively held the position of deputy governor (*shugodai*) of Owari Province after the Shiba received governorship of Owari and Echizen in 1398. The early origins of the Oda before they came to Owari are unclear, though the family name seems derived from the Oda Estate in Echizen Province. Later genealogies claim that the family was descended from the Taira, enemies of the Minamoto line from which the Ashikaga claimed descent, but this was more likely to have been a convenient invention for Oda Nobunaga, who officially ended the Ashikaga shogunate, than a historical reality.[25]

Unlike the Asakura and the Ōtomo, the Oda were not torn asunder by the conflict of the Ōnin War; the Oda family took advantage of the weakness of the Shiba to claim rule of Owari for themselves (while still allowing the weakened Shiba to move in and out of Owari for decades), but the two main lineages largely cooperated and shared various positions in the province, at least until the rise of Nobunaga in the 1550s. He overthrew the main line of the family, a betrayal of sorts, and initiated an expansion of his family's power and influence that was exceptional and unprecedented among warlords of this period. In other respects,

---

[23] Toyama Mikio, *Ōtomo Sōrin* (Yoshikawa Kōbunkan, 1975), 7–8.

[24] Toyama, *Ōtomo Sōrin*, 8.

[25] For a thorough discussion of the early history of the Oda family, see Okuno Takahiro, "Shoki no Oda shi," in *Sengoku daimyō ronshū, vol. 17: Oda seiken no kenkyū*, ed. Fujiki Hisashi (Yoshikawa Kōbunkan, 1985). See also Jeroen Lamers, *Japonius Tyrannus: The Japanese Warlord Oda Nobunaga Reconsidered* (Hotei Publishing, 2001), 19–21.

however, the Oda greatly resembled their peers in origin, in rule, and in their reliance on provincial and palace cities for the agglomeration of power.

The Maintenance of Lordly Authority

It is easy to imagine, long after the fact, that power acquired is easily perpetuated, but the many transitions of this era were anxiety-provoking at the least. But we can read what David Spafford has called "the disorientation experienced in several warrior houses in those tumultuous years [and] the precariousness of settlements and the complexity of feelings that followed other takeovers"[26] in a range of documentary sources from the sixteenth century. Indeed, responses to this sense of a world turned upside-down varied enormously, though the theme of tweaking the administrative tools from previous generations is fairly consistent among the Asakura and their peers.

The origin of the authority of political and military leaders in the medieval period was the court system, appropriated by the first warrior government, of appointing governors to provinces to oversee both regional administration and extraction of resources from agricultural land. The power of the lord of a province in theory emerged from the title and privileges of the bureaucratic post, and not from any direct relationship with a particular territory and/or its population of local rulers and agriculturalists. As the influence of the shogunate waned, however, the structures of political power changed across the regions of Japan, with some governors managing the challenges to their authority from local leaders, organized rebellions, and regional rivals, and thus successfully transitioning into warlords who were empowered by their local resources and networks. In other regions, governors were overthrown by their vassals or by lower-ranking military officials (such as provincial rulers, or *kokujin*, or overseers, *daikan*), and the new governance structures were completely disconnected from the old shogunal administrative system. Still others found their armies defeated and their domains consumed by the expansion of neighboring military leaders.

Through these varied processes, a new crop of leaders emerged, with the most famous being the Hōjō in eastern Japan, the Takeda in Kai and Shinano, the Uesugi in Echigo, the Imagawa along the Tōkaidō, the Rokkaku in Ōmi, the Mōri and the Ōuchi in the San'in/San'yō region, the Chōsokabe in Shikoku, and of course the Asakura in Echizen.

---

[26] Spafford, "An Apology of Betrayal," 352.

Japanese historians disagree, however, about the definition and key characteristics of Sengoku warlords, in terms of their emergence, their maturation, and whether they morphed into early modern feudal lords. The arguments of scholars such as Katsumata Shizuo, Kurushima Noriko, Asao Naohiro, Fujiki Hisashi, and Kuroda Motoki vary depending in part on the particular warrior family examined and the particular region of the country under analysis.[27] These disagreements also tend to reinforce an understanding of Sengoku power as meaningful primarily to the degree to which it was or was not transitional, reducing the period to a bridge between the medieval and early modern.[28] I am not interested in adjudicating these debates, which are too specialized to be of interest here, but rather in acknowledging the diversity of Sengoku rulers in terms of the remarkably different trajectories by which they came to power.

One of the key issues that late medieval warlords confronted in the face of civil wars and both external and internal threats to stability was the mobilization of warriors from within the territory being governed. To combat invasions, a warlord needed an army, and to stabilize the province and create a hierarchical social organization that would provide a sense of belonging and hopefully also loyalty, a warlord needed a bureaucratic structure to recruit warriors from across the region and manage their deployment as well as their rewards. One solution was the "surrogate parent, surrogate child" (yorioya yoriko) system, whereby the warlord designated powerful warrior leaders, often from the corps of hereditary vassals, as surrogate parents to lower-ranking warriors, who were referred to as surrogate children and who were understood to report to and respond to the military commands of the surrogate parent rather than the lord of the domain.[29] This system resulted in further empowerment, particularly in military terms, for the commanders under the

---

[27] See Murai Ryōsuke's dense summary of these historiographical debates in *Sengoku daimyō kenryoku kōzō no kenkyū* (Shibunkaku Shuppan, 2012), 3–20.

[28] Murai divides these positions into what he calls continuity (*renzokusei*) theory and disconnect theory (*danzetsusetsu*); both end up participating in a teleological narrative of Japanese history that accepts developmental stages of progress as a model for understanding history. Murai Ryōsuke, *Sengoku daimyō kenryoku kōzō no kenkyū*, 3–20.

[29] See Wakita Haruko, *Taikei Nihon no rekishi, vol. 7: Sengoku daimyō* (Shogakkan, 1993), 166–167, for an overview of *yorioya yoriko*; see Ikegami Hiroko's discussion in the context of the retainer bands of the Hōjō: "Sengoku daimyō ryōkoku ni okeru shoryō oyobi kashindan hensei no tenkai," in *Sengoku daimyō ronshū, vol. 1: Sengoku daimyō no kenkyū*, ed. Nagahara Keiji (Yoshikawa Kōbunkan, 1983), 377–388. In English, John Whitney Hall describes this system as it evolved in Bizen Province in "Foundations of the Modern Japanese Daimyo," 324–325; and Jeffrey Yoshio Kurashige considers it under Hōjō rule in "Serving Your Master: The Kashindan Retainer Corps and the Socio-Economic Transformation of Warring States Japan" (PhD dissertation, Harvard University, 2011), 54–57.

warlord in an increasingly decentralized system. This represented a risk, but also the possibility of more rapid expansion and more efficient mobilization of large numbers of soldiers.

In the late fifteenth century, the Asakura needed not only to recruit warriors to their cause but also to dislodge the extant loyalty to the Kai, the previous deputy governors (*shugodai*) who themselves had hoped to supplant the Shiba and to become the rulers of Echizen. The Asakura accomplished this by disrupting the old title system (*myō taisei*) that guaranteed certain amounts of taxes paid on the still lingering aristocratic estates (*shōen*) and replaced it with a direct proprietor system that allowed them to provide immediate financial incentives to their warrior followers.[30] Extant documentary evidence does not make it clear if the Asakura used the "surrogate parent, surrogate child" system to recruit soldiers, but it seems likely considering the size of their army. They could call upon 5,000 soldiers based in and around Ichijōdani, 3,000 under Asakura command in Tsuruga, and 2,000 based in Ono. The Asakura also had six main units throughout Echizen province, each of which consisted of 2,000 men.[31] In total, the Asakura could therefore deploy 22,000 soldiers, a number that seems unlikely until we remember that indeed armies of this size were marched into the titanic battles of the second half of the sixteenth century, which will be explored in more detail in Chapter 6.

Another approach to preventing destabilization was the use of tax reports (*sashidashi*) to survey agricultural productivity, which eventually led to increasingly broad and systematized land surveys (*kenchi*) to organize resource extraction. Unlike the imperial estate system, which similarly accounted for land and removed tax income to elites in the capital, tax reports and land surveys allowed warlords to capture, control, and profit from land in their immediate domain, though not all domains were geographically contiguous, as Spafford has explored.[32] Perhaps earliest to employ the land survey were the Hōjō in eastern Japan, who in 1506 launched the first survey of agricultural lands in their territories, accounting for type of product and adjusting the taxation rate accordingly.[33] Yet this was not standard across the domains of Sengoku warlords, with many relying on older, preexisting systems to account for the

---

[30] See Kanda Chisato, "Echizen Asakura shi no zaichi shihai no tokushitsu," in *Sengoku daimyō ronshū, vol. 4: Chūbu daimyō no kenkyū*, ed. Katsumata Shizuo (Yoshikawa Kōbunkan, 1983), 179–223.

[31] Fukui Ken, *Chūsei*, 664.   [32] Spafford, *A Sense of Place*, 23.

[33] See Ikegami's discussion in "Sengoku daimyō ryōkoku," 297, as well as Kurashige, "Serving Your Master," 46, and Michael Patrick Birt's rather technical explanation of the role of surveys in Hōjō land administration: "Warring States: A Study of the Go-Hojo

size and scope of agricultural lands and their taxation rates.[34] The Asakura made use of tax reports but do not appear, based on extant documentary evidence, to have engaged in land surveys.[35] Instead, it was Nobunaga and then Hideyoshi who deployed surveys on increasingly large scales and transformed what had been a Sengoku warlord tool of local rule into an instrument for flattening regional power differentials and aggregating power to themselves.[36] In this sense, historians have broadly understood land surveys to be one of the multifunctional bureaucratic techniques that the early modern Tokugawa shogunate inherited from the preceding Sengoku period. It is also worth noting that the mobilization of military service and the extraction of tax revenue were related; many of the low-level warriors who served in the warlord's armies, and who were recruited through "surrogate parent, surrogate child" relationships, were also agriculturalists who received significant tax breaks for their military service.

Yet another technique that many Sengoku warlords employed to legitimate their rule and authorize their administration was the development and promulgation of provincial codes (*bunkokuhō*), often in the form of house precepts or recorded sayings. For example, Imagawa Ujichika (1473?–1526), the ruler of a large swath of territory in central Japan, including at various points Suruga, Tōtōmi, Mikawa, and Owari Provinces, recorded his thoughts on the administration of this territory just months before his death, with the goal of authorizing his successor as well as preserving the practical knowledge that came with the experience of rule.[37] The text was successful (it is sometimes cited as an example of how the Imagawa transitioned from governors to warlords), and was indeed revised and expanded by his son, Yoshimoto, in 1553. The codes include commentary on proper administration of land transfers, organization of the military, propriety and behavior, regulations on violence, and so on. Many examples of these kinds of codes are extant – the Date

Daimyo and Domain, 1491–1590" (PhD dissertation, Princeton University Press, 1983), 73–89.

[34] See Murai Ryōsuke's helpful discussion of Ikegami and her critics on the issue of *kenchi* in *Sengoku daimyō kenryoku kōzō no kenkyū* (Shibunkaku Shuppan, 2012), 6–8.

[35] Fukui Ken, *Chūsei*, 672–674.

[36] See Asao, "The Sixteenth-Century Unification," 44, on Nobunaga's use of tax statements and land surveys; also see Berry's discussion of the surveys of the Imagawa in *Hideyoshi*, 29–30, and of Hideyoshi, 111–126.

[37] "Imagawa kana mokuroku," in *Chūsei hōsei shiryō shū*, vol. 3, ed. Satō Shin'ichi, Ikeuchi Yoshisuke, and Momose Kesao (Iwanami Shoten, 1965), 115–134. For an English discussion of the Imagawa code, see Ronald K. Frank, "Battle for Minds: Regulating Buddhism in Sixteenth-Century Japan," *Asia Pacific: Perspectives* 5.1 (December 2004): 12–17.

in 1536, the Takeda in 1547, the Yūki in 1556, the Chōsokabe in 1596 – yet historians in some cases doubt the authenticity of these texts as Sengoku documents, pointing instead to the zeal of early modern warrior families for producing sources to enhance the military and administrative pedigrees of their families. A bewildering variety exist as well, such as the Rokkaku family version, which was originally compiled by provincial warriors and then authorized by the warlord's approval in 1567.[38]

Several documents that we can broadly understand as provincial codes are also associated with the Asakura family, though the exact origins of these texts are unclear. The most famous is *The Collected Sayings of Asakura Eirin (Asakura Takakage jōjō)*, attributed to the leader of the family during the Ōnin War, Eirin.[39] This text consists of sixteen injunctions of varying lengths followed by a longer concluding text; as a result, the document is sometimes referred to as the "17 articles of Asakura Eirin." The original is no longer extant, and the various manuscript transcriptions that do exist have differing titles and some minor variations in the contents, but this is not uncommon for the provincial codes of Sengoku warlords. The oldest of the transcriptions appears to be the 1669 copy in the Meiji University library, titled *The Wall Writings of Asakura Eirin (Asakura Eirin kabegaki)*. The sayings are largely practical, focusing on guaranteeing the continuity of the Asakura family as well as their continued governance of the province of Echizen. Overarching themes of the text include the following: avoid nepotism and reward merit; invest in military readiness rather than social prestige; treat retainers properly to engender social cohesion; do not trust neighboring warlords; and practice measured compassion for all within the domain. Several of the individual injunctions in this text are remarkably similar to lines in other Sengoku provincial and house codes, including those attributed to Ise Sadachika, Hōjō Sōun, Tako Tokitaka, and Uesugi Sadamasa. Although we do not know the exact process by which this text was written or recorded, it possesses an undeniable composite quality, reading like a pastiche of the personal sayings of one ruler alongside inherited aphorisms, recently learned techniques, and general

---

[38] David Eason has argued that the conventional view of these texts as an expression of elite warrior dominance in the coercive mode is not supported by the sources themselves. See Eason, "The Culture of Disputes in Early Modern Japan, 1550–1700" (PhD dissertation, UCLA, 2009), 22.

[39] This is not, however, the earliest provincial code attributed to an Asakura leader. The 1910-published collection *Asakura sōsho* contains a *kakun* known as *Hirokage kakun* that claims to have been authored by Asakura Hirokage (1255–1352) in the fourteenth century. The text was probably authored by samurai scholars in the Hagino clan, in Fukui, based on other *kakun* that were becoming increasingly de rigueur in the eighteenth century. See Fukui, *Asakura shi no kakun*, 4–5.

political principles bundled together into one document. The research of historians in Japan does suggest, however, that the core provisions in this text were recorded by Asakura Eirin himself, even if parts of the extant text were edited or added by later generations or indeed after the Asakura family was destroyed.[40]

Another well-known provincial code associated with the Asakura is attributed to the inveterate military man and significant leader in the family, Asakura Norikage (1474–1555, the youngest child of Eirin), better known by his Buddhist retirement name of Sōteki. He was born to the high-ranking second wife of Eirin. Her previous child had been adopted into another warrior family and then murdered by one of his adopted brothers, who reportedly resented the noble standing accorded the new arrival. After giving birth to Sōteki, she gave him the same name as her deceased son (Norikage) and doted upon him. He was raised, in his own words, to be selfish (*wagamama*); yet his mother also taught him to make a name for himself, to study culture and the military arts in equal measure, and to be devoted to Buddhism.[41] Although he never occupied the position of lord of the domain, Sōteki put his mother's teachings into practice in a distinguished career in which he served three different Asakura warlords and participated in twelve military campaigns against religious uprisings, neighboring military forces, and internal rebellions. Sōteki was famous as a specialist in long campaigns involving sieges and protracted negotiations, and he became well known among the warlords of the region as well as the elites of Kyoto.[42] He also maintained a close relationship with the poet Sōchō, who mentions him numerous times in *The Journal of Sōchō* (*Sōchō shuki*). Most notable, perhaps, is the following passage:

A Poem on Asakura Norikage's Hawks

In the garden of his residence, Asakura Tarōzemon Norikage had for four or five years set up nests for hawks. Last year for the first time two, one large and one small, hatched chicks. It was a very rare event. The retired abbot of Ikkeken at Kenninji temple wrote of the chicks in his *Yōyōki*, and various poems in Chinese and Japanese were written about them as well. I therefore composed this:

| *mata kikazu* | Unheard of before: |
| *togaeru yama no* | bringing chicks up from nestlings |

---

[40] The most thorough and recent examination of the *kakun* of the Asakura is found in Fukui, *Asakura shi no kakun*.
[41] These details come from the mortuary text for Sōteki's mother, which is quoted in Fukui, *Asakura shi no kakun*, 20.
[42] Fukui, *Asakura shi no kakun*, 23.

mine narade	not in the mountains
sudatasesomuru	where they go to molt,
niwa no matsu ga e	but in the boughs of a garden pine![43]

Sōchō also notes that both he and Sōteki had donated funds to the reconstruction of the main gate at Daitokuji, one of the main Zen temples in Kyoto that had been partially destroyed in the civil wars of the age. Sōteki's success here at breeding falcons is yet another sign of his almost unbelievable polymathy. If his remarkable success in many ventures wasn't recorded in both a wide variety of sources as well as some particularly reliable ones, such as Sōchō's account, it would indeed be difficult to accept. Yet perhaps Sōteki simply embodied the ideals and aspirations of his status group. Raised in privilege and backed by significant wealth and other material resources, he thrived in the realm of military accomplishment – including not only warfare but leadership and of course hunting with raptors (*takagari*) – as well as the realm of culture, seen in his close association with Sōchō and in the writings attributed to his brush.

The original text of *The Anecdotes of Asakura Sōteki* (*Asakura Sōteki waki*) is no longer extant. Instead, a number of transcriptions exist that are largely similar to one another, with the exception of one or two anecdotes. According to prefatory remarks, the text represents the stories of Sōteki as recorded by his vassal Hagiwara Munetoshi (d. 1570), who worked as Sōteki's secretary in the latter part of his career, though Munetoshi seems likely to have written the book after Sōteki's death in 1555. Furthermore, considering that the warlord Imagawa Yoshimoto is mentioned by name in the text, and Yoshimoto famously died in an attack by Oda Nobunaga's army in 1560, it seems likely to have been written before that year.[44] Historians have hypothesized that the frequent use of phrases such as "his lordship shared this during idle chatter" (*jōjō onzatsudan no koto*) indicates that the text represents not a specific lecture imparted by Sōteki during his final campaign, but rather an odd assortment of aphorisms absorbed during Munetoshi's many years of service. Historians have also hypothesized that Munetoshi must have interviewed Asakura vassals and indeed Yoshikage – the Asakura lord at the time of Sōteki's death – to produce the text.[45] One of the goals of the writing was surely the preservation of the wisdom of the generations of Asakura leaders for the current head of the family, as well as the amplification of the reputation of the lord of the domain.

---

[43] Translated in Horton, *The Journal of Sōchō*, 45.   [44] Fukui, *Asakura shi no kakun*, 28.
[45] Fukui, *Asakura shi no kakun*, 28.

The contents of the *Anecdotes of Asakura Sōteki* are dominated by passages related to war: accounts of Sōteki's own experiences in battle, instructions for leading an army and engaging in efficient wartime communication, stories of the actions of previous Asakura rulers, and so on. Also common are passages related to lord–vassal relations, in which Sōteki instructs the reader in the proper methods of managing retainers and their families. Much of this material is similar to the aphoristic exhortations found in other provincial codes, though this text seems to be largely original in its form, if influenced by other codes in its overall shape. But it is the passages that relate the particular experiences of Sōteki and other members of the Asakura family that are most original and therefore most valuable. His account of his relationship with the last Asakura lord, Yoshikage, and his sense of gratitude for his appointment is notable.[46] His description of the decision to retire and shave his head, becoming a member of a Buddhist order and taking the name "Sōteki" in the process, is likewise informative. And in one of the final passages, when he discusses his hope to study etiquette under a Zen abbot from Daitokuji to help with his tendency to feel anxiety,[47] he conveys an experience that seems to transcend time and space in its universality. The text is useful for its emphasis on the methods of perpetuating the power of the Asakura while also reminding us of their humanity. The dissemination of these kinds of documents among Asakura family members and high-ranking vassals created a sense of shared values, strengthened the community, and provided concrete guidance to a warrior organization that needed strong leadership.

One final technique of maintaining lordly authority that I would like to address here is the management of the Asakura's relationship with the Ashikaga shogunate, nominally the warrior authority of the realm despite the plentiful evidence to the contrary. The Sengoku period is often described in English literature as an age of completely decentralized politics, when the notion of a single warrior government with authority over the entire archipelago had functionally vanished. On the surface this claim is accurate; the Ashikaga were unable to issue directives to the assorted warlords who ruled domains across Japan in this period and were frequently manipulated and constrained by warlords seeking to gain an advantage over their rivals. Simultaneously, however, many warlords continued to turn to the Ashikaga as a source of symbolic authority, striving to draw some form of political legitimacy from the system of ranks and appointments that itself represented an extension of the power

---

[46] Anecdotes 49 and 83.   [47] Anecdote 76.

of the imperial court. The Asakura, perhaps because of their relative proximity to the capital, continued to pursue the approbation of the elites in Kyoto even as they fiercely maintained their political independence and military autonomy.

This relationship was maintained on both sides through acts of what I have elsewhere referred to as *samurai sociability*, meaning ritualized exchanges of gifts and participation in cultural rituals that reaffirmed connections, hierarchy, and cycles of obligation and exemption.[48] Such activity is apparent in every generation of Asakura rulers from the time of their elevation to the status of rulers of the province, up until their destruction at the hands of Oda Nobunaga. In fact, much of the energy of the final leader of the Asakura, Yoshikage, was expended in his final years engaging in social and cultural rituals that had as their goal the solidification of the Asakura–Ashikaga alliance and the abrogation of Oda claims to central authority. Those efforts failed, not because the social and cultural rituals were ineffective, but because Nobunaga was bolder in his willingness to take risks, to form and then break alliances, and to carefully but consistently advance his own fortunes above the needs of his allies.

The historian Satō Kei has catalogued a range of ritual exchanges between the Asakura and Ashikaga, and several examples will helpfully illustrate the character of this relationship that was maintained in part through gifts and visitations. In the beginning of the Asakura rule of Echizen, for example, when Asakura Eirin was still pacifying regions of the province that had been under the control of his rivals the Kai, he sent a gift of a long sword and cash to Ashikaga Yoshimasa, evidenced by a letter of reply from the shogunal advisor and meddler Ise Sadachika. Such gifts were relatively common in these exchanges, signifying both the status of both parties as elite warriors as well as the financial need of the shogunate. The new Asakura lord, in turn, wanted recognition from the Ashikaga of his position and successes in pacifying his province. This kind of hierarchical reciprocity was key to successful ritual exchanges.[49] More broadly, such rituals helped to maintain the connection between the Ashikaga as nominal warrior authorities and the Asakura as their appointed governors of the province of Echizen, and the Asakura often sent money to the Ashikaga to mark anniversaries. For example, Eirin sent cash as a gift to the shogunate to mark the coming-of-age ceremony of Ashikaga Yoshihisa (1465–1489), Yoshimasa's son and heir (and one

---

[48] Pitelka, *Spectacular Accumulation*.
[49] Satō Kei, "Asakura shi to Muromachi bakufu: orei shinjō o chūshin to shite," in Mizuno and Satō, eds., *Sengoku daimyo Asakura shi to Ichijōdani*, 36.

of the causes of the Ōnin War).[50] This gift would have communicated the Asakura's ongoing support for the Ashikaga, signaled their desire for the support of the shogunate, and displayed the relative economic might of the Asakura as lords of their province.

Another round of gift-giving accompanied the succession of Asakura Ujikage (1449–1486) to the headship of the family when his father Eirin died of illness in 1481. Ujikage first notified the shogunate of his father's illness, and then, after his passing, that he had succeeded his father. Such an announcement was vital to the (largely unsuccessful, at this point) attempts of the Ashikaga to maintain order through the prevention of succession disputes, which so often caused internal strife in warrior families as well as warfare on a much broader scale. Accompanying his formal announcement, Ujikage sent gifts of swords, cash, and Chinese art for Yoshimasa, Yoshihisa, and various members of the shogunal cabinet. Yoshimasa replied with a gift of a sword as well as a formal acknowledgment of the proper succession protocol and procedure.[51]

This established the basic pattern of interaction, with some variations, that would hold until the death of Ujikage in 1486. What is striking if not surprising is the consistency of the idea of mutual benefit in the gifts, letters, and funds exchanged, with the bulk of money, of course, flowing from the Asakura to the Ashikaga, and the symbolic authority of the shogunate flowing in the opposite direction. When Yoshimasa built and moved into his Higashiyama Palace (the silver pavilion), he did so with considerable support from warlords like the Asakura, who contributed cash on multiple occasions, sometimes as gifts seemingly given voluntarily, and in other cases in response to shogunal directives.[52] Ujikage seems to have taken advantage of every opportunity to affirm his relationship to the Ashikaga, and the shogunate under Yoshimasa took the opportunity to raise funds through these kinds of relationships.

There are fewer records of the next generation of the Asakura family exchanging gifts with the Ashikaga, though this may be a result of a general lack of shogunal documentation in the late fifteenth and early sixteenth century, or because of general turmoil on the shogunal line. Asakura Sadakage (1473–1512) did exchange gifts with Ashikaga Yoshitane (1466–1523), for example, the tenth shogun of his family and the sole individual to occupy that role twice. First, he received this post in 1489 when the previous shogun died in battle. He was exiled during a conflict with the Hosokawa clan, but in 1508 was reinstated

---

[50] Satō, "Asakura shi to Muromachi bakufu," 37–38.
[51] Satō, "Asakura shi to Muromachi bakufu," 39.
[52] Satō, "Asakura shi to Muromachi bakufu," 40–41.

when the Ōuchi clan took control of Kyoto. In 1520 he was driven into exile yet again, a kind of living embodiment of the tumultuous fortunes of the Ashikaga family and the sorry state of shogunal authority in the first half of the sixteenth century. The relative lack of Asakura exchanges with the Ashikaga in this period thus may have been a strategic move for a warlord family whose fortunes were in a sense relatively stable, with little to gain from association with such a fragile political institution.

The fourth-generation lord of Echizen, Takakage, became the head of his family somewhat suddenly in 1512 when his father died in the midst of a falconry outing. Takakage was nineteen at the time, the eldest son, and well positioned to immediately take over the rule of the province, which he would lead effectively for almost four decades. He engaged in several exchanges of gifts and letters with Ashikaga Yoshiharu (1511–1550), the twelfth shogun of his line and one who had little success establishing himself as a real political power because of his lack of military strength. Takakage sent him a gift when he entered Kyoto in 1534, receiving not only a letter of reply from the shogun but a gift of a lacquered palanquin as well.[53] He replied with a follow-up gift that indicated his willingness to provide military support to the shogun, and several years later he was rewarded, perhaps, with an appointment to the ranks of the Shogunal Advisory Council (*shōbanshū*), a high-status post that had lost some of its luster in an era when the shogun himself was frequently chased out of Kyoto. Still, it is perhaps the most tangible sign that the labor expended by the Asakura in these frequent missives to the Ashikaga and reciprocal gift giving could lead to palpable improvements in their ranking with the fragile warrior hierarchy. This same quest to cement their status as influential friends of the shogun is clearly one of the causes of their ultimate downfall, as we will see in Chapter 6.

Conclusion: Places of Power

A key element in the administrative and military strategies of most rising warrior leaders in the late medieval period was the agglomeration of power in a residence – sometimes a castle, sometimes a palace – served by a town or small city. Provincial warriors (*kokujin*), governors (*shugo*), and other late medieval warrior leaders constructed fortresses in the fifteenth century. The fortresses of governors (*shugosho*) – who often resided in Kyoto, but also maintained provincial residences in some cases – are perhaps the clearest antecedent to sixteenth-century warrior

[53] Satō, "Asakura shi to Muromachi bakufu," 48.

palace cities. Shugo fortresses often included a large hall surrounded by moats or trenches, as well as a residence adjacent to a shrine/temple complex, near the smaller domiciles of vassals. One well-known example is Kasugayama Castle (present-day Jōetsu, Niigata Prefecture), most famous as the home base of the Sengoku warlord Uesugi Kenshin, but originally built by the Uesugi in the late fourteenth to early fifteenth century, when they first entered the province of Echigo as the shogunally appointed governors.[54]

Fortified urban centers also appear in the histories of uprisings and leagues that played such an important role in medieval social and political history in Japan. In the case of provincial uprisings (*kuni ikki*), in which local rulers (*kokujin*) banded together to resist the rise of warlords, the extraction of taxes by shrines and temples, and other intrusions into provincial affairs by what were seen as outside elites, fortified centers often played a key role in their military actions and also stimulated and protected mercantile activity at the regional level.[55] A group of fortified centers from the Fugenji valley in Minamiyamashiro, for example, seem to have been linked together into a kind of networked defense structure that helped to secure the famous Yamashiro provincial uprising, which ruled the province from 1485 to 1493.[56] Although the history of the castle town in Japan is often superimposed on the teleological chronology of progress toward the unified early modern state, with one shogunal castle in Edo and one castle in theory symbolizing the authority of each domainal lord, in the medieval period interlinked fortresses and urban centers could and often did represent resistance to consolidation and unification.

How, then, did Sengoku warlords use the palace city (or the castle town) as a technique of aggregating power, particularly in the combination of administrative and military functions in one site? As was true above, a single pattern is impossible to discern, since some Sengoku warlords evolved from long-serving governors and thus had relatively stable headquarters, while others, such as the Asakura, rose to prominence as political and military opportunists, and thus developed their urban and defensive structures relatively later. Yet the theme of concentrating military, administrative, social, and cultural functions in one site is fairly consistent across multiple examples.

---

[54] See Nihon Kōkogaku Kyōkai, ed., *Shugosho kara Sengoku joka e* (Meichō Shuppan, 1994), on the topic of governor fortresses, and 9–52 on Kasugayama Castle.

[55] Kojima Michihiro, *Sengoku/shokuhōki no toshi to chiiki* (Seishi Shuppan, 2005), particularly part 1, 11–76.

[56] Wakita, *Sengoku daimyō*, 178–180; Carol Richmond Tsang, *War and Faith: Ikkō Ikki in Late Muromachi Japan* (Harvard East Asian Center, 2007), 42–43.

For example, the first reference to Ichijō castle/city (*Ichijō jō*) appears in a text authored by the priest Tōshō Shūgen (1391–1462), and reports that Ichijōdani was constructed as the home base of Asakura Iekage, the father of Eirin. Iekage died in 1451, so Japanese historians estimate that the castle was completed around 1450. It appears to have been used as a military fortress early in its history, as the Asakura defended it against an invasion within years of its founding. In the following decade, a city gate (*kido*) was constructed near Abaka, the "Chinatown" mercantile community located at the conflux of the Ichijō and the Asuwa Rivers.[57] This was surely a factor in the success of Asakura Eirin in navigating the tumultuous tides of the Ōnin War, giving him a stable base of operation from which to launch his effort to overthrow the Shiba, remove the Kai, and establish a new administration over Echizen. When the Kai attempted multiple times to dislodge the Asakura by invading from Kaga to the north, the Asakura were able to resist these advances from the defensive position of Ichijōdani. The rise of the Asakura as a regional power overlaps precisely with the establishment of Ichijōdani as a military base and the extension of the site as a multifunctional urban center.[58]

The case of the Oda contrasts in significant ways. In the years after the Ōnin War, when rival branches of the Oda family competed with one another but collectively dominated Owari, they employed a range of castles across the province. Shobata Castle, for example, was constructed by Oda Nobusada (d. 1538), one of the Three Magistrates of Kiyosu (*Kiyosu sanbugyō*) and the head of the secondary Oda lineage, which in fact came to be known as the Shobata line because it was based in this fortress. Oda Nobunaga was born in this castle in 1534, though his father Nobuhide moved the family to Nagoya Castle in 1538. Nobuhide moved his home base two additional times before his death in 1551 – a sign, perhaps, of the ongoing precarity of his position – though it is unclear if Nobunaga accompanied him. Nobunaga himself also led a somewhat peripatetic existence once he became head of his branch of the family, and moved to Kiyosu Castle (built in the early fifteenth century by the Shiba) in 1555 after he and his uncle schemed to eliminate the rightful occupants. Kiyosu served as his center of operations through several

---

[57] Satō Kei, "Jō: Asakura shi no seisui to Ichijōdani," in Mizuno and Satō, eds., *Sengoku daimyo Asakura shi to Ichijōdani*, 17–18; Takashi, "Jōkamachi Ichijōdani no seiritsu to hen'yō," 43–48.

[58] The Asakura are also associated with a significant medieval text on castle construction, *Chikujō-ki*. The historian Lee Butler has prepared a preliminary (unpublished) translation of this manual, and Erdmann discusses it at length in his dissertation, "Azuchi Castle," 252–253 and 302–303.

years of internecine conflicts with his own branch and the Oda family as a whole, as both a military headquarters and a primary residence. In 1563, to support his military advance into Mino Province, Nobunaga constructed a fortress on Mt. Komaki, an eighty-six-meter hill in the middle of the Nobi plain, well situated with views of the entire region, and moved there with his entire administration. Recent excavations of the site indicate that Komaki Castle also had a fairly well developed castle town, with the kind of status differentiation, commoner shops, and warrior neighborhoods seen in better-known sites such as Ichijōdani.[59] Despite his investment in this urban center, Nobunaga's tenure there lasted just a few years, and in 1567 he relocated to Inabayama, the mountain fortress that he captured from the warlord Saitō Dōsan in Mino. Nobunga renamed the location Gifu and expanded it into a larger and more impressive castle, with a stone-reinforced feature known as a "tiger's mouth" entrance (koguchi) or a barbican. Nobunaga lived in this castle despite its somewhat inaccessible location, and developed a commercial district, as well as multiple market sites inside and outside the town gate. Still, after less than a decade, he began work on a new headquarters in 1576, perhaps because of the series of military victories he had enjoyed in the previous years that necessitated a new and grander stage for the pageantry he clearly enjoyed. He moved to the still-under-construction Azuchi Castle just a month after the beginning of construction and ruled from this site, which would develop into one of the largest and most impressive castles and castle towns in all of Japanese history, until his death in 1582.[60] The Oda thus illustrate the trajectory of some warrior families from an old model that prioritized the utility of mobile encampments over permanent headquarters to a gradual embrace of the settled model of the castle town.[61]

One additional example demonstrates the significance of fortified urban centers in the quest to establish independent authority and to agglomerate power by warlords in the sixteenth century, as well as the diversity of such urban structures. The aforementioned Ōtomo family, governors of Bungo Province in Kyushu since the Kamakura period, made the town of Funai (present-day Oita City) their headquarters because it had previously been the provincial office and home to an

[59] Kojima Michihiro and Senda Yoshihiro, "Shiro to toshi," in Iwanami Kōza Nihon tsūshi, vol. 10: Chūsei 4, ed. Asao Naohiro et al. (Iwanami Kōza, 1994), 201–203.

[60] See Lamers's helpful summary of the construction of Azuchi in Japonius Tyrannus, 122–140.

[61] See Spafford's thorough study of these issues in A Sense of Place, particularly chapter 4.

imperial magistrate.[62] Unlike Ichijōdani, with its history of approximately one century, or the various Oda castles and castle towns, which were on average active for a decade or less, Funai served as the headquarters of the Ōtomo as well as a thriving urban center for the entire medieval period, more than 400 years. The main family residence shifted locations numerous times in the history of the city, but by the Sengoku period it was located in a particularly hilly region of the city, and had two semifortified stories. It served as both the residential and administrative center of the Ōtomo, with private living space as well as public and administrative zones, but appears to have been less important as a military base. Like many Sengoku-era warlords, the Ōtomo relied on a separate mountaintop fortress for wartime activities, at least until the late sixteenth century.[63] In a region that was distant from the politics of the capital and that was home to a number of powerful warrior families, the Ōtomo managed an unusually lengthy tenure as governors and then warlords largely through their reliance on a castle town headquarters that fulfilled multiple functions.

Fortresses, residential palaces, and the towns and cities that grew up near them played many roles in the expanding administrations of warlords in sixteenth-century Japan. Fortresses and later castles served in many instances as residences as well as military headquarters, though these functions could also be disaggregated as in the case of the Asakura and the Ōtomo. These sites were home to public reception halls, administrative offices, gardens and tea houses, and other spaces that served to convey messages about the power of the rulers, and also as stages for various social and political rituals. The warlords who in some cases had newly come to dominate their home region, such as the Asakura, or who had long been seen as central authority figures, such as the Ōtomo, concentrated their resources, their activities, and their assets – financial, military, and human – in these urban centers. These distillations of the power of Sengoku warlords represent the trend toward not unification but rather regionalization, the creation of distinct political units at the provincial level.

---

[62] For a brief overview, see Kojima Michihiro, *Shiseki de yomu Nihon no rekishi, vol. 7: Sengoku no jidai* (Yoshikawa Kōbunkan, 2009), 116–121.

[63] Toyama, *Ōtomo Sōrin*, 118–128.

4   The Material Foundations of Faith

> Images and objects are not inessential parts of religion .... Images and objects perform powerful cultural work in mediating individual and social bodies and the sacred, and they often do it far from official religious sites such as altars or temples. Homes, work places, schools, the road, and the individual bodies of the devout are often the places where amulets, symbols, ex-votos, devotional pictures, souvenirs, trophies, emblems, commemorative objects, and mnemonic devices go to work.   —David Morgan, "The Material Culture of Lived Religions"

In nearly every dig in Ichijōdani, and indeed in most late medieval urban centers across Japan, archaeologists find the same type of object in extremely large quantities, yet this product is rarely displayed in museums, analyzed in scholarship, or included in the canon of Japanese art.[1] The object is the handmade earthenware dish (Figure 4.1), a genre of ceramics known as *kawarake*, which played a vital role in the social and cultural life of premodern Japanese everywhere. These earthenware dishes were used in a wide variety of daily contexts: to make offerings at small shrines and altars, to perform auspicious ceremonies, to exchange food or drink in ritualized warrior meetings and banquets, and to burn oil and candles in the dark. Their singular feature was not the complexity of their construction, being made of rough local clay and pinched into a dish shape before being fired to a relatively low temperature (less than 1,000°C, making this a low-fire or earthenware ceramic) by local artisans. Nor was it their appearance or aesthetic; unremarkable in structure and lacking in any decoration, these dishes were mostly uniform without being either symmetrical or

---

[1] Two exceptions in English are Louise Allison Cort's discussion of the fading modern practice of making *kawarake*, "Disposable but Indispensable: The Earthenware Vessel as Vehicle of Meaning in Japan," in *What's the Use of Art? Asian Visual and Material Culture in Context*, ed. Jan Mrazek and Morgan Pitelka (University of Hawai'i Press, 2007), 46–76; and David Spafford's discussion of *kawarake* distribution as a marker of political geography in the late medieval Kantō region, *A Sense of Place: The Political Landscape in Late Medieval Japan* (Harvard Asia Center, 2013), 196–203.

Figure 4.1 Excavated earthenware (*kawarake*) dishes
(Japanese), Ichijōdani.
Used with permission of the Fukui Prefectural Ichijōdani Asakura Family
History Museum.

ostentatiously asymmetrical, and without any glaze or natural ash
deposits to enhance the exterior. Instead, it was their superfluousness
that made them useful or, as Louise Cort put it, "disposable but
indispensable."[2]

These ubiquitous excavated objects serve as a useful reminder of the
central role of ritual practices in the daily interactions of late medieval
Japanese. As we shall see below, excavated earthenware bowls and cups
are voluminous in all dig sites within Ichijōdani, but their relative quantity varies by the status of the occupants of the site, and this data provides
clues about their uses in daily life. The relative invisibility of these
earthenware objects in the art historical canon, in mainstream cultural
history narratives, and in museums and textbooks about Japanese civil-
ization also demonstrates that much of the lived experience of premodern
Japan is elided in our shared master narratives about history. Religious
life, particularly the daily interactions between people, places, and things,
is less well understood than religious institutional history, doctrine, and
heirloom art. The excavated evidence from Ichijōdani and other provincial urban centers allows us to ask questions about belief and daily
practice in a time of warfare and political fragmentation. It also allows
us to consider religious culture without focusing on the ideological
appropriation of religious language by political figures such as the

[2] Cort, "Disposable but Indispensable."

unifiers, a phenomenon that Herman Ooms referred to as "systematic sacralization" and that Kanda Chisato notes was key to the moralistic drive of rulers who waged war to accrue power.[3] Instead, these material remnants of daily religious and ritual practice point toward the agency of believers in urban sites like Ichijōdani, their intentional engagement with religious institutions and ritual cultures large and small, in an effort, it seems, to affect change, purify their interactions, and accrue merit. I pursue this argument without idealizing the archaeological evidence from Ichijōdani as representing a "purer" version of religious practice, or suggesting that politics were absent from the religious patronage of the Asakura and the elites of the city. Indeed, the most intensive consumers of *kawarake* appear to have been the elite warriors who ruled the province from the city of Ichijōdani, as we shall see below.

The producers of earthenware vessels, by contrast, are largely anonymous in the historical record, as are most potters until the late sixteenth and early seventeenth centuries. Yet excavations of Ichijōdani have located the residences and production sites of *kawarake* makers for the first time. One notable site (excavation no. 43, conducted in 1982) of a neighborhood called Fukube revealed the residence and workshop of an earthenware potter, with enormous quantities of low-temperature ceramic shards as well as a large Echizen-ware ceramic vat, probably used to hold the significant quantities of water needed for the hand-pinching process of making earthenware vessels.[4] Archaeologists also excavated two types of kilns from the site, clear evidence that this was the location of both the hand-made production and the firing of these vessels that were so central to religious and ritual activity in medieval Japan.[5] As a

---

[3] Herman Ooms, *Tokugawa Ideology: Early Constructs, 1570–1680* (Princeton University Press, 1985), 63; Kanda Chisato, *Shūkyō de yomu Sengoku jidai* (Kōdansha, 2010), 55–56.

[4] Cort describes the production process, based on fieldwork conducted in the 1970s, as follows: "The old woman, wearing an apron over an everyday kimono, prepared the clay and made preliminary forms for saucers – breaking off a chunk of clay from a large ball, picking out any stones, rolling the clay on a small board into a thick coil, slicing the coil into even segments, and flattening each segment against the board into a disk. She piled the disks in stacks of five. The middle-aged woman, who had short hair and was dressed in slacks, took a disk in the palm of her left hand and shaped it into a saucer by patting the center with the fingers of her right hand, then patting the edges with the heel of that hand .... She lined them up on a long board – three across, seventeen down. The man seated nearby used a strip of banding iron to trim the edges." See Cort, "Disposable but Indispensable," 62–63.

[5] Much of this material is unfortunately still unpublished. For a good summary of the work on kawarake in Ichijōdani, see Abe Akinori, "Echizen ni okeru 15 seiki kōhan – 16 seiki chūyō no doki/tōjiki," in *Hokuriku ni miru kinsei seiritsuki no doki/tōjiki no yōsō: jōkamachi to sono shūhen iseki no hajiki zara (kawarake) o chūshin ni* (Ishikawa Ken Maizō Bunkazai Sentaa, 2019), 19–27.

123

city, Ichijōdani thus had liminal spaces and in-between neighborhoods in which not only commoner craftspeople such as the bead-makers, dyers, carpenters, and metalsmiths lived and worked, but more marginal and possibly itinerant workers such as the relatively low-status earthenware potters could reside and produce their wares. The fact that this atelier was so centrally located also speaks to the significance of the usage of these ritual vessels in daily life.

This chapter considers the religious life of the residents of Ichijōdani starting with the material evidence, which leads us down different roads than a documentary or institutional history might explore. We might ask what it means to turn our attention to religious life as a separate sphere from daily life in this study of Ichijōdani. Separating out religious and ritual practices from other practices, and sacred spaces from secular ones, is perhaps an exercise in futility, and in most instances an anachronistic one at that. Is a flower arrangement in a Chinese vase positioned carefully next to a hanging scroll with the calligraphic poem of a Zen monk an object of devotion or perhaps a tool used in cultural practice? Is a banquet held in a temple for a visiting dignitary an acknowledgment of the principles of Buddhism or an appropriation of a sacred space for a secular purpose? What qualifies an object or a building as religious, or a space as sacred? Andrew Watsky argues that the glorious ornamented constructions seen in the art and architecture of late medieval warlords embodied the period's notions of the sacred. Rulers, he argues, sought to link their rule to traditional understandings of the gods as protective forces through the construction of works that invoked the numinous power of the sacred. Anton Schweizer similarly proposes that the glorious late medieval and early modern architectural and decorative works of warrior leaders represented their "religious commitment, cultural pedigree, and political ambitions" while also functioning to "trigger notional associations and solicit emotional responses" among observers. Pattern, repetition, and design in decoration convey sacred meaning:

The very presence of rich ornamentation is pivotal to indicating the function of a given building; that the subject matter of the base modules of repeating patterns is equally of relevance; that the seeming redundancy of the same repeated patterns in itself communicates specific significance; and, lastly, that pleasure indeed is an important component of ornament – yet not in the sense of indeterminate delight but rather as an integral part of the message.[6]

[6] Andrew M. Watsky, *Chikubushima: Deploying the Sacred Arts in Momoyama Japan* (University of Washington Press, 2004), 24–25; Anton Schweizer, *Ōsaki Hachiman: Architecture, Materiality, and Samurai Power* (Reimer, 2016), 17–18 and 127.

In the case of Ichijōdani, it is likely that some religious structures of the city, and certainly the palatial residence of the lord, conveyed similar sacred messages through rich ornamentation and decorative density. As we will see below, the archaeological evidence demonstrates that many of these sites were key locations on the larger map of Asakura politics and cultural patronage, and regularly hosted powerful visitors, functioned as venues for performances and ritual sociability, and played intimate roles in the ritual life of the ruling family and their vassals. Some were large complexes with multiple buildings and grand entry gates, while others were of high quality but tucked away in more private and intimate locations, at the base of the mountains. However, the destruction of the city in 1573 erased the very ornamentation that is so richly analyzed in the works of Watsky and Schweizer, reducing the decorative programs and complex articulations of sacred meaning to ash. What endures, strikingly, are the much humbler and more durable edifices of religious practice, which I will refer to as the material foundations of faith. I hope to suggest here that the idea of the sacred – and by extension the power of ornamentation that scholars have celebrated in studies of late medieval art and architecture – rests on a bedrock of faith with two primary layers: first, belief in the power of ritual action, and second, the hope to inter- vene in the cycle of samsara through acts of material memorialization. This core conceptual substructure of late medieval faith, laid bare by the incineration of the capital of the Asakura and the subsequent excavation of its remains, is a striking and valuable piece of evidence in our attempt to study the lived experiences and worldview of sixteenth-century urban residents.

Religious Institutions in Ichijōdani

The city of Ichijōdani was punctuated by religious sites, and the list of temples and shrines is longer and more complex than I can fully explore in this monograph. Surveying a few key sites will help provide an over- view of the prominence of such locations in the city. In 1975, relatively early in the long (and still ongoing) research excavation of locations in Ichijōdani, archaeologists excavated a temple site known as Saigōji (Figure 4.2), in the Akabuchi neighborhood across the river from the Asakura residence (Map 1.5).[7] The complex was protected on the north- ern and southern sides by earthen walls, and the western side was

---

[7] Fukui Ken Kyōiku Iinkai, *Tokubetsu shiseki: Ichijōdani Asakura shi iseki VII* (Fukui Ken Kyōiku Iinkai, 1976), covers sites 15–17. The Akabuchi neighborhood, which contains Saigōji, is site 17. The full excavation report for site 17 is Fukui Kenritsu Ichijōdani

Figure 4.2 Photograph of the excavation site of Saigōji.
Used with permission of the Fukui Prefectural Ichijōdani Asakura Family
History Museum.

naturally marked by the slope of the mountain; it is likely that an additional wall demarcated the eastern edge of the compound. The complex
occupied an area of approximately 1,200 square meters, with a main gate
in the southern wall and a rear gate in the northwest corner. Ditches also
marked the outside of the compound, beyond the earthen walls. Inside
the grounds, supplicants would have encountered a main hall (hondō)
with three bays and a roofed entrance. Another large building, roughly
the same size as the main hall, was located to the west inside the
compound. A covered corridor extended out from the main hall, and a
belfry stood in front of it.[8] Behind the complex to the north was an
earthen wall, next to a number of graves and other memorial markers.
Interestingly, archaeologists have not discovered a fresh-water well on
the property, and none of the structures shows signs of having served as
a residence.

Asakura Shi Iseki Shiryōkan, *Ichijōdani Asakura shi iseki hakkutsu chōsa hōkokusho
VIII* (2000).
[8] Suitō Makoto, "Ichijōdani no shinkō sekai," in Ono, ed., *Jitsuzō no Sengoku jōkamachi*,
153; Fukui Kenritsu Ichijōdani Asakura Shi Iseki Shiryōkan, *Ichijōdani no shūkyū to shinkō*
(Fukui Kenritsu Ichijōdani Asakura Shi Iseki Shiryōkan, 1999), 24.

Although it has become common to refer to this temple as Saigōji, in truth scholars are not sure of the precise Chinese characters used to refer to it in writing, and can only hypothesize about its institutional affiliation. The first site report from 1975 employed the katakana writing system to name the temple, thus avoiding the problem of selecting Chinese characters for its name. A late Edo-period landscape painting of the valley, however, names this site 西光寺, read as "Saigōji" (roughly translatable as "temple of western light"). To complicate matters, a mortar made of local stone was excavated in a later dig at the site, and was inscribed with the name 西巌寺, which would probably be read as "Saigonji" (roughly translatable as "temple of western sternness"), which might also represent the name of the complex. The sectarian affiliation is also unknown, though the presence of the inscription "Namu Myōhō Renge Kyō" on numerous small stone pagodas and other objects on the site has led archaeologists to hypothesize that this was a Nichiren Buddhist temple.[9]

Saigōji yielded an interesting variety of objects in the various excavations that have occurred over the years, including a fragment of a wooden support post that formed part of a gate inside the complex. At the bottom of this object, a carefully carved square hole is still visible, part of the joinery techniques that late medieval carpenters used to fit together wooden pieces in the construction of structures. Stone buddhas and pagodas have also been found in large numbers, which I will discuss further below. Echizen ceramic jars were also excavated in some quantity, but these were not used for storage of foodstuffs; instead, this particular style of jar, excavated from the northern edge of the property, served as a cinerary urn and held the cremated remains of deceased parishioners. In addition, various Chinese ceramics were discovered, including incense burners, iron-glazed (*tenmoku*) tea bowls, and high-quality tea caddies (*chaire*) and tea jars (*chatsubo*) of the kind that warrior collectors considered to be among their most prized possessions.[10]

Archaeologists excavated another temple complex in the Akabuchi neighborhood in the 1980s, which was probably part of the larger Saigōji institution. Located across from Saigōji on the main east–west route through the district, the complex covers an area of approximately 1,850 square meters, making it larger than its neighboring temple, but also more heterogeneous, with townhouses along the northeastern and northwestern edges, a large warrior residence to the southwest, and a wider variety of buildings and spaces across its large and seemingly organic layout. The complex was divided into sections by ditches that

[9] Fukui, *Ichijōdani no shūkyū to shinkō*, 24.   [10] Fukui, *Ichijōdani no shūkyū to shinkō*, 25.

served as boundary markers and also perhaps as diversions for rainwater runoff. The main hall of this temple complex was located squarely in the middle of the largest section, a 112-square-meter structure with a small garden off its southwestern corner.[11]

To the west of the main hall was a cemetery, which yielded an interesting variety of objects. Stone pagodas and buddhas, as are found in many sites in the valley, were lined up here. Archaeologists also excavated cremated remains in a variety of wooden boxes, including a circular box and a box shaped like a bucket, totaling eighteen individual remains. A particularly interesting discovery was what appears to be a stone storeroom, which contained sixteen wooden grave tablets. Archaeologists also discovered bundles of wooden talismans (*kokerakyō*) that seem to have played an important role in the religious practices of Ichijōdani residents (Figure 4.3). These talismans consist of thin strips of bamboo on which an excerpt of a sutra passage has been written. The temple likely sold the rights to a talisman to practitioners who visited the complex; the monks then produced them and stored them, effectively banking them at the temple itself. Their function may have been to help practitioners accrue merit (similar to the practice of buying charms or *omamori* at shrines and temples today) or to have been deployed during ceremonies for the dead. Various talismans were discovered, including stupa talismans (*sasatoba*) and pagoda talismans (*sotoba* or *tōba*), and the text on these objects points to the enactment of rituals at the temple such as Seventh Day Death Rites (*shonanoka-ki*) and First Year Memorial Rites (*isshū-ki*).[12]

To the southwest of this cemetery and ritual site, across a ditch, was the largest structure discovered in the complex. This building was built on a strong stone foundation with raised wooden floors throughout. The western edge of the building faced a sizable garden with a pond. The northern corner of the building contained a large pit from which numerous jars were excavated, indicating in all likelihood a kitchen and/or storage area in which sake and miso were brewed and stored, among other foodstuffs. A nearby well provided fresh water. Judging from the shape of the building, which was not rectangular like the main worship hall but instead had numerous jutting corner rooms and what may have been verandas, this structure was a kind of abbot's hall, serving both a residential function for some of the leaders of the Saigōji complex and a

---

[11] This temple includes sites 40, excavated in 1980, and 46, excavated in 1983. See Fukui, *Ichijōdani Asakura shi iseki XIII*, 1981, and Fukui, *Ichijōdani Asakura shi iseki XV* (1983).

[12] Fukui, *Ichijōdani no shūkyō to shinkō*, 28.

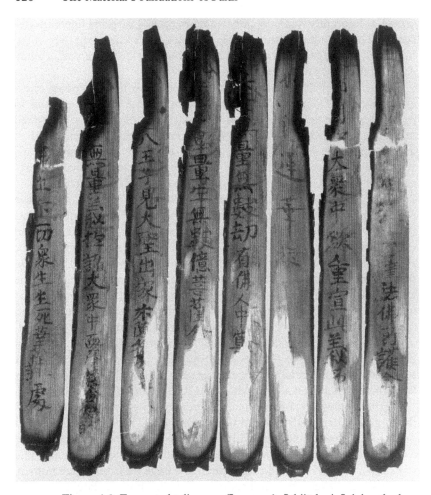

Figure 4.3 Excavated talismans (Japanese), Ichijōdani. Ink brushed on wood.
Used with permission of the Fukui Prefectural Ichijōdani Asakura Family History Museum.

sociocultural function, as a site in which social and cultural rituals could have been staged. As we will see in the next chapter, Ichijōdani was frequently visited by cultural luminaries from Kyoto and other urban centers, many of whom may have visited this and other temple complexes and enjoyed tea, theatrical presentations, meals, and even lodging. It may be that the occupants of the host of buildings around the margins of this complex played subsidiary roles in managing and maintaining these various religious, social, and cultural functions, much as the vassal and family residences around the main Asakura residence held vital roles in running the larger institution of the daimyo administration.

The Asakura, too, constructed and maintained a temple complex close to their residential headquarters, a small gathering of buildings and a garden that served the needs of the family. Known as Nan'yōji and located on elevated ground near the Asakura residence, the temple may have been built as early as the fourteenth century, according to the family history *Asakura-ke denki*.[13] The complex was associated with the younger sister of Asakura Norikage (fifth generation, 1380–1463), perhaps as a mortuary temple. It regularly served as a temporary abode for elite visitors to the provincial city, particularly those connected to or having business with the Asakura family. The courtier and esteemed scholar Ichijō Kaneyoshi (1402–1481), for example, visited Ichijōdani in 1479 and stayed in Nan'yōji. He was visited there by the head of the Asakura clan at the time, Eirin (1428–1481), plus his son and heir Ujikage (1449–1486). The visit was an important opportunity for the Asakura, recently established as the rulers of Echizen, to cement ties with Kyoto elites, and they gave plentifully to Kaneyoshi. Eirin presented the courtier with 200 *kanmon*[14] in cash and ten bundles of cotton wadding, and to Kaneyoshi's entourage he gave additional cash, swords, and other gifts. Kaneyoshi, in return, issued the directive that Eirin should receive the court appointment of a local attendant position, adding to his titles.[15] In short, the site played a role in the sociability of the Asakura, providing a close and secure resting spot for outsiders.

Nan'yōji also famously served as the site of the visit by Ashikaga Yoshiaki before he became shogun, a major moment in the history of the Asakura family and the town of Ichijōdani that I analyze in detail in Chapter 6.[16] Broadly, while Yoshiaki was in Ichijōdani for several months, Asakura Yoshikage invited him to engage in various cultural gatherings. On one occasion, Nan'yōji was the staging ground for a cherry blossom viewing, and the two – accompanied by a small entourage of Yoshiaki's vassals, as well as unnamed Asakura warriors – visited

---

[13] Fukui, *Asakura shi no kakun*, 238.

[14] If we assume (using a very rough but widely accepted conversion estimate for the medieval period) that 1 *kanmon* was equivalent to 1 *koku* of rice, enough to feed one person for a year, 200 *kanmon* is revealed to be a small fortune.

[15] Takeuchi Rizō ed., *Daijōin jisha zōjiki*, vol. 7, pp. 38, 42, 46.

[16] Gyūichi, *The Chronicle of Lord Nobunaga*, 115; Ōta, *Shinchō kōki*, 81.

blossoming cherry trees in the valley and exchanged poems on the beauty of the flowers.[17] It goes without saying that looking back, the beloved poetic theme of the ephemerality of cherry blossoms portended the fall of both houses.

Nan'yōji was excavated in 1989, revealing a site of approximately 5,000 square meters, which contained several small buildings and a garden.[18] The primary structure was a small Buddha Hall (*butsuden*) located in the southern part of the complex, closest to the northern wall of the Asakura residence. The Buddha Hall appears, based on the excavations, to have resembled other medieval structures of this type, consisting of a three-bay-by-three-bay square central room, surrounded by a narrow corridor/veranda (*mokoshi*) that enclosed it. The roof of the building was raised over the central room, with a pent roof over the corridor, making it seem from the outside to possess two stories.[19] The Buddha Hall of temple complexes in medieval Japan, usually Zen temples, typically served as the site of worship of a central image, such as a statue of Sakyamuni, often flanked by other Buddha figures or by two disciples. These images would have been elevated on pedestals, which in turn sat on a raised altar platform; above the platform was a decorated textile, either purple or gold, bearing an inscription. Lacquered tablets with text honoring patrons of the temple were also common, and indeed this complex served the needs of the Asakura family above all other supplicants.[20] It would have taken a member of the Asakura house just a minute or two to walk from the north gate to the Buddha Hall, making this a likely site for daily family worship.

To the east of the Buddha Hall was another small building that likely served as the Abbot's Residence (*hōjō*), which was connected by a covered corridor to a parallel building that seems to have functioned as guests' quarters. Both these structures looked out on a rock garden with a small pond, with the forested hillside serving as the backdrop in a magnificent example of "borrowed scenery" (*shakkei*). The northern half of the complex contained several buildings that were connected to the abbot's residence by covered corridors, and likely functioned as the sites

---

[17] Inoue Toshio, Kuwatana Kōnen, and Fujiki Hisashi, eds., "Asakura shimatsuki, Kaetsutō jōki, Esshū gunki," in *Nihon shisō taikei, vol. 17: Rennyo Ikkô-ikki,* ed. Inoue Toshio and Kasahara Kazuo (Iwanami Shoten, 1972), 360.

[18] The full excavation report, which encompasses sites 64 and 65, is Fukui Kenritsu Ichijōdani Asakura Shi Iseki Shiryōkan, *Ichijōdani Asakura shi iseki hakkutsu chōsa hōkokusho* 12 (2016).

[19] Fukui, *Ichijōdani no shūkyū to shinkō*, 31.

[20] Martin Collcutt, *Five Mountains: The Rinzai Zen Monastic Institution in Medieval Japan* (Harvard Asia Center Press, 1981), 190–191.

of daily living: the presence of a hearth, a well, and a storeroom – perhaps part of a kitchen complex – provide ample evidence for this reading.[21] The entire complex thus can be split along a north–south axis. The relatively public, outward-facing portion served the needs of the Asakura and their elite visitors, who sometimes stayed in the guest quarters. The abbot's residence would have functioned as a semi-public site of social and cultural rituals, including gift exchange, tea ceremonies, and possibly poetry and calligraphy performance. The garden provided the ideal scenery for these encounters. The northern half of the complex was private, plebeian, and largely functional.

Somewhat unusually, excavations of this site did not yield large quantities of objects that would conventionally be understood as religious icons. Likewise, the high-quality, imported Chinese ceramics that archaeologists located in great numbers in Saigōji are not found here. Instead, an impressive cache of earthenware ritual vessels was excavated, which supports the idea that this temple may have functioned in part as a kind of reception hall, a political space used for the necessary social rituals that lubricated elite warrior society. Archaeologists discovered a pit that was filled with discarded earthenware dishes and plates of the sort used at ritual banquets to consume food and beverages from pure, previously unused vessels.[22] The temple thus provides us with an exceptional glimpse inside the "mixed-use" facilities of the residence and surrounding structures.

Another significant temple complex on the outskirts of the town was Nishiyama Kōshōji, located just beyond the lower city gate, nestled in the hills to the west and overlooking the confluence of the Asuwa and Ichijōdani Rivers.[23] This large site, covering 3,200 square meters, was partially excavated in the 1990s, though the full extent is still unknown and much of the attempt to map the original layout relies on speculation. Part of the complex was used as a graveyard, particularly the sloping hillside behind the primary structures. One of the few recognizable structures was a Seven-Year Memorial Tower to Seishun (d. 1535), a disciple of the famous Tendai monk Shinsei (1443–1495). Asakura Eirin reportedly invited Seishun to help revive the temple in the midst of the Asakura campaign to rule the province, and this monument was produced as part of the Buddhist ceremonies in 1542 honoring the seven-year memorial of

---

[21] Fukui, *Tokubetsu shiseki: Ichijōdani Asakura shi iseki* (1994).
[22] Fukui, *Ichijōdani no shūkyū to shinkō*, 31.
[23] The full excavation report, which encompasses sites 86, 87, 90, 132, 135, and 144, is Fukui Kenritsu Ichijōdani Asakura Shi Iseki Shiryōkan, *Ichijōdani Asakura shi iseki hakkutsu chōsa hōkokusho* 11 (2015).

his death. The foundations of several structures were excavated as well, but too little remained to allow an understanding of the function of the different buildings. Archaeologists also excavated a number of stone statues from across the complex, which will be discussed in the next section in this chapter.

Perhaps the most important find in the Nishiyama Kōshōji complex was a large underground storehouse, lined in stone, at the center of the grounds. Although the upper layer of stone showed significant evidence of damage from fire, likely a result of the destruction of Ichijōdani in 1573, many objects were reclaimed from the interior. High-quality imported Chinese ceramics were numerous, including utensils usually employed in tea gatherings and for display and serving during banquets. In addition, a fine celadon water container, originally manufactured in China, was found, an object that would have been used for replenishing the water in an inkstone while writing using a brush. A metal incense burner also survived the ravages of time. We can speculate that the location of this temple outside the city gates allowed it to serve the needs of a larger population of worshippers, including rural residents of nearby communities as well as travelers along the local roads and river ways. Conversely, the temple was more exposed to the potential dangers of bandits or the invading forces of the Asakura's enemies; the storehouse may have been a protection against such predation in a time of war and relative social and political instability.

Another religious site that archaeologists have excavated and that played a significant role in Ichijōdani's history is An'yōji, located to the south of (in other words, *outside*) the upper city gate.[24] This temple complex was part of the Pure Land Seizan Zenrinji sect, which had its headquarters at Eikandō temple in Kyoto. Construction was reportedly initiated by Asakura Norikage (1380–1463) and the temple was completed in 1473; in 1488 it served as the site of a sermon by Shinsei, mentioned above.[25] The temple similarly served as the location for at least two lectures by the aristocrat and Confucian scholar Kiyohara no Nobukata (1475–1550).[26] One of the largest temple complexes in the city, An'yōji seems to have enjoyed a relatively high status among local

---

[24] The full excavation report, which encompasses sites 92, 97, and 98, is Fukui Kenritsu Ichijōdani Asakura Shi Iseki Shiryōkan, *Ichijōdani Asakura shi iseki hakkutsu chōsa hōkokusho* 13 (2016).

[25] Primary source references to the early history of the temple, most of which come from Edo-period collections, can be found in Fukui Ken Kyōiku-cho Maizō Bunkazai Chōsa Sentaa, *Tokubetsu shiseki: Ichijōdani Asakura shi ikseki hakkutsu chōsa hōkoku 13* (2016), 51–57.

[26] Fukui, *Ichijōdani no shūkyū to shinkō*, 34.

religious sites, most notably in the second half of the sixteenth century when it became the location for the housing of Ichijōdani's most elite visitor, Ashikaga Yoshiaki. An'yōji thus uniquely came to house on its grounds a palace (*gosho*) of the sort usually found in Kyoto.

Preliminary survey and excavation of the site began in 1970,[27] while primary excavation began in 2007 and the main site report was published in 2016. The excavated area consisted of approximately 4,200 square meters. Archaeologists discuss the site in two sections: the palace area to the north and the temple precincts to the south, though in fact the entire area was technically part of the An'yōji complex. The palace was protected to the north by a large earthen wall and to the east by stone walls erected along the slope of the mountain. Visitors would have entered the palace from the west, where a gate would have regulated access from the main road through the valley. Excavations did not reveal the exact layout of the original structures of the palace, and further investigations are planned. In addition, some descriptions of buildings from contemporaneous sources do survive. The temple precincts to the south included a stone wall on the mountain slope to the east, several clusters of stone pagodas and stone Buddhas, and standard walls around the compound. Only two structures have been identified, but future excavations are likely to further clarify the layout of buildings. A range of objects excavated from these two locations in the temple complex reinforces the separation of the palace precinct from the temple precinct. Ritual earthenware dishes (*kawarake*) of the sort discussed at the opening of this chapter make up approximately 60 percent of the excavated ceramics in the temple portion of the site, which is consistent with other temple locations and low- to mid-ranking warrior residences in the city. But in the palace portion, earthenware dishes comprise 75 percent of excavated ceramics, a clear sign of increased ritual activity of the kind seen only in high-ranking warrior residences and social/cultural sites.

Yoshiaki, whose career and relations with the Asakura will be discussed further in Chapter 6, arrived in Ichijōdani in late 1567, and stayed in the city for nine months during a tumultuous time for his family and indeed for warrior institutions in Kyoto. He departed Ichijōdani only in the seventh month of 1568, in the company of four of Oda Nobunaga's vassals, to finally act on their long-discussed plan to install Yoshiaki as shogun and to pacify the region around the capital. Yoshiaki saw this as the beginning of the fulfillment of his ambition to reestablish the Ashikaga shogunate as the legitimate ruling institution of Japan, while

---

[27] Fukui Ken Kyōiku Iinkai, *Ichijōdani Asakura shi iseki: Gosho/An'yōji* (1971).

Nobunaga seems to have considered his role as protector of Yoshiaki to be his own ticket to power as a potential ruling hegemon. Ichijōdani thus served as one of the staging grounds for the launch of the process that would "ultimately lead to Japan's military pacification, political unification and social transformation."[28]

One of the oldest religious institutions in the valley is the Abaka Kasuga Shrine located just to the north of lower city gate. According to early modern documents, the shrine was founded in 1068, and gradually fell into disrepair over the course of the early medieval period. Asakura Hirokage (1255–1352) reportedly felt great reverence for the shrine and funded its refurbishment, which was completed in 1353. Later generations of the Asakura and their vassals similarly patronized the shrine and paid for its reconstruction, and on occasion used it as the site of cultural rituals, including the performance of Noh plays associated with *kami* worship (*shinji nō*), a form of drama in which the main character of the play (known as the *shite*) is a god. This shrine is still active, however, and thus has not been excavated.[29]

This is only a handful of the temples and shrines that operated in Ichijōdani at the height of the city's activity; numerous additional religious sites have been discovered by archaeologists, though not yet fully excavated, analyzed, or published. What is also missing from this summary is a sense of the belief structure that drove the construction, refurbishment, and patronage of these religious institutions. For the Asakura family itself, we can use contextual evidence to fill in some of the gaps in the material record. For example, numerous sources attest to the Asakura family's devotion to Akabuchi Daimyōjin, which they considered to be their tutelary deity. This faith had its origins in Tajima Province, where the Asakura were said to have originated, and focused on the worship of marine deities. At one point the Asakura apparently built and maintained an Akabuchi Shrine inside the city gates at the base of the mountains on the western side of the valley. In addition, a small shrine building dedicated to Akabuchi may have existed inside the Asakura palace complex. Last, an Akabuchi Shrine also seems to have been maintained inside the mountaintop fortress of the Asakura, indicating that this tutelary deity was worshipped and installed at every key location for the ruling family: in the city they ruled, in the residence they habitually occupied, and in the fortified retreat they could retire to in times of military emergency. The most dedicated worshipper of Akabuchi in the Asakura family appears to have been Yoshikage, the last lord, who commissioned the origin scroll

---

[28] Lamers, *Japonius Tyrannus*, 59.   [29] Fukui, *Ichijōdani no shūkyū to shinkō*, 57–58.

Akabuchi Daimyōjin engi (which describes the origins of the Kusakabe clan in Tajima, putative ancestors of the Asakura) in 1560. He patronized not only his family's local Akabuchi shrines, but the "original" Akabuchi Shrine in Tajima as well, sending prayers, charms, medicine (in particular, *goō* or *ushi no tama*, a rare and sacred bezoar from the gut of an ox that was believed to have life-saving powers), and other votive offerings.[30] It is perhaps not surprising that his final hour in Ichijōdani, before he fled the advancing armies of Oda Nobunaga and lost his own life, was spent in prayer at Akabuchi Shrine.

The Asakura took part in other traditions of worship as well, including worship of the sun goddess, Amaterasu. The cult of Amaterasu was focused on the Grand Shrine of Ise, a major institution funded in part through estates that it held in various provinces across the archipelago. In Echizen, a so-called shrine kitchen (*mikuriya*) dedicated to Ise had been founded in the Heian period in what is now Fukui city, and continued throughout the medieval period to provide offerings (particularly seafood because of its proximity to the coast) that were transported to the Grand Shrine of Ise. This estate also became the home of Shinmei Shrine – dedicated to the worship of Amaterasu – and according to a range of documentary evidence, several Asakura lords patronized this shrine and the "shrine kitchen," including Asakura Hirokage (1255–1352), Iekage (1402–1451), and the final Asakura lord, Yoshikage, who made offerings to Amaterasu through the shrine after the Asakura defeat at the Battle of Anegawa.[31] Similarly, the Asakura worshipped the deity Hachiman, whose cult had spread among the warrior class to the point that he was understood to be the patron god of war. According to the records of a small Hachiman shrine now located in Fukui city, the shrine was previously located inside the city gates of Ichijōdani. Asakura Yoshikage was deeply interested in the worship of Hachiman and may have patronized this shrine; he was profoundly affected by his encounter with a statue of Hachiman from the Kyoto temple Shōbōji and commissioned a reproduction (*utsushi*) that unfortunately is now lost, likely destroyed in the fires of 1573.[32]

---

[30] Fukui, *Ichijōdani no shūkyū to shinkō*, 47.

[31] On "shrine kitchens," see Ōzeki Kunio, "Shinryō," in *Encyclopedia of Shinto*, accessed November 18, 2019: http://k-amc.kokugakuin.ac.jp/DM/dbSearchList.do;jsessionid= A0BA4F8FB9EC495A13E343380954F59C?class_name=col_eos&search_condition_ type=1&db_search_condition_type=0&View=0&focus_type=0&startNo=1& searchFreeword=shinryo&searchRangeType=0. On the history of Shinmei shrine, see the shrine's website, accessed November 18, 2019: www.shinmei-jinja.jp/yurai/. See also Fukui, *Ichijōdani no shūkyū to shinkō*, 47–48.

[32] Fukui, *Ichijōdani no shūkyū to shinkō*, 48–49.

The Asakura thus engaged with a range of religious and ritual practices as evidenced by extant documentary evidence and some excavated archaeological materials. As the most powerful, the wealthiest, and the most networked residents of Ichijōdani, they had what we might think of as the largest spiritual toolkit, with access to not only local religious institutions but various religious traditions from across the archipelago. It may be that the diverse local residents of Ichijōdani also participated in the worship of Akabuchi Daimyōjin, the war god Hachiman, and other traditions such as the Kumano faith, but we lack substantive evidence of such practices. Instead, the destruction of Ichijōdani left behind the barest traces of a lively, ubiquitous ritual culture that seems to have undergirded all of the religious institutions and faiths of not just the city but the region. It may be that the stripping away of the city's palace, shops, and residences in effect exposed the core, skeletal structure of religious practice in medieval Japan, as we shall see below.

Stone Buddhas and Stone Pagodas

Scattered across the temple complexes mentioned in this chapter, as well as along trails in the woods and in clearings in the valley, are thousands of small stone statues, sculptural images associated with Buddhism. Some appear in the shape of Buddhas (*sekibutsu*), while others appear as simple tablets in the shape of a pagoda (*itabi* or *sekitō*). Some even appear in the more symbolically complex form of a five-ringed tower (*gorintō*), a form of miniature pagoda popular in Shingon and Tendai Buddhism. These objects are usually associated with death or, more broadly, with the marking of a grave, or perhaps in some instances with the memorialization of a life. They also represent, alongside the earthenware ritual ceramics that archaeologists find in such large quantities in almost all sites across the valley, our best record of the lived religious practices of the residents of late medieval Ichijōdani over a period of a century. It goes without saying that these are the most durable products of the sacred world of the city, indestructible by fire and largely immune to the destruction wrought by armies intent on the elimination of their enemies.

Carved of the most durable material readily available in the medieval world, stone buddhas (Figure 4.4) and stone pagodas (Figure 4.5) represent a powerful intervention into the core soteriological concern of Buddhist faith: escaping from the cycle of birth, death, and rebirth. Commissioning or producing a carved stone buddha or pagoda to mark the death of a loved one represents both an act of memorialization and a virtuous practice that would accrue merit for the deceased. Yet at the same time, the permanence of the stone statute seems to suggest a

Figure 4.4 Stone buddha (*sekibutsu*) from the grounds of
Seigenji, Ichijōdani.
Photograph by author.

Figure 4.5 Stone pagoda (*sekitō*) from the grounds of
Seigenji, Ichijōdani.
Photograph by author.

resistance to the core Buddhist notion of ephemerality. The desire to memorialize the deceased implies the immutability of attachment, the difficulty of letting go, and the need of the living to maintain contact with a representation of the dead. The Buddhist teacher Nichiren resolved this tension by glossing the creation of monuments and memorials as a means of overcoming the dualism of sentient and nonsentient things: "when we sentient beings die, a *stūpa* (*toba*) is erected and consecrated with an eye-opening ceremony (*kaizen kuyō*): this is the realization of Buddhahood of dead beings, and that corresponds to the realization of Buddhahood of plants."[33] Perhaps the permanence of stone markers was the point, as a contrast to the fragility of life and the goal of breaking through the cycle of *samsara*.

Whether the intention was to grasp onto the memory of the deceased or to ritually mark the possibility of the realization of Buddhahood, the breadth and density of stone Buddhas and pagodas across Ichijōdani points clearly to a key phenomenon of medieval religious practice in Japan, namely, the transformation of Buddhism from an elite culture in the Heian period to a widely available and largely accessible set of overlapping practices throughout the medieval period. Janet Goodwin has examined the rise of a medieval culture of mortuary commemoration among nonelites in Japan, beginning with the larger shift in Buddhist practice from rituals that were largely restricted to elite patrons to forms of Buddhist practice that were aimed at commoners, including those without education or economic means. Buddhist mortuary rites became more widely available in a variety of formats in the Kamakura period, and the commissioning of stone sculptures, though still expensive, in theory was not restricted to aristocrats or wealthy warriors. In fact, new forms of collectivity enabled engagement in religious rites that might otherwise have been inaccessible. In some communities, people formed collectives around the idea of "karmic affinity" (*kechien*) to fund stone Buddhas and pagodas, providing a sense of belonging while also allowing the opportunity to participate to those without the individual means to pay for rites and sculptures.[34]

In Ichijōdani, stone Buddhas and pagodas appear in clusters in nearly every neighborhood, totaling more than 2,800 objects.[35] Most numerous

---

[33] Translated in Fabio Rambelli, *Buddhist Materiality: A Cultural History of Objects in Japanese Buddhism* (Stanford University Press, 2007), 49.

[34] Janet R. Goodwin, "Shooting the Dead to Paradise," *Japanese Journal of Religious Studies* 16.1 (1989): 64–68.

[35] I have tabulated these figures based on the "Stonework Digital Archives" database maintained by the Ichijōdani Asakura Shi Iseki Shiryōkan: http://asakura-museum.pref .fukui.lg.jp/045_stoneworks/.

are the five-ringed towers, particularly those that are carved out of a single block of stone: 1,577 of these objects survive. By contrast, only 91 five-ringed towers made of multiple stones – an inherently complicated and fragile structure – survive. Stone Buddhas are the second most numerous, at 860 extant objects. We see a precipitous drop-off in shape variety after these two main categories, with only 132 *itabi*, which are stone steles in the shape of a pagoda, often with an image as well as an inscription carved into the flat surface. The remaining stone shapes include umbrella stupas (*kasatōba*) and gravestones, among other varieties.

All these shapes correlate with our understanding of medieval mortuary ritual practices, and help provide a glimpse into the religious activities of Ichijōdani's diverse community. The five-ringed tower, for example, derives its religious significance from the long history within the Buddhist tradition of the stupa as a reliquary, a container for holy objects or even bodily fragments associated with the historical Buddha. The earliest stupas in South Asia were religious sites for pilgrimage and enactment of ritual while also serving as not just containers for relics but in many cases as depositories of individual reliquaries that in turn held relics.[36] The stupa spread across the region and developed increasingly complex forms and decorative programs. In East Asia, stupas grew into multi-tiered architectural structures, most commonly referred to in English as pagodas. These wooden towers with multiple eaves continued to function as reliquaries, often containing not only relics associated with the Buddha but various religious treasures. Alongside the construction of pagodas that played a key role within the larger Buddhist temple complex, the construction of stone stupa markers of various shapes and sizes became popular as a form of memorialization.

The five-ringed tower is a striking variety of the stupa or pagoda form that became widespread in Japan at the end of the Heian period,[37] in association with the esoteric Buddhist schools, Tendai and Shingon. Each layer or level of the tower represents an element from Buddhist cosmology, articulated in the form of a different shape. Stone and wooden five-ringed towers can be found in various contexts in Buddhist temples in Japan, almost always connected to mortuary practices. In the case of the five-ringed stone stupas found throughout Ichijōdani, most of them are concentrated on the edges of the town's more remote Buddhist temple complexes, particularly Nishiyama Kōshōji outside the city gates, a small Tendai temple in the southwestern

---

[36] Gustav Roth, Franz-Karl Ehrhard, Kimiaki Tanaka, and Lokesh Chandra, *Stupa: Cult and Symbolism* (International Academy of Indian Culture and Aditya Prakashan, 2009).
[37] Ishii Susumu and Suitō Makoto, *Sekibutsu to sekitō* (Yamakawa Shuppansha, 2001), 39.

corner of the valley called Seigenji, and a Jōdō Shinshū temple in the southeastern corner of the valley called Jōkyōji. While some of these stupa markers are found inside the city gates, primarily on the edges of the town's temple precincts, the fact that the majority are located on the margins of the community points to their association with the other-worldliness of death and the universal tendency to push graveyards away from the centers of habitation and industry.

Stone Buddhas are also found in large numbers, a trend that is consistent with patterns across Japan in the medieval period. Nationally, stone Buddhas not only proliferated but also became smaller after the fourteenth century, perhaps as a result of a more diverse range of patrons or groups of patrons commissioning the production of more cost-efficient (smaller, and often group-funded) memorial statues.[38] Of course, stone Buddha statues in Ichijōdani and across Japan in the medieval period are not identical, but fall into particular categories. One common form is the Nyorai Buddha, the Japanese version of the Tathagata category, reserved for the highest rank of Buddhas in Mahayana Buddhist cosmology. In True Pure Land Buddhism, for example, the Amida Nyorai (Amitābha) was a common stone Buddha that would have been associated with the recitation of the nenbutsu. A notable and identifiable example from Ichijōdani was excavated from Nishiyama Kōshōji and bears the inscription "Zenkōji Nyorai," a reference to the celebrated Amida icon housed at the famous and influential Zenkōji temple in Shinano province (present-day Nagano).[39] This was a powerful image, since Amida's forty-eight vows to convey all sentient beings to the Pure Land was a significant source of hope as well as a useful reminder of the spiritual force of Buddhist practice.

Another popular form was the Jizō Bosatsu or Kṣitigarbha Bodhisattva, a saint-like figure who was highly revered in premodern Japan and associated with the protection of women and travelers; in the Edo period, these figures became associated with the protection of children as well, both living and dead. Many stone statues around Ichijōdani are identifiable as Jizō, and many more may have been intended as Jizō images but are no longer clearly marked as such. Furthermore, Jizō and Amida images are often paired in a single stone bas-relief statue. Two early examples – one in poor condition and inscribed with the date 1534 and one in exceptional condition and inscribed 1536 – come from Seigenji.[40] Both show Amida Buddha standing on the right, arms open in the mudra

---

[38] Ishii and Suitō, *Sekibutsu to sekitō*, 22–23.
[39] Ichijōdani, "Stonework Digital Archives," Ko-00013.
[40] Ichijōdani, "Stonework Digital Archives," S-00190 and S-00580.

of welcome, and Jizō standing on the left, with his right hand holding a staff and his left hand holding a wish-granting jewel, a potent relic known as *hōju no tama*. This was a powerful combination of images from Buddhist cosmology: Amida Buddha was of course primarily associated with the Western Paradise, while Jizō, who often attended Amida, was associated both with relieving the suffering of the denizens of the Buddhist hells and with helping Amida to deliver pious practitioners to the Western Paradise. Jizō's staff symbolized the power of Buddhism to awaken believers to the reality of their suffering, while the jewel was believed to grant wishes and bestow blessings. This pair of images would have thus provided potent succor to parents mourning a lost child, or to any bereaved individual or group seeking to improve the fortunes of the soul of deceased loved one. Jizō images may also represent the religious agency of women in Ichijōdani, as some scholars have argued that the Jizō cult was primarily advanced by the activities of women.[41]

The Kannon Bosatsu, or Avalokiteśvara Bodhisattva, was also a popular choice for stone statues, sometimes appearing as a single image and sometimes as part of a group of Buddhist figures. Kannon was one of the most revered figures in popular Buddhism in Japan, closely associated with the ideals of mercy and compassion. An undated example excavated from Kōshōji, for example, seems to have been associated with a Buddhist funeral, and shows Kannon standing alone.[42] Another example dated to 1552 from the Koyasu neighborhood, home to the Imamura family of Asakura vassals, pictures two versions of Kannon flanking two iterations of Amida, though it is difficult to determine which manifestations because of damage to the statue.[43]

We do not have direct documentary evidence regarding the uses and intentions of these stone pagodas and Buddhas. Most are made from a type of volcanic stone known as *shakudani* that was mined from Mt. Asuwa in Echizen and known for its bluish color. Likewise, most of the stone objects do bear inscriptions, including dates, certain key phrases associated with mortuary rituals, and the names of the patrons. Though these spare texts help us to locate these works in the larger matrix of cultural practice, what we might think of as the subjective aspirations of the Ichijōdani residents who commissioned these works remain elusive. More broadly in the Japanese Buddhist tradition, image-making was closely associated with the accumulation of merit, or the production of

---

[41] See, for example, Milla Micka Moto-Sanchez, "Jizō, Healing Rituals, and Women in Japan," *Japanese Journal of Religious Studies* 43.2 (2016): 307–331.
[42] Ko-00009.   [43] TK-00127.

karmic virtue through ritual acts.[44] Thus, the commissioning of a stone Buddha or stupa by a bereaved family member or by a collective may have represented an attempt to gain benefit in the grand karmic journey toward enlightenment through the arrangement of proper funerary rituals. Or, depending on the practitioners and the particular school of Buddhism they followed, the focus may have been not on merit-making for the living but on merit-making for the dead. As George Tanabe notes, "Benefits and blessings, the related virtues of merit, are enjoyed as rewards for one's efforts, but they can also be dedicated or transferred to others. Like economic transactions, merit can be transferred from one account to another .... The best reason for transferring merit to the deceased is to help them gain rebirth in the pure land."[45] Thus, the stone pagoda or Buddha could have served as a "gathering place for the family, a place for sutras to be read, a place for offerings to be made on behalf of the deceased."[46] For many residents of Ichijōdani, we can imagine that both personal karmic benefit and merit for the deceased comingled as goals of the commissioning of a stone stupa or Buddha.[47]

Yet Fabio Rambelli reminds us that the "traditional distinction between an elite tradition dealing with texts and doctrines and a popular tradition dealing with objects and rituals"[48] is problematic. The separation of the Buddhist practices of elites, focusing on "the quest for ultimate salvation," has been heavily researched by scholars in the field of religious studies as well as in art history, while ostensibly plebeian Buddhist practices and their material remnants have been largely ignored. Ichijōdani's unusually thorough excavation allows us to glimpse the materiality of mortuary practice in at least one late medieval urban center without relying on the traditional distinction mentioned by Rambelli. Indeed, the proliferation of stone funerary markers in both elite neighborhoods of Ichijōdani as well as more marginal and distant locales implies that the interest in such memorialization extended throughout the social hierarchies of the city.

What goals beyond merit-making, then, might the diverse range of Buddhist practitioners in Ichijōdani have shared when they

---

[44] See George J. Tanabe, Jr., "Merit and Merit-Making," in *Encyclopedia of Buddhism*, vol. 2, ed. Robert E. Buswell, Jr. (Macmillan Reference, 2004), 532–534.

[45] Tanabe, "Merit and Merit-Making," 532.

[46] Karen M. Gerhart, *The Material Culture of Death in Medieval Japan* (University of Hawai'i Press, 2009), 107.

[47] See also Akiko Walley's work on merit-making through the commissioning of Buddhist art, including inscriptions on Buddhist objects: "Inscribing and Ascribing Merit: Buddhist Vows and the Hōryūji Shaka Triad," *Harvard Journal of Asiatic Studies* 73.2 (2013): 299–337.

[48] Rambelli, *Buddhist Materiality*, 5.

commissioned and activated stone stupas and Buddhas as part of the city's mortuary culture? Here I turn to scholarship on the idea that images and objects in Buddhism could serve as more than receptacles for ritual action, and instead as powerful agents in the interactions between believers and the divine. As James Dobbins has noted, in True Pure Land Buddhism, it was widely believed that "Amida's presence can be found in the simple and the mundane,"[49] and thus the images of stupas and Buddhist figures must be seen as more than mere representations. The five-ringed tower, even if carved out of a single block of stone, points to the idea of a reliquary that holds sacred remnants of the historical Buddha himself, and in fact can be conflated with the body of the Buddha, serving simultaneously as object of worship and a sacred subject. The object thus is made from an inanimate material, stone, but simultaneously holds (at the symbolic level) the material remnants of the most powerful and divine holy being in the Buddhist cosmology. And the process of transformation from profane to sacred, from stone into reliquary, from attachment-obsessed human to enlightened Buddha, is bound up in this object that begins as a mere rock but endures as a sacred ritual work.[50] The object in some sense contains the Buddha. Likewise, images of Buddhas and Bodhisattvas are not understood to be passive objects in the Buddhist tradition; rather, they are "real presences to the point of indicating them as future buddhas" that can, according to Buddhist belief, be animated and display the behavior and actions of sentient beings: crying, talking, moving, and generally communicating with believers.[51] For believers performing rituals in front of a stone pagoda or Buddha on the outskirts of the valley or tucked behind a temple complex in town, merit-making would likely have been a primary concern, but so too was the possibility that in the moment of prayer, the Buddha in the statue looked back.[52] Belief in the compassion of the Buddha and bodhisattvas surely motivated believers to commission stone statues and perform rituals across the valley.

[49] James Dobbins, "Portraits of Shinran," in *Living Images: Japanese Buddhist Icons in Context*, ed. Robert H. Sharf and Elizabeth Horton Sharf (Stanford University Press, 2001), 33.
[50] Rambelli's discussion of the Buddhist system of objects was useful in thinking through these issues. *Buddhist Materiality*, 81–87.
[51] Rambelli, *Buddhist Materiality*, 83.
[52] See also Halle O'Neal's study of Buddhist palimpsests, which similarly functioned "to embody what has been lost, to provide a visible point of access for the bereaved, and to better target the merit generated by copying the words of the Buddha for the benefit of the deceased." Halle O'Neal, "Inscribing Grief and Salvation: Embodiment and Medieval Reuse and Recycling in Buddhist Palimpsests," *Artibus Asiae* 79.1 (2019): 5–28.

One other possibility worth considering is that the erection of stone pagodas and Buddhas functioned for some Ichijōdani residents as a means of ameliorating anxieties about death and the afterlife, particularly the possibility that the dead could transform into vengeful spirits (*onryō*). As Brian Ruppert has noted, "the construction of stūpas, as well as the mortuary practices conducted at them, offered a means to cope with increasing worries about problems such as those raised by the vengeful spirit of the exiled Sugawara no Michizane."[53] Extant documentary and material evidence shows that diverse populations in medieval Japan believed that an unnatural or particularly tragic death created the possibility that the spirit of the deceased would be unable to find its proper resting place and could become vengeful, causing material harm through natural disaster, bad governance, and other forms of adversity. So, death on the battlefield, as the result of an execution, by suicide, or during travel away from home could lead to a spiritual force that would wreak havoc on the temporal world. These beliefs were widespread and in many cases institutionalized. The Kamakura Shogunate, for example, went to great lengths to pacify the spirits of the many warriors who died during the Genpei War (1180–1185). In the century following the end of the war, the shogunate dedicated enormous numbers of stone pagodas to mollify the wandering spirits from the war, including 84,000 in the year 1225 alone.[54] Similarly, the temple Amidaji (present-day Shimonoseki City, Yamaguchi Prefecture) was repurposed as a mortuary temple for the boy emperor Antoku and the thousands of Taira soldiers and family members who drowned themselves at the end of the Genpei War in 1185, precisely the kind of violent and unnatural death that could lead to vengeful ghosts. This temple housed a range of artworks dedicated to the life and death of Antoku. The complex served as the primary site for various rituals that commemorated the deaths of him and his followers while also placating their spirits.[55] Of course, Amidaji and the pacification of the spirits of Antoku and the Taira warriors was distant from the urban context of Ichijōdani in the sixteenth century. The underlying belief structure, however, helps us to understand the power of erecting

---

[53] Brian O. Ruppert, "Beyond Death and the Afterlife: Considering Relic Veneration in Medieval Japan," in *Death and the Afterlife in Japanese Buddhism*, ed. Jacqueline I. Stone and Mariko Namba Walter (University of Hawai'i Press, 2008), 107.

[54] Ruppert, "Beyond Death," 120.

[55] See Naoko Gunji, "Amidaji: Mortuary Art, Architecture, and Rites of Emperor Antoku's Temple" (PhD dissertation, University of Pittsburgh, 2007); and, more recently, "Horrified Victors: Spirit Pacification of Heike Losers," in *Lovable Losers: The Heike in Action and Memory*, ed. Mikael S. Adolphson and Anne Commons (University of Hawai'i Press, 2015), 166–184.

stone stupas and Buddhas as a means of accomplishing multiple goals in both the temporal and spiritual realms.

Archaeological materials also show that such commemorative activities changed over time. Although only one-third of extant stone pagodas and Buddhas bear an inscription, using the dates that are available it is possible to graph the general trends in the dedication and placement of these stone markers over approximately 100 years. In fact, using this data, archaeologists can divide the history of the Asakura occupation of the valley into three periods.[56] The first begins with the Asakura settlement of Ichijōdani before the Ōnin War and ends around 1504. In these thirty-odd years, only a handful of stone stupas and Buddhas were dedicated and inscribed, probably a reflection of the fact that the Asakura themselves were largely focused on their conflict with the Shiba and the Kai during this early era, and both the city and their administration would not have been particularly settled. The second period extends from 1504 to 1532, when the number of stone stupas and Buddhas steadily grows. Although the Asakura continued to face challenges during this period, notably, aggression from the Single-Mind league (*ikkō ikki*) adherents in Kaga Province to the north, these three decades by and large represented the establishment of steady governance in Ichijōdani and Echizen Province as a whole. Last, in the period from 1532 to 1573, the number of statues increases to as high as thirty or forty in certain years, and mostly stays above ten per year for these four decades. This is the era of Asakura rule and Ichijōdani prosperity in all of its pomp, when the Asakura maintained fairly equanimous relations with neighboring warlords and trade and travel within the province were mostly stable.

It seems appropriate to return to the function of stone stupas and Buddhas in their original social context; these were, after all, markers of death, even though they emerged directly from the concerns and aspirations of the living. In general it is difficult to connect specific excavated objects to known historical events from Ichijōdani's single century of habitation; however, a small but significant number of stone stupas and Buddhas inscribed with death dates from the day 1570/6/28 can be clearly linked to a major conflict in the history of the Asakura: the Battle of Anegawa. The role of this battle in the tumultuous final years of the Asakura family will be examined in more detail in Chapter 6, but for now it is worth noting that the Asakura joined with their allies the Azai in a conflict with Oda Nobunaga and his junior ally Tokugawa Ieyasu in the

---

[56] Suitō, "Ichijōdani no shinkō sekai," 149.

shallows of the Ane River near Lake Biwa (close to present-day Nagahama City, Shiga Prefecture). *The Chronicle of Lord Nobunaga* claims that more than 1,100 "warriors of standing" from the ranks of the Azai and Asakura died in the battle, which resulted in a victory for Nobunaga.[57] In Ichijōdani, the cost of the conflict is legible to some degree in seven extant stone stupas and Buddhas: six five-layer stupas and one Jizō Bodhisattva statue, all dated to the day of the battle. It is very unusual to find more than one stone marker made on a particular day, so scholars agree that these memorialize a small number of the fallen who resided in Ichijōdani. Of course the number of stone death memorials that have been found is a tiny fraction of the population that lived and died in this regional center over the century of its activity. Somehow, though, the diminutive stone stupas and Buddhas that dot the edges of temple complexes and mark the interstitial spaces between urban land and the surrounding mountains seem like entirely fitting markers of a city that definitely came to its own end in 1573.

Conclusion: Material Foundations

The dead can be found in many places around Ichijōdani. To the north of the urban center, outside the lower gates of the city, is a location called Fushano that seems to have served as the primary crematory.[58] Located along a creek flowing down from Ichijōdani mountain, the site originally included a structure of some kind that likely contained two rooms: a staging area where the wooden coffin containing the corpse would have been placed during the final Buddhist memorial service preceding the cremation, and a large rectangular furnace made of stone walls on a flat stone base. When excavated, the furnace was filled with soot, bone fragments, and shards of earthenware vessels that were used to hold ashes after cremation. Archaeologists found significant quantities of cremated human remains in the site, as well as fragments of various ritual implements associated with funerary services and a variety of Chinese specie, currency to help the dead on their way. These ritual objects imply that the crematorium was not only the site of cremation, but may have served as the stage for the cremation ceremony (*dabi no gi*) at which Buddhist functionaries recited prayers while the body and wooden coffin were immolated.[59]

---

[57] Ōta, *The Chronicle of Lord Nobunaga*, 148.   [58] Excavation no. 48, excavated in 1984.
[59] Karen Gerhart narrates an elite example of such a ceremony in *The Material Culture of Death in Medieval Japan*, 56–57.

Another notable concentration of human remains can be found at Saigōji, the large temple in central Ichijōdani. At the back of the complex, archaeologists found an unusual graveyard filled with small wooden buckets and circular boxes (*magemono*) containing the remains of children, including not only cremated remains with a handful of bone fragments, but entire skeletons. Like the Jizō statues found around the valley that are often associated with the deaths of children, these material remains point to the important function that death rituals and their associate forms of material culture played in helping to grant some kind of closure to the living after the deaths of family members, old and young.

Religious practice in Ichijōdani was not exclusively focused on death, of course, or on problems related to merit-making and the karmic cycle. Archaeologists have excavated good-luck charms and small wooden figures, some obviously made in the tradition of celebrating and enhancing fertility, others seemingly appeals to the gods for a long and successful life.[60] And the earthenware vessels used in ritual contexts that are found in so many excavations remind us that the everyday experiences of eating, of exchanging cups of alcohol, of giving and receiving gifts, and of lighting a candle at night would have been understood as life-enhancing activities disconnected from the concerns over death marked by the many stone Buddhas and pagodas. Although the sacred realm was clearly omnipresent in Ichijōdani and the institutional and doctrinal layers of religious belief and meaning no doubt complex, the material foundations of religious practice that I have highlighted in this chapter – the earthenware vessels used in rituals and the carved stone death markers – expose the most fundamental concerns of medieval faith.

---

[60] Ono Masatoshi, "Shōfuku no shakushi," in Ono, ed., *Jitsuzō no Sengoku jōkamachi: Echizen Ichijiodani*, 168–169.

5   Culture and Sociability in the Provinces

What is materiality? What is sociality? Perhaps these are two different
questions. Perhaps materiality is a matter of solid matter. And sociality
has to do with interactive practices .... Perhaps. But perhaps not.
Perhaps materiality and sociality produce themselves together.
Perhaps association is not just a matter for social beings, but also one
to do with materials. Perhaps, then, when we look at the social, we are
also looking at the production of materiality. And when we look at
materials, we are witnessing the production of the social.   —John Law
          and Annemarie Mol, "Notes on Materiality and Sociality"

On the eighth day of the third month of 1568, Ashikaga Yoshiaki – the
heir to the shogunate in Kyoto – paid a visit to the residence of a
distinguished and influential member of the Asakura family, Kōtokuin
(d. 1573), who was the mother of the current lord of the province. She
had married into the Asakura family from the Wakasa Takeda lineage, a
branch of the famous family of warriors that claimed descent from the
Minamoto clan, and she was the senior ranking woman in Ichijōdani at
the time. Yoshiaki, who was visiting Ichijōdani while attempting to gain
backing for his plan to invade Kyoto and reestablish the shogunate, was
required to engage in a circumspect political dance with the Asakura. On
the one hand, he was essentially at the mercy of his hosts; although he
traveled with an entourage of warriors and advisors, and had the backing
of many in Kyoto, including members of the imperial family, he was
reliant on the benevolence of the Asakura, who had total control of the
province of Echizen and complete command over the city of Ichijōdani.
On the other hand, Yoshiaki was the heir to the highest-ranking warrior
lineage in the land, and his mere presence in the provincial palace city
transferred significant cultural capital to the Asakura and their vassals,
elevating them in the eyes of not only their subjects but more importantly
their elite peers across Japan. He needed military support, and could
offer significant cultural and ritual benefits in exchange. Formal visits
(*onari*) such as this were thus calculated, choreographed, and highly

political affairs that also resulted in culturally rich and pleasurable social gatherings.

The precise agenda of the gathering is not recorded in extant documents, but we know from the records of similar events (including other visits by Yoshiaki during his time in Ichijōdani) that the Ashikaga lord likely sent a representative ahead of time to verify that the route from his temporary residence to Nakanogoten, the palatial residence of Kōtokuin, was properly guarded and ready for his progress. He then traveled in a palanquin at the center of a procession of dozens of guards and attendants. Arriving at Nakanogoten, he greeted his hosts and then engaged in a ceremonial exchange of sake, which was the typical social ritual that warriors in this period practiced to mark an occasion as symbolically significant. We know that the primary purpose of the visitation was to enact a ceremony in which Yoshiaki, as a representative of the Ashikaga, elevated Kōtokuin to the second rank as a Buddhist nun, a courtly honor for her and the Asakura family. When the ceremony ended, it was evening, and all present then participated in an elaborate banquet that lasted throughout the night.[1] Such events involved significant exchanges of both rounds of alcoholic beverages and food, as well as gifts such as swords, ceramics, specie, and horses. Like the potlatch ceremonies of the indigenous nations of the Pacific Northwest in North America, these medieval provincial banquets were singular opportunities for relationships to be formed, social status to be clarified, wealth to be displayed, and power to be not only exhibited but deployed on the human bodies present.[2] The ritualization of these social interactions is a perfect illustration of Catherine Bell's conception of strategic activities that are built from interactions between people in a bespoke "symbolically constituted spatial and temporal environment."[3]

This chapter explores the performative and artistic landscape of Ichijōdani to argue that provincial cities were vital and active centers of cultural production and consumption, part of a distributed network of makers and performers who themselves played a major role in the politics of the late medieval period through their staging of lectures, performances, and other cultural gatherings. I show that the specificity of a city like Ichijōdani – the particular historical moment, the natural and built environment, and the political agency of the participants – made the cultural activities that took place in the city uniquely meaningful.

[1] Inoue et al., eds., "Asakura shimatsuki," 360.
[2] Sakurai Eiji, "Enkai to kenryoku," in *Utage no chūsei: ba, kawarake, kenryoku,* ed. Ono Masatoshi, Gomi Fumihiko, and Hagihara Mitsuo (Koshi Shoin, 2008), 219–240.
[3] Bell, *Ritual Theory,* 93.

The "distributed sociability" of culture and performance in this historical moment should not be measured against periods of centralized rule and thus judged to be an aberration, but rather understood – as I argue throughout this book – as a distinctive moment in Japan's history when regional communities enabled vibrant ways of living that have been insufficiently acknowledged as constitutive elements of Japanese culture and tradition.

The ingredients required for Ashikaga Yoshiaki's visitation to Kōtokuin to be successful, for example, included proper urban infrastructure, palatial residences with tea rooms and gathering spaces, and elegant and carefully manicured gardens – all of which could in theory be found in Kyoto. Yet the reality was that the imperial capital after the Ōnin War of 1467–1477 was at times unable to facilitate the very gatherings that were a necessary condition for warrior and aristocratic elites to conduct their business. In the provinces, the practices of entertainment, pageantry, and sociability that the Ashikaga shoguns had refined in the fifteenth century were not simply copied, but further expanded and articulated. This was accomplished through the activities and networking of a diverse cast of scholars, priests, aristocrats, poets, and actors who traveled between cities, to be sure, but also set down roots in places like Ichijōdani, using the city and its surrounding valley as a home and source of creativity. The site-based sociability this chapter explores was not a mimetic shadow of the real culture operating in Kyoto, but rather was the key to the very functioning and operation of the provincial warrior power that defined the last century of the medieval period.

Sociable Exchange: Poetry, Scholarship, and Painting

Ichijōdani, located just three or four days' travel to the north of the capital region, was both remote and accessible, provincial and urban, and thus an attractive destination for travelers from Kyoto as well as tourists, refugees, and other wanderers of the roads in the sixteenth century. The capital of Echizen itself served as a powerful draw for a range of elite, cultured visitors from Kyoto and beyond, and the Asakura and their vassals played a role in attracting cultural practitioners to Ichijōdani as well. The Asakura were frequent visitors to Kyoto and other urban centers, and some individuals in the family were deeply connected to contemporaneous cultural trends, interested in the benefits of artistic patronage, and determined to make their home base an attractive, meritorious, and lively center for the province they had come to rule. This warrior cosmopolitanism was strikingly clear in the mid-fifteenth century, when the Asakura resided largely in Kyoto and were active patrons of and participants in cultural networks in the capital; the poet Sōtetsu (1381–1459), for example, mentions Asakura Eirin nine times in his diary between 1458 and 1459, a reflection of Eirin's prominence as a regular host of a *waka* gathering in the city.[4] After seizing power from the Shiba and focusing their time and energy in Ichijōdani, the Asakura continued to actively network with Kyoto elites to expand their opportunities for cultural patronage, and then worked to bring new artists and performers to the city on a short-term, a long-term, and in some cases a permanent basis. This is a helpful reminder that cultural developments can bubble up from the activities of a diverse community like Ichijōdani, but they can also emerge from relatively top-down initiatives such as the intentional promotion and financing of the Asakura.

One example of the draw of Ichijōdani is seen in the activities of the linked-verse (*renga*) poet Saiokuken Sōchō (1448–1532), a peripatetic Zen monk with deep connections to Daitokuji in Kyoto, where he studied, as well as to Suruga (present-day Shizuoka), his birthplace and longtime residence. Sōchō visited Ichijōdani on numerous occasions and developed a close relationship with the Asakura that involved considerable exchange of ideas, favors, requests, and of course poetry. Sometimes Sōchō called on the Asakura in Ichijōdani for his own purposes: to seek funding for some new construction project at Daitokuji, for example. At other times, the Asakura sent for him because of some need of their own: "We were met by a mountain ascetic sent by Asakura Tarōzaemon Norikage. I read the letters he brought, and we then accompanied him to lodgings in Hirao. The next morning I wrote a reply."[5] Sōchō's visits could be short, lasting just a few days, or quite long, born of deep friendship and, we can imagine, the pleasures of life in a thriving but manageable urban center. His longest documented stay with a warrior in his many travels around Japan appears to have been the four months he spent with Asakura Norikage in 1523.[6]

Ichijōdani and provincial urban centers like it could thus serve as a refuge as well as a source of support for monks, poets, and other creative individuals on the road in the sixteenth century. This is a reminder that the networks that were once concentrated in Kyoto, which at the height of the Ashikaga shogunate served as the primary residence for the most

---

[4] See Suegara Yutaka, "Ichijōdani ni bunka o tsutaeta hitobito," in Fukui Kenritsu Ichijōdani Asakura Shi Iseki Shiryōkan, *Sengoku no manabiya: Asakura bunka, bunbu o kimeru* (Fukui Kenritsu Ichijōdani Asakura Shi Iseki Shiryōkan, 2013), 5.

[5] Horton, *The Journal of Sōchō*, 19. Also, H. Mack Horton, *Song in an Age of Discord: The Journal of Sōchō and Poetic Life in Late Medieval Japan* (Stanford University Press, 2001), 69.

[6] Horton, *Song in an Age of Discord*, 73.

senior warrior elites from around Japan, spread into the provinces when these leaders returned to their home domains and ruled as local power-holders rather than servants in the shogunal structure. This is not quite a "nationalization" of culture of the sort that can be seen in Japan during the Edo period, when governance was relatively stable and the system of alternate attendance cycled people, ideas, and products in and out of the provinces and the largest cities. Indeed, the question of whether or not "Japan" as a unified entity existed in any meaningful sense in the sixteenth century (whether Sengoku should be translated as "the nation at war" or as "warring states") is a matter of considerable debate. Still, the ways in which cultural production and consumption opened up geographically and economically in this period, examined below through various examples including Noh, tea, poetry, and painting, point to major late medieval transformations in the relationships between a broad range of people and what we now think of as the canonical cultural heritage of premodern Japan.

Another member of the cultural elite whose pursuit of patronage led him to Ichijōdani was the poet Jōkōin Gyōken (active in the late fifteenth century). A Buddhist monk, Gyōken studied under Gyōkō (1391–1455), a Nijō school *waka* poet, and then was adopted by him and made heir to his lineage as well as holder of an official position editing poetry collections for the imperial court. However, the Ōnin War forced Gyōken and his son Gyōsei to flee Kyoto, and he made his way to Ichijōdani to seek patronage from the Asakura, staying for more than a decade. He appears as a fairly regular participant in *waka* poetry gatherings in Ichijōdani between 1477 and 1490. Surviving instructional texts also point to his activity as a poetry teacher for the Asakura and their vassals. In 1491, for example, he instructed Kanemasa Yoshitsugu, a warrior who served the Asakura, in the *Collection of Ancient and Modern Poems* (*Kokinshū*) according to an annotated version of the text in the collection of the Yōmei Bunko. In 1495, he wrote out a copy of Fujiwara Teika's *Essentials of Poetic Composition* (*Eiga no taigai*) at the request of a certain Ichijōdani resident named Fujiwara no Arimune.[7] Several additional undated texts, including a copy of *Wise Answers to Foolish Questions* (*Gumon kenchū*),[8] were also transcribed by Gyōken for patrons in Ichijōdani. Asakura patronage of the Jōkōin house continued, it seems, for several generations, with references to the relationship continuing as late as 1560.

The 1560s seem to have been an unusually fertile period for poetic exchange and production in Ichijōdani. Perhaps the most famous

---

[7] See Fukui, *Sengoku no manabiya*, 25, colophon in figure 6, and the discussion on 81.
[8] Figure 7, Fukui, *Sengoku no manabiya*, 26, figure 7, and 81–82.

example was the well-documented Meandering Stream Banquet
(*Kyokusui no en*) that the Asakura held on 1562/8/21.[9] Like many of the
social and ritual practices patronized by the Asakura, this event was a
reference to the sociability of the imperial court, but it also gestured at a
much broader East Asian tradition of social and cultural practice that
would have been known to all those participating. Meandering Stream
Banquets had their roots in Chinese purification rituals held in the
spring, with a long and well-documented history. The event was usually
held on the third day of the third month. On this occasion, nobles and
commoners alike gathered alongside local streams and celebrated the
arrival of spring through the consumption of alcoholic beverages.[10]
Perhaps the most famous iteration of this custom was the Orchid
Pavilion Gathering of 353, during the Six Dynasties era of Chinese
history. This banquet was held in Shaoxing and involved many of the
greatest poets of the day. One of the participants, the calligrapher and
politician Wang Xizhi (321–379), recorded a preface to the larger collection of poems from the event, and his text is considered one of the finest
works of Chinese calligraphy, though it survives today only in copies.
Painters also took up the theme of the Orchid Pavilion Gathering,
memorializing these spring purification rituals as embodiments of elite
poetic culture and its Daoist influences.[11]

Some version of this practice made its way to Japan and was embraced
by court nobles in the Nara and early Heian periods. In this adapted
Japanese version, aristocratic participants sat alongside a garden brook,
composed a Chinese-style poem (*kanshi*), and then drank a cup of sake
that had been periodically placed in the water to float downstream.[12] In
competitive versions of this event, participants had to compose a poem
before the cup arrived at their position; failure to do so necessitated
taking a sip of sake and then placing the cup back in the stream.
Asakura Yoshikage wanted to revive this practice and opted to restate it
as a celebration of the arrival of autumn rather than spring.[13]

---

[9] Inoue et al., eds., "Asakura shimatsuki," 355–357.
[10] Ōhira Kei'ichi, "Kyokusui no en saikō: Ō Gishi ga Rantei de kyokusui no en o moyōsu
   made, soshite sono go," *Hyōfū* 41 (November 15, 2004): 97–110.
[11] See Marshall P. S. Wu, *The Orchid Pavilion Gathering: Chinese Painting from the University
   of Michigan Museum of Art* (University of Michigan Press, 2000). Also Hui-Wen Lu, "A
   Forgery and the Pursuit of the Authentic Wang Xizhi," in *Visual and Material Cultures in
   Middle Period China*, ed. Patricia Buckley Ebrey and Shih-shan Susan Huang (Brill,
   2017), 193–225.
[12] Shirane, *Japan and the Culture of the Four Season*, 243, n. 14.
[13] Satō Kei, "Shiryō shōkai, 'Echizen Ichijōdani kyokusui no en shika,'" *Ichijōdani Asakura
   Shi iseki Shiryōkan kiyō* (1993): 1–9.

The peripatetic poets of the late fifteenth and sixteenth centuries are, of course, fairly well known, and have been well documented in English-language scholarship by H. Mack Horton and David Spafford. The draw to travel to the provinces extended beyond the realm of poetic practitioners, however, and also included a range of other cultural and social experts. A particularly notable example was the courtier Kiyohara no Nobukata (1475–1550), one of the leading scholars of his age and a prominent Confucianist.[14] Nobukata was not from a particularly influential aristocratic house; the Kiyohara (sometimes also known as the Funabashi-Kiyohara because Kiyohara no Hidekata changed the family name to Funabashi in 1601) had traditionally served as low-level court officials with minor clerical duties.[15] Nobukata, however, who was adopted into the Kiyohara family from the Yoshida family, developed significant expertise in the Chinese classics as well as Yoshida Shinto and even the Japanese literary canon, and lectured widely to warriors, Buddhist priests, and members of the court, including several emperors.[16] Nobukata developed enough of a name for himself that he later became the target of attacks by Tokugawa-period scholars such as Yamazaki Ansai (1618–1682), who excoriated Nobukata's praise of *The Tale of Genji* and *The Tales of Ise*. Nobukata appreciated how these classics deployed "ritual decorum and humaneness,"[17] which Ansai interpreted as evidence of how these works had seduced intellectuals of previous eras. Nobutaka transcribed, commented on, and amassed a significant collection of Chinese texts that became part of the patrimony of the Funabashi-Kiyohara family, and which in the 1950s were institutionalized as the Seike Collection held by Kyoto University Library.[18]

Nobukata's first trip to Echizen occurred in 1529, after he took Buddhist vows at Daitokuji and nominally retired from the headship of his house. He was hosted by Asakura Takakage (1493–1548), the penultimate Asakura ruler of Echizen, who invited him to lecture on the topic

---

[14] Tanaka Naoko, *Muromachi no gakumon to chi no keisho: ikoki ni okeru seito e no shiko* (Bensei Shuppan, 2017), 158–169.

[15] Kesao Ihara, "Historical Materials about Jigekanjin Officials in the Medieval Imperial Palace," *REKIHAKU* 156 (2009): 1–5.

[16] Satō Kei, "Kiyohara no Nobukata no Echizen gekō to Asakura shi," in Fukui Kenritsu Ichijōdani Asakura Shi Iseki Shiryōkan, *Sengoku no manabiya: Asakura bunka, bunbu o kimeru* (Fukui Kenritsu Ichijōdani Asakura Shi Iseki Shiryōkan, 2013), 10. On Confucian-Shinto syncretism and its reliance on Nobukata, see Bernhard Scheid, "Shinto as a Religion for the Warrior Class: The Case of Yoshikawa Koretaru," *Japanese Journal of Religious Studies* 29, nos. 3–4 (Fall, 2002): 299–324.

[17] See Haruo Shirane, ed., *Early Modern Japanese Literature: An Anthology, 1600–1900* (Columbia University Press, 2008), 359–360.

[18] See https://rmda.kulib.kyoto-u.ac.jp/en/collection/seike.

of government. Over the course of his stay of approximately two months, he also lectured to the Asakura lord on the written Shinto purification rituals of the Nakatomi school; when recited, these texts were believed to grant merit that increased with frequent repetition. He continued his travels in the region and then returned to Kyoto, only to come back to Echizen again briefly in 1530 on his way to the Noto Peninsula. Next, in the 1540s, Nobutaka renewed his activities in Ichijōdani, lecturing on the *Nihon shoki* and Nakatomi purification rituals multiple times in 1542 at the invitation of two Nichiren Buddhist institutions in the valley. In 1543, Asakura Takakage invited Nobukata to lecture to his pages (*koshō*) on Chinese classics such as *Mao Poetry*, the *Analects*, and the *Six Secret Teachings*. He stayed in Ichijōdani for several months, lecturing again on the *Nihon shoki*. In 1545, he returned to Ichijōdani and stayed for two months, and according to extant documents he lectured at least thirty-seven times on the *Mengqiu*, a Tang-dynasty Confucian primer. Just two months later, he returned to Ichijōdani yet again, and over the course of a further two-month stay he lectured on the *Classic of Filial Piety*. After a brief return to Kyoto, he came back to the valley in early 1546 and stayed for nine months, lecturing now on the *Doctrine of the Mean* and the *Mencius*.[19] In 1547 he returned to continue lecturing on the *Mencius*, and by the end of that year he had completed his own commentaries on this massive classical text; Nobukata's commentary on the *Mencius* was widely read and is still extant in Kyoto University's Seike collection.[20] For the scholar, therefore, these visits to Ichijōdani and invitations to lecture on the Chinese classics were not merely remunerated teaching opportunities but instances for the articulation of analyses of these key texts in the Confucian tradition that when documented would become some of Nobukata's most lasting contributions to the premodern scholarly tradition. In fact, it is likely that Nobukata's most important works were written in Ichijōdani, as he spent the majority of his final years in the Echizen capital, lecturing on the *Nihon shoki*, the *Great Learning*, the *Doctrine of the Mean*, and the *Tales of Ise*. He passed away in Ichijōdani in 1550 at the age of seventy-six, having made the city a kind of second home.[21]

Some members of the Kyoto court, such as the courtier Asukai Masayasu (1436–1509), also had strong connections to Ichijōdani.

[19] Satō, "Kiyohara no Nobukata," 12.

[20] See *Mōshisho*, vols. 1–14, digitized at the Kyoto University Library, accessed May 10, 2019: https://rmda.kulib.kyoto-u.ac.jp/item/rb00012999#?c=0&m=0&s=0&cv=0&r=0&xywh=-2514%2C-124%2C8143%2C2477.

[21] Yonehara Masayoshi, *Sengoku bushi to bungei no kenkyū* (Ōfū, 1994), 268–274; and Satō, "Kiyohara no Nobukata," 12.

Figure 5.1 Members of the Asukai house practicing kickball, 1799,
Pictorial Guide to Gardens in Kyoto (*Miyako rinsen meishō zue*).
Used with permission of the Smithsonian Institution.

The members of the Asukai family were well known in Kyoto as the
dominant masters of the practice of performative kickball (*kemari*), which
was highly valued and extremely competitive among the aristocracy
(Figure 5.1). The Asukai held imperial documents that officially recognized their position as superior masters of this ritual, and they were
entitled to pass down secret teachings of the practice in their family.[22]
The Asukai were also distinguished *waka* poets and had historically
been involved in the compilation of major court poetry anthologies,
such as the *New Collection of Poems Ancient and Modern* (*Shin kokinshū*)
of the Kamakura period and the *New Poetry Anthology of Ancient and
Modern Times Continued* (*Shinshokukokin wakashū*) of the Muromachi
period.[23]

---

[22] Lee Butler, *Emperor and Aristocracy in Japan, 1467–1680* (Harvard University Asia
Center, 2002), 74 and 174.
[23] In fact, the earliest visits of the Asukai to Echizen predated the rise of the Asakura and the
establishment of Ichijōdani as the capital of the province; Asukai Masayori (1358–1428),
for example, visited in 1427 to verify his family's estate holdings in the region.

Asukai Masayasu came to Echizen during the difficult years immediately following the Ōnin War. His first known journey to Ichijōdani was in 1477, just as the conflict in Kyoto was coming to a close but violence and upheaval were still spilling over into the provinces. Again he returned in 1478 and 1479, followed by a hiatus that may have been related to disruption in his own family, which resulted in his formal departure from the Asukai lineage after failing to be named heir in 1482. Traveling as an independent man of culture to Ichijōdani, where his fields of knowledge in kickball and poetry would have given him a highly elevated status and opportunities for patronage, was therefore a savvy move for a struggling member of the Kyoto elite. Indeed, he is known to have spent time in the Echizen capital an additional four times, in 1485, 1494, 1501, and 1508, making the valley one of his final destinations before his passing in 1509.[24]

Masayasu's primary goal in visiting Ichijōdani was to provide instruction to the Asakura and their vassals, seen in a number of sources. In the aristocratic diary *Record of Lord Kaneaki* (*Kaneaki kyōki*), for example, the author Hirohashi Kaneaki notes that on the morning of 1478/8/15 Masayasu traveled to Echizen, invited by Asakura Eirin to lecture.[25] Material and documentary evidence similarly can be found in a series of works by Masayasu that he gifted to members of the Asakura family. One example is a scroll with calligraphy in Masayasu's own hand that records twelve poems from the various imperial collections of *waka*. Masayasu presented this work to Asakura Sōteki in 1494 when Sōteki was seventeen years old.[26] Similarly, in 1508, Masayasu transmitted a secret text of the Asukai family to the sixteen-year-old Asakura heir at the time, Magojirō (later known as Eirin, 1493–1548). The document, *Asukai Masayasu's Secret Hereditary Writings on Kickball*, concentrates the methods and techniques of *kemari* into twelve articles, ostensibly based on the early thirteenth-century writings of the Asukai family founder.[27] Such instruction, however, was not limited to members of

---

[24] Miyanaga Kazumi, "Tenji gaisetsu," in Fukui Kenritsu Ichijōdani Asakura Shi Iseki Shiryōkan, *Sengoku no manabiya: Asakura bunka, bunbu o kimeru* (Fukui Kenritsu Ichijōdani Asakura Shi Iseki Shiryōkan, 2013), 14.

[25] Hiroshi Kaneaki, *Kaneaki kyōki*, entry for 1478/8/15. In the National Museum of Japanese History diary database, accessed on August 25, 2019. www.rekihaku.ac.jp/up-cgi/getdocrd.pl?tn=88&ti=88&h=./history/w11564068515_18867&ch=1&p=param/kaneaki/db_param&o=81&k=20&l=&sf=0&so=.

[26] See figure 1 in Fukui Kenritsu Ichijōdani Asakura Shi Iseki Shiryōkan, *Sengoku no manabiya: Asakura bunka, bunbu o kimeru* (Fukui Kenritsu Ichijōdani Asakura Shi Iseki Shiryōkan, 2013), 22–23 and 78.

[27] The text, *Asukai Sōyo kemari hidensho*, is reproduced in Fukui, *Sengoku no manabiya*, 24–25, and transcribed on 79–80. "Sōyo" is the retirement name of Masayasu, so I opted to translate the title using the latter name for clarity.

the Asakura family. Masayasu also worked closely with select vassals of the Asakura residing in Ichijōdani. For example, he transmitted his own writings on kickball to Sugiwaka Yoshifuji, an intendant (*daikan*) who served the Asakura and, like them, was devoted to the mastery of the courtly ritual.

It is perhaps worth pausing to consider the attractiveness and utility of kickball for the elite warrior population of Ichijōdani. The custom of kicking and juggling a leather ball originated in China, and then blossomed and evolved in the early practices of refined sociability of the court in Japan. According to one legend, the powerful Fujiwara family itself was named, in effect, for the dedication of its founder, Kamatari (614–669), to the game; it was his determination to rush into a wisteria field (*fuji wara*) to retrieve a misplaced ball that earned his lineage its famous moniker.[28] Over time, this prerogative of members of the imperial court became increasingly formalized and rule-bound, without losing its competitive or athletic nature. The court of play was ideally rectangular in shape and marked at each corner by a different kind of tree (willow, cherry, pine, and maple). Eight players, dressed in fine robes, participated in the event, sometimes performing a kind of collective style and athleticism, and in other instances kicking the ball a regulation height in the air to demonstrate mastery of difficult techniques. A scorekeeper would keep track of the successful moves of each player, and assistants would retrieve stray balls.[29] In the Kamakura period, some warriors developed an interest in kickball, including Minamoto no Yoriie, the second shogun, but it remained primarily a court pursuit.

In the Muromachi period, kickball became fashionable with several of the Ashikaga shoguns as they determinedly and self-consciously modeled their cultural and political practice on the high-status work of the Kyoto court. Ashikaga Yoshimitsu, for example, widely seen as the most successful of all of the Ashikaga shoguns, famously hosted the emperor at the shogunal palace in a striking ritual reversal of the usual roles of superior and inferior. Multiple times during the sixteen days of activities, kickball competitions were held alongside *waka* poetry gatherings and musical performances.[30] Perhaps because of the example of Yoshimitsu, kickball was widely adopted alongside other arts as an ideal practice for a civilized warrior leader. The aristocrat and scholar Ichijō Kaneyoshi (1402–1481), for example, wrote in his essay "To Unify the Nation and Restore Civil

---

[28] Stephen Carter, *Householders: The Reizei Family in Japanese History* (Harvard University Asia Center, 2007), 33.

[29] Butler, *Emperor and Aristocracy in Japan*, 74.

[30] See Matthew Stavros with Norika Kurioka, "Imperial Progress to the Muromachi Palace, 1381: A Study and Annotated Translation of *Sakayuku hana*," *Japan Review* 28 (2015): 3–46.

Society" – a didactic text meant to guide the young Ashikaga Yoshihisa as he took up his duties as shogun – that along with praying to the war god Hachiman, honoring his parents, and upholding compassion, Yoshihisa should "pursue the Ways of Japanese poetry, kickball, and other arts, according to your own preferences."[31] The providers of training in these arts were none other than the elite aristocratic families of the imperial court, experts in what Christian Ratcliff called "cultural service,"[32] such as the Asukai. For the Asukai, therefore, teaching the Asakura and their vassals the intricacies of the practices of kickball and *waka* was the fulfillment of their imperial duty as well as an opportunity to express their elite status and receive material support in exchange. For the Asakura, conversely, engagement with kickball and *waka* represented the fulfillment of their aspirations to attain the goal (mentioned by Asakura Sōteki in his *Evening Chats*) of ruling with civility, in the mode of an educated and cultured monarch, and to use the tools of cultural patronage both for self-improvement and for the creation of social bonds with their vassals.

A different example of the fertile exchange that occurred in Ichijōdani under the patronage of the Asakura is found in the activities of the Gozan Zen monk Gesshū Jukei (d. 1533), best known as the author of *Collected Writings of Gen'un (Gen'un bunshū)*. Jukei was an extremely active literatus who enjoyed close interactions with a wide range of medieval elites.[33] He was, for example, close to the courtier Sanjōnishi Sanetaka, a famously influential calligrapher, author, and scholar who served as a kind of advisor and lecturer to the emperor and his circle on poetry and the classics.[34] Jukei was based in Kyoto, but he spent substantial periods of time in Ichijōdani on at least seven documented occasions between 1487 and 1520. He was invited directly by the Asakura, probably as a result of their support for the influential (and understudied) Wanshi school of Zen Buddhism, a Sōtō lineage that put as much emphasis on literature as the Rinzai lineage Gozan schools.[35] Jukei's writings are filled with references to Ichijōdani, found in texts ranging from inscriptions on

[31] Stephen D. Carter, *The Columbia Anthology of Japanese Essays: Zuihitsu from the Tenth to the Twenty-First Century* (Columbia University Press, 2014), 88.

[32] Christian Doran Ratcliff, "The Cultural Arts in Service: The Careers of Asukai Masaari and his Lineage" (PhD dissertation, Yale University, 2007).

[33] See the biographical summary in Tamamura Takeji, *Gozan zensō denki shūsei* (Shibunkaku Shuppan, 2003), 160–161. See also the discussion of his role in the dissemination of medical knowledge in Tanaka, *Muromachi no gakumon*, 77–94.

[34] On Sanetaka, see H. Mack Horton, "Sanjonishi Sanetaka," in *Dictionary of Literary Biography, vol. 203: Medieval Japanese Writers*, ed. Steven D. Carter (Gale Group, 1999). On Jukei's relationship with Sanetaka, see Asakura Hisashi, "Gesshū Jukei koron: kaken no gakufū," *Chūsei bungaku kenkyū* 17 (1991): 34–52.

[35] See Martin Collcutt, "Zen and the *Gozan*," in *The Cambridge History of Japan, vol. 3: Medieval Japan*, ed. Kozo Yamamura (Cambridge University Press, 1990), 633–634.

Zen memorial portraits to poetic notations on fans and other forms of painting. Jukei's writings therefore serve as a kind of textual map of the web of cultural, political, and social connections described throughout this chapter.

Collected Writings of Gen'un[36] helpfully illustrates some of the practices and networks of association and patronage that enlivened the city. Many notations related to Echizen or the Asakura record requests for names from residents of Ichijōdani; Jukei responded by bestowing a sobriquet with auspicious Buddhist and poetic associations. In one instance, a request arrived for a name for a youth, and Jukei responded by granting the name "Tōun/Munekumo" (棟雲). In another example, a request came to Jukei for an elegant name for a page, and he awarded the name of "Arikazu" (有和).[37] On another occasion, he was asked to write a passage mourning the death of an Ichijōdani resident he had socialized with; Jukei recorded that he had been looking forward to returning to the city to see this associate, but that he suddenly died because of the spread of a disease in the region, inspiring feelings of grief and compassion.[38] In 1520 Jukei was asked to write the preface for a volume being prepared in association with memorial ceremonies for Asakura Norikage (1380–1463). Around this same time, the current head of the Asakura – Takakage – asked Jukei to write the inscription on a newly commissioned painting of the Eight Views of the Xiao and Xiang Rivers by the Soga school painter Bokkei, discussed further below. In a similar example, the Asakura vassal Uozumi Kageharu submitted a request to Jukei to write the inscription on a memorial portrait[39] for his father. This is a tiny sample of the huge range of similar labors he performed in Ichijōdani and for Echizen-based patrons over his decades of affiliation with the Asakura.

Jukei's activities as the author of the Zen inscriptions on memorial portraits and as the provider of Buddhist names for young and old alike reflect the key role that cultural and social rituals played in regulating the rhythms of life and death for the residents of Ichijōdani. In this regard, the activities of painters in Ichijōdani are worth examining in some detail. Painting, it seems, was dear to many of the Asakura leaders, to the point that some even took up the brush and practiced painting under the guide of watchful tutors on a regular basis.[40] They also extended their support

---

[36] See Gesshū Jūkei, "Gen'un bunshū," in *Zoku gunsho ruijū*, vol. 13–1 (Zoku Gunsho Ruijū Kanseikai, 1959), 287–439.
[37] Gesshū Jukei, "Gen'un bunshū," 337 and 339, nos. 54 and 57.
[38] Gesshū Jukei, "Gen'un bunshū," 346, no. 67.
[39] Gesshū Jukei, "Gen'un bunshū," 378, no. 136.
[40] Toda Hiroyuki, "Soga ha no kaiga," in *Sengoku daimyō Asakura shi to Ichijōdani*, 186–187.

and protection to a group of painters affiliated with the tradition of Chinese ink painting, known as the Soga school. The most famous name affiliated with this school is Soga Jasoku, who is mentioned in several early modern commentaries on painting, including the influential seventeenth-century text *A History of Painting in Japan* (*Honchō gashi*). According to that source, Jasoku was from an Echizen family of warriors, but studied painting in Kyoto under the preeminent ink wash landscape painter Shūbun and trained in Zen under the equally famous master Ikkyū. Some paintings exist that are attributed to Jasoku and that could date to the period of the activity of Shūbun and Ikkyū, such as *Birds and Lotus*, an ink painting in the format of a hanging scroll in the collection of the Princeton Art Museum (Figure 5.2). Better known are various paintings in Daitokuji attributed to Jasoku, particularly *fusuma* paintings in the sub-temple Shinjuan that is affiliated with Ikkyū. Scholars in Japan have argued, however, that Jasoku may have been a professional title for masters of the Soga school, and the sobriquet was perhaps used by various painters between the fifteenth century and the late sixteenth century, when this influential line of artists was extinguished in the city they had made their home.[41]

Thus, references and attributions to Soga Bokkei, for example, who is understood to have been the first-generation painter of the school, may overlap with some of what is claimed in later sources about Jasoku's biography. Bokkei's birth and death dates are unknown, but his earliest known painting is dated 1452, putting his period of activity squarely in the mid- to late fifteenth century. Whether he came from Echizen originally is not verifiable using extant documents. It is clear, however, that the Asakura had significant contact with Ikkyū, and that Ikkyū and Bokkei collaborated in various projects. Unfortunately, Bokkei's link with the painter Shūbun is harder to verify. We must ask which Shūbun is being referenced. Two painters with homophonous sobriquets (周文 and 秀文) appear in the historical record as Chinese-style ink painters of the fifteenth century. The former Shūbun appears to have been trained at Shōkokuji, one of the Gozan Zen temples in Kyoto, and became an official painter to the Ashikaga in the mid-fifteenth century.[42] The biography of the latter is less clear; according to some sources, Shūbun was a migrant from Ming-dynasty China or perhaps Yi-dynasty Korea who

---

[41] Quitman E. Phillips, *The Practices of Painting in Japan, 1475–1500* (Stanford University Press, 2000), 35.

[42] See, for example, the painting "Winter and Spring Landscape," attributed to Tensho Shūbun in the collection of the Cleveland Museum of Art, The Norweb Collection 1958.476, referenced in the Cleveland Museum of Art, *Handbook of the Cleveland Museum of Art* (Cleveland Museum of Art, 1966), 278.

Figure 5.2 *Birds and Lotus*, ca. fifteenth century, attributed to Soga Jasoku. Hanging scroll, ink on paper.
Used with permission of the Princeton University Art Museum.

settled in Echizen and married a woman of the Asakura family.[43] And of course it is possible that these two names refer to the same painter.

---

[43] A helpful analysis of the documentary and visual evidence can be found in Elizabeth Lillehoj, "Reconsidering the Identity of Ri Shūbun," *Artibus Asiae* 55.1–2 (1995): 99–124.

Regardless, Soga Bokkei seems to have trained in some fashion under an ink painter called Shūbun, and produced work that was clearly influenced by the Ming and Yi traditions of ink wash painting.

Among extant works are several portraits of Ikkyū and a handful of landscape paintings.[44] One particularly well-documented example is the painting "Fish-Basket Kannon" attributed to Bokkei with an inscription by Ikkyū. This hanging scroll is now in the collection of the Cleveland Museum of Art; it depicts a standing woman framed by an almond-shaped halo. Wearing a white blouse and pants, with a dull blue shawl wrapped around her waist, the woman stands barefoot with her hands clasped, gazing into the distance. On her left arm hangs a basket holding seaweed, and below the basket an ornate Buddhist prayer bead string is visible hanging down the outside of her left pants-leg. The calligraphy above the figure identifies her as the "fish-basket Kannon," an incarnation of the beloved Bodhisattva who ministers to common people in mortal form: "A fisherman's wife by the river and sea, one whole life of song."[45] According to Chinese Buddhist tales, she appeared as a beautiful woman in a fishing village and was propositioned by many young men; to choose among them, she demanded that they recite sutras until only one remained. The theme of the cosmic power of the Buddha and Bodhisattvas to reach out to and teach even the most rural commoners is rendered here without patronizing the peasantry; indeed, the radical compassion of Guanyin, as she was known in Chinese, or Avalokiteśvara in Sanskrit, was powerful precisely because it was accessible and seemingly infinite in its application. The provincial leaders of Ichijōdani were hardly poor fishermen, yet this painting is an apt representation of the collaboration between the Soga painters, with their deep connections to Ikkyū and the Gozan network of Zen temples in Kyoto, and the Asakura and their vassals in Echizen.

Following Bokkei, Soga Sōjō became the leading painter of the Soga school. His exact dates are unknown, but he was active in the late fifteenth and early sixteenth century, went by the name "Jasoku," and worked for the Asakura while maintaining close contact to Daitokuji in Kyoto. In fact, the first character of his name, Sō, or Mune, was historically associated with the Daitokuji priesthood.[46] Three paintings (in the Metropolitan Museum of Art, Nezu Museum of Art, and a private collection) are reliably attributed to Sōjō, and a number of others bear his name but raise some questions, including works in the

---

[44] Toda, "Soga ha no kaiga," 193.
[45] Sonja Arntzen, *Ikkyū and the Crazy Cloud Anthology: A Zen Poet of Medieval Japan* (University of Tokyo Press, 1986), 89.
[46] Toda, "Soga ha no kaiga," 194–195.

Daitokuji sub-temple Shinjuan. Sōjō was followed by his son Shōsen, who was active in the first half of the sixteenth century and, according to the writings of Gesshū Jukei, directly worked within the Asakura household.[47] Again, a handful of works are attributed to Shōsen, who seems to have painted primarily landscapes, but the reality is that the bulk of his work, and indeed many of the paintings of the entire Soga school, were likely lost in the obliteration of Ichijōdani in 1573. A whole school of medieval Japanese painting that seems to have been widely respected and largely influential in its day is barely visible to us because of the wars of the latter half of the sixteenth century, wars of "unification" that are still understood primarily as generative rather than destructive.

The Performance of Power

One of the cultural forms that became increasingly prominent over the course of the medieval period was theater, the performance of narrative tales accompanied by song and dance. The best-known articulation of this diverse performative tradition is Noh or *nōgaku*, made most famous through the plays of Zeami (1363–1443), an actor and playwright who captured the attention of Shogun Ashikaga Yoshimitsu and helped to propagate interest in Noh among members of the warrior class. The Noh theater is often referred to as *sarugaku* in medieval documents, a reminder of its roots in rural, popular performances. Noh/*sarugaku* flourished in Ichijōdani under Asakura rule, and indeed played a major role in the articulation of lordship through performance and patronage that was key to the successful rule of late medieval provincial warlords.

The first records of professional performers in Ichijōdani appear not long after the Asakura successfully wrested control from the Shiba following the Ōnin War. In a record from 1479, it is noted that performers from the Kongo troupe – one of the main Noh schools based in Kyoto – traveled to Echizen. In 1484, another source records that Kanze Koreshige of the Kanze troupe traveled to Ichijōdani as part of a performance campaign aimed at raising funds to reestablish the occupational association (*za*) of his troupe.[48] From this time on, it seems that Noh performers frequently came to Ichijōdani from Kyoto, and both the Asakura lords and their vassals were regular patrons of the tradition; in fact, the popularity of Noh led to the emergence of Echizen-based actors who also performed for the residents of Ichijōdani. In the fifth injunction left by Asakura Eirin, in fact, the first lord of the Asakura explicitly

[47] Toda, "Soga ha no kaiga," 197.   [48] Fukui, *Asakura shi no kakun*, 53.

addresses the dangerous attraction of the theater as well as its opportunity:

Do not amuse yourself by repeatedly inviting the four Kyoto Sarugaku troupes to put on a show. Instead, if you use those funds to pay for a talented Sarugaku actor from within the province to go to Kyoto and study performance, won't that be better for posterity? Still, do not seek to entertain yourself with nighttime performances of Noh inside the castle [palace] grounds.[49]

For Eirin, therefore, patronage of the theater was an acceptable and even noble pursuit for a leader, but the funding and influence of the lord should benefit the people of the province rather than solely produce pleasure for those in power. Paying to educate a local actor who will return and benefit all the residents of Ichijōdani was a practical invest-ment in the future cultural life of the city.

Eirin was not the only Asakura lord to patronize Noh. The third Asakura warlord, Sadakage (1473–1512), was known for his close connec-tion to Konparu Zenpō, perhaps the most influential playwright of his day and one of the major medieval figures after Zeami in the history of the transformation of Noh into an elite cultural form. For example, according to an anecdote recorded in *Miscellaneous Comments by Zenpō* (*Zenpō zōtan*), Sadakage watched a performance of the Noh play *Yashima* by Zeami, which is based on *Tales of the Heike* and focuses on an encounter with the ghost of Minamoto no Yoshitsune, a well-known and salient tale for any warrior leader. The Asakura lord discussed the play with Zenpō and complimented the main actor in terms that impressed the playwright with the warrior's deep knowledge of the craft.[50] The fourth generation lord of Echizen, Asakura Takakage, similarly watched a performance of the Noh play *Sekidera Komachi*, also by Zeami, which depicts the Heian-period poet Ono no Komachi at the end of her life. The Asakura lord reportedly requested that this play be performed, and considering the dense inter-textuality of its text – which requires deep knowledge of Buddhism, *waka* poetry, and the cultural milieu of the *Tale of Genji* – we can get a glimpse of the cultural and educational profile of the Asakura.[51] On another occasion, Takakage ordered that a Noh play be performed at a shrine following a military victory as a form of semi-public prayer.[52] The Asakura's vassals

[49] Fukui, *Asakura shi no kakun*, 53.
[50] Soga Takashi, *Sengoku bushō to nō* (Yūzankaku, 2006), 13. See also Omote Akira and Masayoshi Itō, *Konparu kodensho shūsei* (Wanya Shoten, 1969), 87, 367, 378, 386, and 444.
[51] Soga, *Sengoku bushō to nō*, 14.
[52] Miyanaga Kazumi, "Asakura shi to Echizen Sarugaku," *Ichijōdani Asakura Shi Iseki Shiryōkan kiyō* (1995): 27.

appreciated Noh as well, and a number of accomplished and well-known actors emerged from their ranks in the sixteenth century, some of whom indeed went to Kyoto to study with the four main troupes as suggested by Eirin.[53]

Perhaps the most ardent supporter of Noh in the history of Ichijōdani was the final Asakura lord, Yoshikage, who deployed this as well as a range of additional social and cultural ritual forms in his interactions with the elites of his day. He regularly held Noh performances in Ichijōdani, making good use of Nan'yōji, the family temple just to the north of the main Asakura residence. In the late 1560s, for reasons that will be explored further in the next chapter, Yoshikage held a series of fourteen Noh performances in the city, including such classic plays as *Okina*, the ancient and mysterious work that is more akin to a religious ritual than a narrative drama; *Takasago*, by Zeami, about a separated but loyal couple symbolized by an evergreen pine; *Nonomiya*, in which a wandering monk encounters the melancholy spirit of Lady Rokujō, the abandoned and scorned lover of Prince Genji; *Shakkyō*, which includes a famous lion dance; *Dōjōji*, in which a vengeful woman hides under a temple bell and transforms into a poisonous snake; *Kantan*, about a man who finds knowledge in a dream made possible by a mysterious Daoist pillow; *Sakuragawa*, by Zeami, which explores the love between a mother and son, separated by circumstance, against a backdrop of cherry blossoms and the theme of the transience of life; *Kurama tengu*, in which the warrior Minamoto no Yoshitsune, as a boy, is trained by a mountain goblin in the arts of war so that he will be able to defeat the Taira clan in the great war to come; *Kagetsu*, about the reunion of a father and son; and *Seiōbō*, based on a Chinese myth about the Queen Mother of the West.[54]

What was the attraction of *sarugaku* and Noh for the Asakura and their vassals? The reductive explanation is that these provincial samurai were copying the activities of their betters in the capital. This is the implication of the aforementioned interpretation of Ichijōdani as a "little Kyoto" that gazed from afar on the tattered splendors of the imperial city and tried to reproduce them in the countryside. This explanation is dissatisfying because it ignores the shift in political power, the profoundly different social and economic context, and indeed the words of the warriors themselves who were engaged in these cultural activities, not just as patrons but as practitioners. Instead, we should see the relationship of the Asakura with the diverse cultural forms of *sarugaku* and Noh, which were certainly concentrated in Kyoto, but which also thrived and in fact

---

[53] Miyanaga, "Asakura shi to Echizen Sarugaku," 24–25.
[54] Soga, *Sengoku bushō to nō*, 15–17.

had their origins in provincial regions, as generative rather than mimetic. The warriors of Ichijōdani participated fully in the cultures of poetry and scholarship, of painting and Zen practice, and indeed in Noh and *sarugaku*. They were actors, in both senses of the word, on the stage of late medieval culture.

Tea and Ceramics

The Asakura, perhaps not surprisingly considering their deep involvement in poetry, scholarship, and the performing arts as described above, were also central to the growing field of tea culture. This key development of late medieval culture is perhaps best approached from the angle of the acquisition and display of artworks, notably ceramics, from China, Korea, and Japan. One point of origin for warrior involvement in collecting ceramics is located in the fifteenth century, when Ashikaga shoguns and other powerful warrior leaders began to devote increasing resources to the creation of secular spaces for social gatherings.[55] Their activities were modeled on those of the imperial court, the ultimate repository of political and cultural legitimacy in Japan, and the power that the Muromachi Shogunate sought to appropriate.[56] The Ashikaga shoguns – particularly the third shogun, Yoshimitsu (1358–1408); the sixth shogun, Yoshinori (1394–1441); and the eighth shogun, Yoshimasa (1436–1490) – hired cultural advisors (*dōbōshū*) to acquire and display Chinese things (*karamono*), along with other forms of curatorial and creative work. Among the Chinese works valued by the Ashikaga shoguns and their advisors were calligraphy and paintings by Chinese Chan monks, ceramic tea bowls, and lacquer vessels.[57] These shoguns also invested in the construction of new palaces with rooms that were deliberately designed to allow diverse forms of aristocratic sociability. Spaces known as gathering rooms (*kaisho*), for example, were useful for meetings of elite warriors, aristocrats, and townspeople to drink tea, engage in linked-verse poetry, and enjoy banquets. Many rooms included structures such as built-in desks (*oshiita*) for scholarly writing implements, decorative alcoves (*toko*) for hanging scrolls and flower arrangements,

---

[55] This section was previously published as part of the essay "Chinese Ceramics and Warrior Sociability in Sixteenth-Century Japan, 53–70.

[56] Matthew Stavros, *Kyoto: An Urban History of Japan's Premodern Capital* (University of Hawai'i Press, 2014), particularly chap. 5.

[57] Shiga Tarō, "Muromachi shōgunke no shihō o saguru," in *Muromachi shōgunke no shihō o saguru* (Tokugawa Bijutsukan, 2008), 158–169.

and staggered shelves (*chigaidana*) for incense burners, tea containers, and other small ceramic vessels.[58] These palatial structures put the display of Chinese ceramics at the very center of the social life of elite warriors.

The primary record of this Ashikaga culture of sociability is *The Manual of the Attendant of the Shogunal Collection* (*Kundaikan sōchōki*), a text that is often cited as one of the foundational works in tea culture as well as a landmark in the history of Japanese painting (Figure 5.3).[59] It also should be understood as a record of warrior social and ritual culture. Attributed to one of the Ashikaga cultural advisors, Sōami (d. 1525), *The Manual* presents detailed information on the proper display of Chinese art, with great attention paid to protocols for the arrangement and display of hanging scrolls and ceramics in particular. It paints a picture of the palaces of the Ashikaga that is distinctive in its detail, and both inspiring and somewhat intimidating to contemporaries in its articulation of elite decorative conventions. Who could have competed with the Ashikaga? Yet Sōami might have written the guide in response to the dissolution of the collection he had helped to manage. Under the eighth Ashikaga shogun, Yoshimasa, Kyoto descended into a destructive and unnecessary civil war that leveled much of the city and rapidly spread into the provinces, unsettling the structures of authority that his predecessors had endeavored to construct.[60] Yoshimasa did nothing to intervene and died in 1490, securing his legacy as a remarkable cultural patron but a thoroughly unsuccessful ruler or, as Donald Keene wrote, "the worst shogun ever to rule Japan."[61] His successors were unable to end the spread of war or to reestablish their own family as a stabilizing force in warrior politics, and the collection of artworks they had assembled and displayed began to disperse. The spread of this collection created an opportunity for Sōami, who wrote *The Manual* in response to the need of new owners of Chinese art objects from the Ashikaga collection to appropriately utilize their acquisitions in social gatherings and rituals of display and exchange. Drawing on his memories and perhaps on notes left by his predecessor Nōami (1397–1471), he drafted and sold copies of *The Manual*. The first documentary reference to it appeared in 1511, and as Sōami or others produced more manuscript copies, it was mentioned in letters and diaries with increasing frequency, until the rise of the new

---

[58] Yukio Lippit, *Painting of the Realm: The Kano House of Painters in 17th-Century Japan* (University of Washington Press, 2012), 113–119.
[59] Lippit, *Painting of the Realm*, 119–125.
[60] Donald Keene, *Yoshimasa and the Silver Pavilion: The Creation of the Soul of Japan* (Columbia University Press, 2003).
[61] Keene, *Yoshimasa and the Silver Pavilion*, 166.

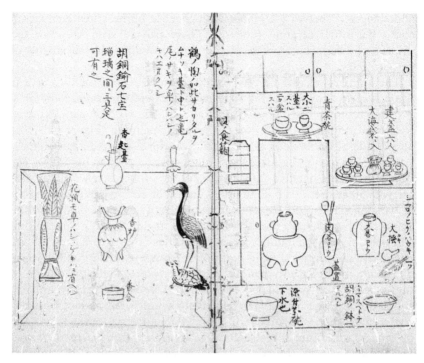

Figure 5.3 Page from *The Manual of the Attendant of the Shogunal Collection* (*Kundaikan sōchōki*).
Used with permission of the Ehime University Library.

generation of commoner tea masters and warrior collectors in the second half of the sixteenth century.[62]

The Manual and related contemporaneous display records make it clear that the Ashikaga shoguns routinely exhibited Chinese ceramics in the course of their social gatherings, particularly the reception rooms in which the shogun and his peers ritually greeted and entertained visitors. *The Manual* contains sections titled "Tea Bowls" (*chawan mono no koto*), "Ceramics" (*tsuchi no mono*), "Tea Leaf Jars" (*ha cha tsubo no koto*), and "Tea Caddies" (*suricha tsubo no koto*), all of which focus primarily on Chinese wares owned by the Ashikaga. The first section discusses celadon bowls and porcelain bowls imported from China, including Ding-ware porcelain works and what may be Longquan celadons. The second section focuses on conical tea bowls known as *kensan* (today

---

[62] Yano Tamaki, *Kundaikan sōchōki no sōgō kenkyū* (Bensei Shuppan, 1999), 6–11 of the research section.

Figure 5.4 Excavated iron-black glazed stoneware bowl (Chinese, Jian ware), Ichijōdani.
Used with permission of the Fukui Prefectural Ichijōdani Asakura Family History Museum.

known as Jian-ware ceramics, and referred to as *tenmoku* in Japan) that were produced in Fujian and decorated with iridescent glaze (*yōhen*). The text also mentions oil spot glazed (*yuteki*) tea bowls, a *kensan* variety, which became one of the most coveted forms of tea bowls among commoner tea practitioners (Figure 5.4).[63] The fourth section discusses tea caddies, providing object sketches and descriptive terminology such as "eggplant-shaped" (*nasu*) and "with shoulders" (*katatsuki*) that would become common in tea writings. The third section of the text, on tea jars, is brief and somewhat unusual: "Some tea jars have been highly valued since ancient times. Their lordships [the Ashikaga shoguns] own some examples. However, they are not displayed in gatherings. One hears that there are many famous objects (*meibutsu*), but these days they are over-priced."[64] This comprehensive text provided the requisite knowledge for provincial warrior leaders to fully engage in the rituals of sociability pioneered by the Ashikaga shoguns.

Warrior elites not only collected these distinctive forms of Chinese ceramics, but in fact named them – not yet a common practice in tea

---

[63] Yano, *Kundaikan sōchōki no sōgō kenkyū*, 345 of the sources section.
[64] Murai Yasuhiko, *Chanoyu no koten, vol. 1: Kundaikan sōchōki, Okazarinosho* (Seikai Bunkasha, 1983).

culture – and valued them at unusually high prices.[65] A prominent example of such a work is the Chinese-manufactured tea jar named Shōka (Pine Flower), a nationally designated "Important Cultural Property" in the collection of the Tokugawa Art Museum. We can speculate that a ceramics workshop in southern China, perhaps one of the Foshan kilns in Guandong Province, produced Shōka in the thirteenth or fourteenth century, since it closely resembles the shape and size of jars that were made there and in surrounding kilns and then exported through the active port of Guangzhou.[66] The container, which is 39.7 centimeters tall, is similar in shape and volume to Chigusa and other famous tea jars of this era. The clay is gritty and rough, with horizontal lines that point to the coil construction and paddle-and-anvil technique a potter used to create the cylinder, layering coils of clay and then flattening and thinning the walls to make the large but lightweight form. The potter then attached the thrown neck of the jar and the thick, sturdy mouth, as well as the four lugs on the jar's shoulder. The white slip was then applied to the upper body and neck of the jar, followed by a layer of ash glaze that, when fired, would transform into a translucent, glassy sheath, revealing the interplay of slip and clay in an attractive brown pattern. The drips of unglazed slip in the lower third of the jar add a distinctive character to the piece, and perhaps inspired its name.

Although not listed in the extant documents associated with the Ashikaga, later sources claim that Shōka was at one point owned by Ashikaga Yoshimasa, and thus began its known career as a famous object, or *meibutsu*, in the Ashikaga collection. After the Ōnin War, the Shibashi family (warrior retainers to the Ashikaga) acquired Shōka and either gifted or sold it to the tea master Murata Jukō, widely considered the founder of the "rustic style" of tea, known to us as *wabi* tea as practiced by most modern tea schools. Later the jar came into the collection of another Sakai tea master, a doctor named Kitamuki Dōchin, who is mentioned in several of the earliest tea diaries as the owner of the distinctive piece. In 1542, for example, the Nara-based lacquerware merchant Matsuya Hisamasa (d. 1598) recorded that he had visited the home of Dōchin in Sakai for a tea gathering and encountered the "large jar Shōka," along with a painted hanging scroll by the Chinese Chan monk Muqi and a Shigaraki water container among other

[65] Tokugawa Yoshinobu, *Chatsubo* (Tankōsha, 1982), chap. 8 of research volume, 77–87.
[66] Li Baoping and Li Jianan, "Chinese Storage Jars in China and Beyond," in Cort and Watsky, eds., *Chigusa and the Art of Tea*, 74–75.

notable utensils.[67] The jar appears again in tea diaries in 1553 and 1559, and in 1576 as the property of Dōchin.[68] In 1577 the jar returned to warrior ownership, which I discuss below.

Most historians of tea ritual have ignored the origins of the practice in the sociability of medieval elite warriors. It may be that the dominance of commoner schools of tea in the Tokugawa period, and the continuing influence of their descendants in modern Japan, has biased historians to emphasize non-samurai participants as innovators who somehow worked against the powerful warrior patrons who sustained them. Certainly, the standard narrative of the development of rustic tea (wabicha) posits a genealogy extending from Sōami to the sixteenth-century tea master Sen no Rikyū (1522–1591) and from Rikyū to the Sen tea schools in early modern and modern Japan. This is anachronistic and ignores that fundamental role of warriors at every stage of the development of tea. Particularly key were the daimyo, described by Melissa McCormick as "powerful and culturally ambitious warriors ... who had spent some time in the capital" and whose efforts "provided the engine for new representations of imperial life and the capital in medieval Japan."[69]

The Asakura, like many Sengoku warlords, sought to appropriate the social and cultural practices of the Ashikaga even as the structures of Ashikaga rule were weakened by civil war. They acquired a large collection of Chinese art, as noted in such records from the sixteenth century as the Yamashina family diaries and the Chinese poetry anthology Collection of Literature of the Five Phoenixes (Kanrin gohōshū).[70] In addition, the Asakura are explicitly mentioned in the prologue of an extant version of The Manual of the Attendant of the Shogunal Collection as having sponsored the writing of at least that copy by Sōami.[71] For provincial warlords like the Asakura, Chinese ceramics represented a form of cultural capital as well as an opportunity to perform the civilized graces of the capital. The Asakura used their collection in social gatherings at their palatial residence in the heart of the city both to reify their wealth and status to warriors from their own region and to entertain visiting warlords and notables from the capital city who were passing through. At the end

[67] Nagashima Fukutarō, annot., Matsuya kaiki, in Chadō koten zenshū, 3rd ed., vol. 9, ed. Sen Sōshitsu (Tankōsha, 1977), 7.
[68] Tokugawa, Chatsubo, research volume, 347–350, summarizes the references to Shōka in the primary sources.
[69] Melissa McCormick, "Genji Goes West: The 1510 Genji Album and the Visualization of Court and Capital," Art Bulletin 85.1 (March 2003): 80.
[70] Fukui Kenritsu Ichijōdani Asakura Shi Iseki Shiryōkan, Hana saku jōkamachi Ichijōdani (Fukui, 2005), 104–105.
[71] Yano, Kundaikan, 53. Also Mizuno Kazuo, "Ichijōdani no bunka," in Sengoku daimyo Asakura shi to Ichijōdani, ed. Mizuno Kazuo and Satō Kei (Kōshi Shoin, 2002), 150.

of the fifteenth century, for example, Shirakawa Masaasa, a warlord from northern Japan, stayed in Ichijōdani with his army of nearly 700 men. A more famous example occurred in 1567, when the Asakura hosted and entertained Ashikaga Yoshiaki before he returned to Kyoto. Such occasions called for banquets, tea gatherings, and poetry exchanges at which the family's collection of Chinese art was displayed.

The documentary evidence regarding the Asakura is of course supported by the archaeological evidence from Ichijōdani.[72] The residential palace of the Asakura had a teahouse with decorative features in the *shoin-zukuri* style that incorporated built-in innovations of Ashikaga palaces, such as the decorative alcove and staggered shelves. The teahouse faced a strolling garden with a pond. Excavations yielded substantial quantities of high-quality tea utensils, particularly ceramics, which in some cases exceeded the number noted in the documentary record. The range and depth of the collection are notable. Excavated wares include Ding porcelains, Longquan celadons, Jingdezhen "shadow blue" porcelains, Jian-ware tea bowls, and many other varieties of luxury ceramics from China. Additionally, archaeologists found inlaid Goryeo celadon from Korea. Among the excavated imported wares, some pieces were already antiques at the time of their usage in the sixteenth century, having been imported to Japan hundreds of years earlier.[73]

One particularly abundant site in Ichijōdani is a former elite warrior residence (site 57) not far from the Asakura palace, probably the home of a retainer of the warlord. Archaeologists unearthed a range of Chinese ceramics from this site, including porcelain and celadon dishes, Jian-ware tea bowls, and one medium-sized and two large tea-leaf storage jars (Figure 5.4).[74] These materials indicate that not only the Asakura but also their elite retainers collected a range of high-quality Chinese ceramics. If the distribution of such wares was widespread among aspirational samurai, which seems to be the case, owning such objects was probably necessary in order to participate in the social activities of their masters.

[72] Mizuno Kazuo, "Ichijōdani Asakura shi iseki shutsudo ibutsu," in Mizuno and Satō, eds., *Sengoku daimyo Asakura shi to Ichijōdani*, 253–270.

[73] For a summary of excavated tea ceramics, see Masatoshi, *Jitsuzō no Sengoku jōkamachi*, 111–113; for a brief discussion of the Asakura tea house, see p. 182. For more detail, see Masatoshi, *Sengoku jōkamachi no kōkogaku*. Color images of some of the best examples of excavated ceramics can be found in Fukui, *Hana saku jōkamachi Ichijōdani*.

[74] Fukui Kenritsu Asakura Shi Iseki Shiryōkan, *Tokubetsu shiseki Ichijōdani Asakura shi iseki hakkutsu chōsa hōkoku VI* (Fukui Kenritsu Asakura Shi Iseki Shiryōkan, 1988), 35–50, as well as accompanying plates and diagrams.

Another site that has yielded Chinese ceramics, including tea wares, is the former location of Saigōji, the temple located in the Akabuchi neighborhood and discussed in Chapter 4. A notable piece (reconstructed from shards) is a large tea jar comparable in size and decoration to Shōka and others in circulation during this period.[75] In Kyoto, warriors often organized tea gatherings, poetry gatherings, and other social occasions at Buddhist temples, which frequently had purpose-built tearooms and gardens. As mentioned previously, the excavation of Saigōji in Ichijōdani points to similar use of temple spaces for the display of Chinese ceramics in the provinces as well.

The activities of the Asakura are also illustrated by two genres of collecting records that appeared in the sixteenth century, presumably part of a response to the dissemination of the ideas and practices in *The Manual*. The first type, memoranda of imported artworks, catalogued works that are often referred to as "famous objects" (*meibutsu*), and became popular among both commoner and warrior tea practitioners in this period.[76] One of the earliest known examples of such a text, *Record of Praiseworthy Famous Objects* (*Seigan meibutsuki*), enumerates 414 objects by category and provides such details as the location of previous and current owners. Many of the listed objects were in the collections of provincial warriors – the Hosokawa, Asakura, Takeda, Miyoshi, and others. The largest category of objects in the *Record* are Chinese paintings and works of calligraphy, followed by what appear to be Chinese ceramics: 26 large tea jars, 38 tea caddies (Figure 5.5) "with shoulders" (*katatsuki*), and 34 Jian-ware tea bowls of various types.[77]

The second genre, the tea diary (*chakaiki*), emerged in the first half of the sixteenth century and has been thoroughly explored by tea historians as the canonical textual form in the development of *chanoyu*. The *Gathering Records of Tennōjiya* (*Tennōjiya kaiki*) of the Tsuda family of Sakai, for example, begins in 1533, and *Gathering Records of Matsuya* (*Matsuya kaiki*) of the Matsuya family of Nara begins in 1548. These texts record warlord participants in tea gatherings and note numerous famous objects that these warlords acquired, owned, and used in the

---

[75] See the color photo in Ono, *Jitsuzō no Sengoku jōkamachi*, 13. A fine Jian-ware tea bowl and tea caddy were excavated as well. See Fukui *Ichijōdani no shūkyō to shinkō*, 25.

[76] See the discussion of texts from this period such as *Ōgo dōgu nedan zuke*, *Noto meibutsuki*, and *Chanoyu zu* in Yano Tamaki, "Meibutsuki no seisei kōzō: Jikken to henshū no hazama," in *Chadō gaku taikei, vol. 10: Cha no koten*, ed. Tsutsui Hiroichi (Tankōsha, 2001), 71–72.

[77] Transcribed in Tsutsui Hiroichi, "Seigan meibutsuki," in Tsutsui, *Cha no koten*, 373–402.

Figure 5.5 Excavated iron-black glazed tea caddy (*chaire*)
(Chinese, Jian ware), Ichijōdani.
Used with permission of the Fukui Prefectural Ichijōdani Asakura
Family History Museum.

context of tea culture. The warlord Matsunaga Hisahide, who was centrally involved in the betrayals, wars, and capital politics of the 1560s,
reportedly owned at least fifty-nine famous objects, eight of which had
been part of the Ashikaga collection and many of which were Chinese-
manufactured ceramics.[78] These warlord participants, like the Asakura,
made the most of the overlapping worlds of tea practice and ceramics
acquisition and display to articulate a public program of lordship that
evolved the model established by the Ashikaga. As the hosts of tea
gatherings; the collectors of paintings, ceramics, and other artworks key
to tea practice; and the primary coordinators of semi-public and public
cultural rituals at which these objects were deployed, the Asakura
engaged in what the epigraph to this chapter calls "the production of
the social": a deep and meaningful association between people and things
in a particular place at a particular historical moment that has inherent
historical value.

Arranging the Landscape of Ichijōdani

Excavations of Ichijōdani have yielded remarkable examples of shards of
ceramic containers for the arrangement and display of flowers.
Archaeologists were able to reconstruct several examples of lustrous
celadon containers using unearthed shards from the ruins of the
Asakura residence, for example, which help us to picture how the lords

---

[78] Takemoto Chizu, *Shokuhōki no chakai to seiji* (Shibunkaku Shuppan, 2006), 102–107.

Figure 5.6 Celadon flower container (*hanaire*) (China, Southern
Song Dynasty, twelfth to thirteenth century).
Used with permission of the Fukui Prefectural Ichijōdani Asakura
Family History Museum.

of Echizen used Chinese-manufactured ceramics to display beautiful
arrangements of locally harvested flowers to entertain guests, decorate
their living and working spaces, and mark and celebrate seasonal change.

One fine example of a Song-dynasty Chinese piece used for flower
display from Ichijōdani is a mallet-shaped vase with a clearly defined
body, angular shoulders, and finely sculpted handles (known as "ears" in
Japanese ceramic parlance) in the shape of mythical carp or perhaps
phoenix (Figure 5.6). Not all residents of Ichijōdani had access to
imported Chinese celadons, of course, and we find many other types of

ceramics used for flower display and arrangement among the excavated materials from across the city. Most common are Echizen ceramic vases, which would have been both much more abundant in the shops of the city as well as available for a considerably lower cost.

These excavated ceramics serve as useful evidence of the ways in which practices such as ceremonial tea gatherings, banquets, poetry salons, and other participatory performances of culture shaped the lives of the residents of the city. The connection of these objects to the tradition of flower arrangement is no accident; flower display connects all of the cultural and social practices discussed in this chapter, with its origins in the courtly culture of seasonal celebration, or what Haruo Shirane has called "the ubiquity of nature and the seasons" in canonical forms of Japanese culture, particularly literature.[79] Yet this raises the question: How do we recover the role of nature and the seasons in the lives of Ichijōdani's residents? A celadon container without flowers is, after all, empty, beautiful as the work of a ceramic artisan but reduced to a nonfunctional, historical relic. More broadly, we might ask how the natural environment shaped not just the lives of the residents of Ichijōdani but the city itself.

Perhaps flower arrangement, and more generally the culture of social gatherings and rituals such as tea ceremonies, can in fact serve as a window into the negotiated relationship between the residents of the city and the environment that constrained and in a sense enlivened it. The flowers and tree branches displayed in the imported Chinese celadon vases of the Asakura residence, as well as those arranged in the Echizen-ware containers of vassals and commoners living in town, grew along the banks of the Ichijō river, in the gardens of Ichijōdani residences, and in the fields of farming communities to the north and south of the city. Tea practitioners of the late medieval period often discussed the flowers they preferred to display in their tea gatherings, and based on extant records it is likely that plum blossoms (*ume*), camellia (*tsubaki*), chrysanthemum (*kiku*), willow (*yanagi*), and daffodil (*suisen*) were commonly cultivated and displayed in Ichijōdani's tea rooms and banqueting halls, as they are the most frequently mentioned blossoms in sixteenth-century tea diaries.[80]

In addition, looking at both the archaeological evidence and the local ecology of the valley today, scholars speculate that various trees were prominent in and around the city in the sixteenth century. Pines (*matsu*), of course, are common throughout the region, are among the most

[79] Shirane, *Japan and the Culture of the Four Seasons*, 1.
[80] Fukui, *Hana saku jōkamachi Ichijōdani*, 18–19.

Figure 5.7 Elm tree, dating to the Muromachi period
(1336–1573), Ichijōdani.
Photograph by author.

represented trees in visual media from the late medieval period, and were often found both in gardens and throughout the valley. Chestnut trees (*kuri*) were also widespread, producing edible nuts that were harvested in the fall. Chinese hackberry (*enoki*), a deciduous tree in the hemp family, was widely used in gardens, and its bark may have also had medicinal uses. Also common was the native Japanese elm (*keyaki*), grown in gardens, harvested for wood for furniture, and generally appreciated across Japan.

In fact, a remarkable specimen of Japanese elm that local experts have dated to the fifteenth or sixteenth century still grows to the southwest of the main gate and entrance to the Asakura residence (Figure 5.7). I always visit this tree on my trips to the valley and walk around its trunk, marveling at its longevity in a place where so much that was living was burned to ash. How can we take seriously the idea of the tree as a historical actor in the events of the fifteenth and sixteenth century, as a witness to and participant in the "small universe" of Ichijōdani? The natural environment did more than just shape and constrain the growth of the urban community; the flora and fauna, the river, the rocks and earth were constituent elements in the life of the city. This Asakura elm is not, of course, the only surviving remnant of the ecology that the devastating fires of Nobunaga's armies destroyed. A number of relatively small ecosystems, or what we might think of as buried biospheres, have been excavated and carefully studied by archaeologists alongside trees and shrubs that continue to grow and that may date to the late medieval period. Most notable is Nakanogoten, the garden attached to the residence of Asakura Yoshikage's mother, Kōtokuin, which likely also served as the residence for some of the Asakura lord's wives. Excavations revealed a remarkable variety of plants, and careful study of their arrangement has yielded a comprehensive inventory and map of the original site.[81]

The Nakanogoten garden provides us with a rare glimpse of the lived experience of Ichijōdani residents by exposing the intersection of the valley's biodiverse environment, the culture and technology of garden design, and the use of this space for rituals of sociability by the members of the Asakura family. Such interactions were not limited to the Asakura; although many of the cultural activities explored in this chapter were restricted to the warrior elites of the city, excavations of the neighborhoods of urban commoners in Ichijōdani show that enjoyment of tea culture, gardening, and flower arrangement was widespread across the social hierarchy. Usage of outdoor spaces for ritualized sociability was also common, and included the hills and mountains that frame the valley, which Fujiki Hisashi has argued served vital roles in maintaining, supplying, and enlivening towns and cities during the medieval age.

We tend to assume, anachronistically and narcissistically, that the only actors that matter in this relationship are the humans who shaped those outdoor spaces. The Asakura ruled the city, designed the garden, and chose which trees and plants to cultivate and which ones to remove. Yet the survival of the rocks and much of the flora of the garden, like the late medieval elm mentioned above, points to the "small agency" of these natural elements of the city of Ichijōdani, their role in an assemblage of forces that collectively make the place and indeed constitute its history. Jane Bennett refers to Charles Darwin's fascination with the particularly small agency of a type of tiny, wriggly nonhuman actor: "that the exertions of worms contribute to human history and culture is the unplanned

[81] Fujiwara Takeji, "Ichijōdani Asakura shi iseki no shūkei ni tsuite," in *Sengoku jōkamachi Ichijōdani ni kan suru gaisetsu/ronshū* (Fujiwara Takeji, 2014), 39–61.

result of worms acting in conjunction and competition with other (biological, bacterial, chemical, human) agents."[82] The trees, rocks, and bushes carefully arranged in Nakanogoten garden similarly acted in conjunction and competition with agents around them; they settled and aged, shifted position, impressed visitors with their intrinsic qualities, and shaped the perceptions and experiences of the humans who spent time among them.[83] We see this relationality throughout the medieval world of poetry, literature, and painting, where birds and insects, flowers and tree branches, streams and rivers, and the power of the weather are ubiquitous forces in both the experience and the articulation of emotions, indeed of human subjectivity.

ki o kiru ya shimo no tsurugi no sayamakaze

Will it fell the trees? the frost-sword gusts of the mountain wind[84]

Even the fires set by the armies of Nobunaga, it turns out, were unable to fell the trees of the city.

---

[82] Jane Bennett, *Vibrant Matter: A Political Ecology of Things* (Duke University Press, 2009), 96.

[83] For a thorough exploration of the role of geography and the environment in the historical events of the Sengoku period, see John Elijah Bender, "Wind, Forest, Fire, and Mountain: The Evolution of Environmental Management and Local Society in Central Japan, 1450–1650" (PhD dissertation, University of California at Santa Barbara, 2017).

[84] Esperanza Ramirez-Christensen, *Murmured Conversations: A Treatise on Poetry and Buddhism by the Poet-Monk Shinkei* (Stanford University Press, 2008), 89.

The meaning of the word "ruin" has its origins in the idea of fallen stones. When we frame an object as a ruin, we reclaim it *from* a fall into decay and oblivion and often *for* a form of cultural attention and care that elevates the value of that object.   —The Getty Research Institute, "Irresistible Decay"

Ichijōdani was largely open and outward-facing in its urban disposition, and the Asakura chose to engage with the political trends of the day rather than isolate themselves in their provincial home. We have seen that the city was deeply connected to other urban centers and regions in Japan through the circulation of goods, such as the widespread dissemination of Echizen ceramics, and the movement of people, such as the scholars and poets who traveled from Kyoto and elsewhere to interact with the Asakura and their vassals. The city's connections were not limited to the archipelago but extended beyond Japan to include both regional and global associations. Although the Asakura were among the most characteristic and iconic "Warlords of the Age of Warring States" (*Sengoku daimyō*), this phrase perhaps implies an attitude of separation and a posture of generalized hostility to the outside world that does not capture the complex diplomatic efforts and cultural exchanges that characterized sixteenth-century Echizen. But this diplomatically engaged, open quality also exposed the Asakura and the lively city they oversaw to broader destructive forces.

Certainly, at the beginning of the Asakura rule of Echizen in the late fifteenth century, it must have been hard to imagine – as the capital city of Japan was embroiled in civil war and conflict increasingly spilled out into the provinces – that the Asakura family not only would successfully maintain their domain but would create in Ichijōdani a political center and thriving urban community that would continue to grow for 100 years. A Korean scholar and politician, Sin Sukju, writing in *Records about All Countries in the Eastern Sea* (Korean: *Haedong jegukgi*; Japanese: *Kaitō shokokuki*) in 1471, mentions that regular diplomatic and trade missions to Japan would sometimes proceed directly to provincial ports rather than entrepots such as Sakai in order to avoid the pirates of the inland sea.[1] Echizen is one of the provinces named in Sin's discussion of the regions and domains of Japan, and archaeological evidence from the province indicates that East Asian maritime vessels did call on the province's ports.

Indeed, according to the chronicle *Account of the Asakura* (*Asakura ki*), in 1551 a Chinese ship arrived in the port of Mikuni harbor (present-day Fukui harbor). The captain of the ship was named Nanshan, and his vessel carried 120 sailors.[2] Although the contents of the vessel were not recorded, it seems likely based on the excavations of Ichijōdani and other provincial cities that it held Chinese and Southeast Asian ceramics and other goods that were regularly shipped in large quantities throughout the region. And we must not forget that Ichijōdani had its own community of Chinese artisans and merchants, who made the thriving Abaka neighborhood perhaps the most important and interconnected district in the wider city. Through the activities of these diverse merchants of Ichijōdani, the city was coupled to not just the larger province of Echizen but the broader regional network of trade.[3]

Another piece of evidence for the interconnection between Ichijōdani and the larger sphere of East Asian trade and warlord networking is seen in the activities of the last Asakura lord, Yoshikage (Figure 6.1), in the final years before the destruction of his family and of the city. As early as 1566, Yoshikage seemed to have been working toward the establishment of more trading opportunities for Ichijōdani in the northern region of Japan, along the Sea of Japan coast, and with neighboring countries including, perhaps surprisingly, Ryūkyū. Yoshikage carried on a correspondence with the Shimazu family of warlords in Kyushu, who both were well situated to arrange diplomatic (or other) missions to the Ryūkyū Kingdom to the south of Japan and, indeed, worked with other warlords on the planning of such expeditions. Shimazu Takahisa (1514–1571), an internationalist ruler who played a major role in facilitating the spread of Portuguese-style firearms, initially welcomed the activities of European Jesuits in his domain and actively maintained trading relations with Ryūkyū; his policies were followed by his heir Yoshihisa, who became

---

[1] Isao Soranaka, "Obama: The Rise and Decline of a Seaport," *Monumenta Nipponica* 52.1 (Spring, 1997): 91.

[2] Fukui Kenritsu Ichijōdani Asakura Shi Iseki Shiryōkan, *Sengoku jidai uchi to soto: Echizen Asakura shi to sono jidai no taigai kōryū* (Fukui Kenritsu Ichijōdani Asakura Shi Iseki Shiryōkan, 2013), 89.

[3] Fukui, *Sengoku jidai uchi to soto*, 87–89.

Figure 6.1 Posthumous portrait of Asakura Yoshikage (Japanese).
Used with permission of Segetsuji.

head of the family in 1566. In 1567, the Asakura lord wrote to Yoshihisa
to discuss their ongoing negotiations after Yoshikage had sent an ambas-
sador to the Shimazu with a proposal. The Shimazu lord had agreed to it
and sent a messenger in reply who brought gifts for Yoshikage, including
a long sword named "Samonji" and a horse. The extant 1567 letter is
Yoshikage's reply, in which he verifies that he received the messenger and
gifts, and is eagerly awaiting the planned mission from Satsuma to

Ryūkyū.[4] Like many late medieval warlords, Yoshikage was thus active in his engagement with the outside world, not only according to the traditional power structures established by the Ashikaga shogunate. Sixteenth-century warlords had to be entrepreneurial and seek connections in diverse networks to guarantee the prosperity and safety of their realm.

Asakura Yoshikage, as we will see below, was both independent and ambitious as a ruler, interested in strengthening and protecting his domain while also taking advantage of opportunities, through alliance-building and cooperation with other rulers across Japan, to expand the fortunes of Echizen province. Yet it may be that Yoshikage's engagement with the outside world exposed the Asakura to broader conflicts of the Japanese archipelago without providing them with the strength – which Nobunaga obtained through vicious campaigns of expansion – to resist the tide of "unification." This had far-reaching consequences for the Asakura, for the city of Ichijōdani, and for our understanding of the chronology of Japanese history. The series of events described in this chapter also produced the ruins – the destroyed palace city – that modern archaeologists have so thoroughly excavated and analyzed, making this study possible.

Asakura Yoshikage and the Zenith of Ichijōdani

Asakura Yoshikage, the fifth and final lord of the family, ruled Echizen from 1546 to 1573, which in every sense but one was the most successful period in the history of Ichijōdani. There were significant threats to Echizen even before the irruption of Nobunaga's campaign to conquer Japan, and Yoshikage and his lieutenants largely dealt with them using a variety of tools available in the late medieval military domain, as we shall see. Concurrently, as indicated by the anecdote about his intercourse with the Shimazu, he worked to expand the opportunities for trade and exchange that would continue to benefit Ichijōdani, and he likewise was active as a patron of the arts for not just his family but the whole community in which he lived. Until the conflict with Nobunaga, Yoshikage was navigating the challenges facing him and his domain with a fluency befitting an independent yet engaged ruler. What, then, led to his death and the destruction of not just his family but the city they had helped to build? Is the disappearance of Ichijōdani the result of political

---

[4] Fukui Kenritsu Ichijōdani Asakura Shi Iseki Shiryōkan, *Asakura shi godai no hakkyū monjo*, letter no. 157, p. 185.

errors on the part of Yoshikage or part of a historical transformation that was somehow inevitable?

Yoshikage was born in 1533, the eldest son of the tenth-generation head of the Asakura (and fourth lord of Ichijōdani), Takakage (1493–1548). Later genealogies list his mother as Kōtokuin of the Wakasa branch of the Takeda family. Yoshikage's father passed away in early 1548 and he thus succeeded to the headship of the family at the age of fifteen.[5] Six months later, he visited Kyoto to engage in the ritual greeting of a new lord with the emperor and the elites of the capital.[6] Records of his activities from this point forward indicate that he enthusiastically assumed the office of lord of Echizen, replying to letters from afar and issuing certificates confirming land rights.[7] He was well supported by a robust band of vassals, generals, and family members.

In 1555, Yoshikage faced what was perhaps the first major crisis of his rule. The province to the north of his domain, Kaga, had been dominated by an independent and at times conflicted Single-Mind rebellion (ikkō ikki) known as the Kaga league. On several occasions, the military conflicts and religious activities of the Kaga league had spilled over into Echizen, where numerous league-affiliated temples were also active, and the Asakura had been either forced or invited to respond with military incursions from time to time. The chief general of the Asakura to that point, the sixth son of Asakura Eirin and perhaps the family's most accomplished military leader, was Asakura Norikage (1477–1555), more commonly known by his Buddhist retirement name of Sōteki. Sōteki had already been dutifully protecting Echizen from internal and external threats for four decades at the time of Yoshikage's succession to the position of lord of the domain, going back to his first battle in 1494 at the age of seventeen. Most recently, in 1544, Sōteki had led a successful invasion of Mino Province at the age of sixty-seven. Both as chief military commander and as an advisor, he loyally supported the young ruler, as seen, for example, in a letter he wrote to the Irobe clan in 1552 seeking their assistance in the purchase of a rare horse for Yoshikage.[8]

In 1555, Sōteki set out on what would turn out to be his final military excursion, when he invaded Kaga and attacked league forces in order to assist in the efforts of Uesugi Kenshin (Nagao Kagetora, 1530–1578) to

---

[5] Recorded in "Asakura ke denki," in Fukui, *Asakura shi no kakun*, 241. For a general description, see Suitō Makoto, *Asakura Yoshikage* (Yoshikawa Kōbunkan, 1981), 46–49.

[6] As recorded in Hanawa Hokinokichi, ed., *Oyudono no ue no nikki*, *Zoku gunsho ruiju*, suppl., vol. 8 (Taiyō Shinsha, 1943), entry for Tenbun 17/9/9, p. 83.

[7] See the earliest known letters by Yoshikage, from 1548 to 1550, in Fukui, *Asakura shi godai no hakkyū monjo*, 124–126.

[8] Fukui, *Shiryō hen: chūsei*, 881–882.

expand his authority across the region. After successfully toppling three mountaintop fortresses and fighting in multiple battles over the course of a month, Sōteki was finally forced to retire from the field because of a mounting illness. Yoshikage was, according to letters he wrote in the aftermath of the victory, thrilled with the larger military outcome. He wrote congratulatory letters to various Asakura warriors because the battle in Kaga had been a success and heads had been taken.[9] Indeed, one war tale records that the Asakura took 680 heads from their enemies. But the cost of this victory was high, as the aging Sōteki had to return to Ichijōdani to nurse his illness; within a month, despite attempts to procure medicine that might assist him, the grand old general who had protected Echizen over many decades passed away. Yoshikage had already appointed another family vassal to lead the war with the Kaga league, Asakura Kagetaka (dates unknown). His results were decidedly mixed, however, until the shogunate intervened and called for the two sides to make peace. For Yoshikage and the entire Asakura house, Sōteki's death was an enormous loss. As the historian Suitō Makoto noted, the death of Sōteki meant that the direct influence of his father Asakura Eirin, who was seen as a kind of second founder of the family because of his role in establishing the Asakura as the rulers of Echizen in the aftermath of the Ōnin War, was now extinguished.[10] Yoshikage still had manifold family members and advisors, but none who could claim both the authority of being Eirin's child and Sōteki's wealth of experience on the battlefield.

Yoshikage does not appear from the extant historical record to have been constrained by the passing of such a key advisor and house leader. Indeed, the next five years of his rule were marked by peaceful relations, growing trade, and increasingly widespread influence for the Asakura family. In 1561, for example, the beleaguered shogun Ashikaga Yoshiteru (1536–1565) wrote to Yoshikage and ordered him to cooperate with the Miyoshi, who were sponsoring (and effectively, manipulating) the shogun in Kyoto. Yoshikage responded deferentially, and also sent a horse to Yoshiteru as requested.[11] Although Yoshikage did not become deeply involved in the struggle between the Ashikaga and the warlords who were vying for control of the shogunate at this time, this incident serves as effective foreshadowing of the conflict that would ultimately bring about the end of Asakura rule of Echizen, and it may be that the possibility of becoming a player in larger affairs was planted in Yoshikage's mind by Yoshiteru's 1561 request.

---

[9] Fukui, *Asakura shi godai no hakkyū monjo*, 136–138.   [10] Suitō, *Asakura Yoshikage*, 60.
[11] Fukui, *Asakura shi godai no hakkyū monjo*, 157–158.

Yoshikage also held a major, festive event in Ichijōdani in 1561, a ritual performance of mounted archery skills that was witnessed by a large crowd and stands out as a significant form of warrior spectacle and sociability.[12] Warriors from the twelfth to the sixteenth centuries trained in three forms of mounted archery that were meant to prepare them for the particular challenges of shooting enemies while on horseback during battle. The first form, known as *yabusame* (tough to translate; literally "flowing arrow horse"), is still widely practiced in Japan today at Shinto shrines, and is understood to be both a form of military training and a kind of entertainment for the gods. The archer rides down a straight track, controlling his mount with his knees while drawing his bow and firing arrows at three targets perpendicular to the horse's path. The second form, *kasagake* ("hat shooting"), consists of courses that mounted archers traverse while shooting a variety of targets; originally these consisted of hats set up as targets on raised mounds, but over time the events evolved into increasingly formal and regularized courses where targets were placed at set distances and archers were allowed only one shot per target. The third and most difficult form, *inuōmono* ("dog-shooting event"), is no longer practiced in Japan,[13] and it was this event that Yoshikage hosted in 1561. It involved setting dogs loose in a fenced-in, circular run. Mounted archers would ride around the edge of the run and attempt to shoot the dogs running inside with blunted arrows.

A pair of painted folding screens from the seventeenth century in the collection of the Freer Gallery of Art and Arthur M. Sackler Gallery at the Smithsonian shows a version of this ritual from the early years of the Tokugawa peace (Figure 6.2). On the left screen, a single dog in a long, rectangular area runs away from a large group of mounted and running warriors who chase him with bows drawn. One warrior has caught up with the dog and looks ready to release his arrow.

On the right screen (the top half of the figure), a single dog has been brought into a circular enclosure by a handler and is about to be released, while one mounted warrior waits inside the circle with a bow in his hand and seventeen mounted archers watch from just outside the perimeter. The two screens flow seamlessly into one another and clearly are meant to be viewed as one image, and indeed the entire picture seems to show a single event, though perhaps at different moments in time. Perhaps most noticeable are the substantial crowds that watch the displays of martial skill from around the enclosure. On the far left side of the lower image is

[12] Recorded in Fukui, *Asakura shimatsuki*, 870.
[13] Doi Tadao, Morita Takeshi, and Chōnan Minoru, trans., *Hōyaku Nippo jisho* (Iwanami shoten, 1980), entry for "Inuvōmono."

Figure 6.2 Painted folding screens, *Dog-Chasing Game* (*inu-o-mono*)
(Japan, seventeenth century).
Used with permission of the Smithsonian Institution.

a covered temporary structure underneath a drooping pine tree, outfitted
with green tatami mats on the floor and gilded folding screens as a
backdrop. This building serves as a viewing platform for what appears
to be an aged warlord and his two sons, an advisor, a page, and a group of
his chief warriors, perhaps his bodyguards. To the right and left of this
structure are small crowds of standing onlookers. The other three sides of
the rectangle are marked by raised viewing platforms where a remarkable
miscellany of people lounge while watching the events. Women under
umbrellas, samurai with their swords carefully arranged at their sides,
fathers holding babies, and Buddhist monks sitting in groups of three or
four all watch the displays of sporting martial skill unfolding
beneath them.

   What was the scale of these public displays? In the pair of screens,
hundreds of onlookers seem to have gathered around the enclosure.

However, according to the record of this event, more than 10,000 people attended Yoshikage's 1561 hunt, dwarfing the gathering represented in these screens.[14] Yoshikage held the event at Ōkubo beach (present-day Sanri beach) on the coast, and the act of departing Ichijōdani and traveling with his army to the event location was in and of itself a powerful display of military authority that attracted huge numbers of onlookers. The soldiers of his army rode in formation in two rows, with archers followed by swordsmen, all displaying gilded weapons and elaborate costumes, including lacquered (*ebōshi*) hats. Individual members of Yoshikage's band of retainers rode proudly and received lavish attention for their bearing and outfits. The account of the event names them one by one, describing their swords and attire in what seems to be a clear indication that this was perhaps the point of the event; rank, wealth, and power were projected to the crowds in this spectacle of warrior rule. The event proceeded despite inclement weather. The Asakura and their men performed mounted archery and took "one thousand dogs" even though the wind was fierce, the waves were large, and rain fell in sheets. The following day the wet weather continued, but the day after that they again held the dog-shooting event. The final day a group of sea divers was summoned, and they retrieved shellfish and seaweed; the participants then enjoyed themselves on their boats until evening and returned to Ichijōdani the following day. The lively picture of a community brought together around an act of samurai pageantry described in the extant account and also seen in the slightly later screen paintings thus illuminates what must have been the most buoyant and celebratory period of the Asakura family's century of rule.

The next several years were relatively quiet for the Asakura and Ichijōdani, and the documentary record is marked by the rhythms of what can only be described as peaceful and normal rule, which is perhaps unusual in a period that saw significant political tumult elsewhere in the Japanese archipelago. Some conflict continued along the border with Kaga, but the Asakura armies seem to have dealt with these clashes in a relatively routine manner. Yoshikage wrote letters clarifying land rights, held memorial celebrations for his ancestors to mark appropriate death anniversaries, sent tribute to the Imperial court, and on occasion hosted poetry salons for his family and retainers.[15] Ichijōdani itself was, to the extent that can be determined from the archaeological evidence, thriving

---

[14] Inoue, "Asakura shimatsuki," 353–355. Of course, this figure often was meant to signify a large number, and probably can't be taken literally.

[15] See the helpful timeline in Fukui, *Echizen/Asakura shi kankei nenpyō*, 180–183.

during this period and was probably at its maximum population of around 10,000 people.

Meanwhile, outside Echizen, considerable upheaval could be found in the capital region as well as in various domains. The aforementioned Ashikaga shogun, Yoshiteru, struggled to regain some autonomy as nominal leader of the military government. Despite being chased out of the capital and then forced to return, clear indications of his lack of authority, Yoshiteru used his remaining powers to grant certain privileges to extend his networks and arbitrate conflicts between warlords. For example, he aligned himself with Uesugi Kenshin of Echigo, who was busy fighting wars on multiple fronts of his large, northern domain. Kenshin visited Yoshiteru in Kyoto in 1553 and again in 1559 and received various symbolic rewards in exchange.[16] Ultimately, Yoshiteru was unable to carve out a truly independent sphere from the manipulation of the powerful and devious Matsunaga and Miyoshi clans, who in 1565 attacked the already politically debilitated shogun. Yoshiteru was surrounded in his own residence and, according to *The Chronicle of Lord Nobunaga*, put up a stout defense: "Yoshiteru was caught by surprise; his fate was sealed. Still, he came out wielding his sword and cut down the attackers, repeatedly forcing them back and causing many a wound. The shogun fought bravely, but he could not prevail against so many; so he set his palace alight and in the end committed suicide."[17] According to the contemporaneous Jesuit commentator João Rodrigues, the effect on the city of Kyoto itself was devastating. After the death of the shogun, "the city was destroyed ... and remained in a wretched state."[18] Importantly for our story, the shogun's younger brother, who had taken Buddhist vows under the name Kakkei and resided at the temple Ichijōin, a monastery of the great Nara temple Kōfukuji, fled into the provinces to avoid assassination himself. This was Ashikaga Yoshiaki, who would soon become the last Ashikaga shogun, and whose relationship to the Asakura played a role in their downfall.

Yoshiaki made his way to Ōmi Province with the assistance of various warlords who still felt some loyalty to the shogunate and seems to have decided around 1566 (when he symbolically exited the priesthood and returned to the world of temporal affairs) to attempt to become shogun himself. To do so, he needed significant military backing because of the hostile forces clustered around Kyoto that had been the undoing of his

[16] Abe Yōsuke, ed., *Sengoku daimyō ronshū*, vol. 9, 297–302.
[17] Ōta, *The Chronicle of Lord Nobunaga*, 116; Ōta, *Shinchō kōki*, 83.
[18] Michael Cooper, *João Rodrigues's Account of Sixteenth-Century Japan* (Hakluyt Society, 2001), 159.

older brother.[19] He did much of the political work of finding a military sponsor by letter, writing regularly to Uesugi Kenshin and Oda Nobunaga. He also parlayed in person with the warlord Rokkaku Yoshikata (1521–1598), who faced considerable turmoil within his own domain from hostile subordinates and thus was unwilling to challenge the Miyoshi in Kyoto. Yoshiaki next traveled to Wakasa Province, and sought the assistance of Takeda Yoshimune (1526–1567), leader of a branch of the more famous Takeda family based in Kai Province, who had a strong historical relationship with the Ashikaga. Yoshimune, too, was unwilling to commit his armies to an assault on the imperial capital when he faced considerable unrest in his own domain.

And so Yoshiaki, along with a retinue of more than a dozen vassals, next turned to the Asakura in Echizen, arriving in the port city of Tsuruga on 1566/9/8 under the protection of Asakura Kagetsune, a retainer of Yoshikage's. It appears that Yoshiaki resided there, in Tsuruga Castle, for fourteen months, issuing letters (including further entreaties to Uesugi Kenshin to pacify the capital) and presumably consorting with local officials. On 1567/11/21, he progressed to Ichijōdani and took up residence in An'yōji. This temple, which had been constructed by Asakura Eirin in the late fifteenth century, occupied a large area south of the outer gates of the city, so it was, on the one hand, technically outside the strict sphere of urban control of the Asakura, and, on the other hand, tucked further into the Ichijō valley and thus safely removed from danger.[20]

Yoshiaki stayed in Ichijōdani for approximately eight months, and in that time he interacted with the Asakura in semi-public rituals of sociability on several occasions. The first of these, on 12/25, consisted of an official visit by Yoshiaki to the Asakura palace, which is well documented and provides a useful overview of the rhythm of this type of late medieval ceremony. After formally receiving Yoshiaki, Yoshikage offered him a gift of a long sword by Sukeyoshi. Next, a banquet began, and as drinks were served, Yoshiaki presented the Asakura with gifts. With the first round of sake, he presented a long sword; with the second, he offered a horse. With the third round, he gave an incense container decorated with gold flowers, followed by a platter decorated with a bird and flower motif for the fourth round. For the fifth round, he presented a long sword by Mitsutada, and a Nobukuni short sword for the sixth. He gave an Ichimonji long sword for the seventh round. For the eighth round, Yoshikage gave Yoshiaki a Sadatsuna long sword. For the ninth round,

---

[19] See Lamers's helpful discussion of Yoshiaki's position in *Japonius Tyrannus*, 54–55.
[20] Inoue, "Asakura shimatsuki," 358–359.

Yoshiaki presented a Nagamitsu long sword. At this point, the two stood, and admired a hanging scroll painting by the Song-dynasty Chinese artist Qian Xuan (1235–1300). For the tenth round of drinks, Yoshikage's son came forward and presented to Yoshiaki a Yasumitsu long sword and a horse. In thanks for offering him many cups of sake and for the gifts received, Yoshikage gave Yoshiaki a Mitsumune long sword. Yoshiaki, in turn, formally gave Yoshikage's cousin Asakura Kagetoshi (1505–1572) permission to take Buddhist vows and don the hood of a priest under the name Isatsu. In thanks the Asakura presented him with 10,000 copper coins. The gathering was reportedly enjoyed by all until late in the evening.[21]

Similar moments of sociability marked the rest of Yoshiaki's stay with the Asakura. While he was busily writing to various warlords entreating them to pacify Kyoto, he was also enjoying the fruits of his stay in Echizen's capital city, often with some benefit for the locals as well. This is apparent, for example, in another formal visitation of Yoshiaki to the residence of Asakura Yoshikage's mother in 1568/3, as mentioned in the previous chapter. During this visit, Yoshiaki promoted Kōtokuin to the second rank as a Buddhist nun, followed by a banquet that extended throughout the entire day and into the night, again with extensive rounds of ritualized drinking and gift exchange.[22] Similarly, a bit later in the third month, Asakura Yoshikage hosted Yoshiaki for a cherry blossom viewing party at Nan'yōji, the temple near the Asakura residence that was frequently used for social and cultural rituals. In this case the young Ashikaga lord joined the Asakura and various vassals for cherry blossom viewing and the composition and sharing of *waka* poetry.[23]

The crowning event of Yoshiaki's time in Ichijōdani, and in some sense the moment when the city and its rulers seemed to receive a kind of elite recognition, occurred on 1568/5/17, when Yoshikage hosted Yoshiaki for a formal visitation to the Asakura palace.[24] The occasion in this instance was the arrival in Ichijōdani of the Kyoto courtier Nijō Haruyoshi (1526–1579), who had come to visit Yoshiaki, perhaps in light of the young Ashikaga lord's recent change in the characters of his given name and participation in the "coming of age" ceremony. It was unusual for a visitation with this level of formality and significance in the life of the heir to the shogunate to occur in a provincial palace rather than in the capital city of Kyoto, which implies a level of trust in the Asakura and in Yoshikage in particular, but also indicates just how isolated the Ashikaga were.

[21] Inoue, "Asakura shimatsuki," 359–360.   [22] Inoue, "Asakura shimatsuki," 360.
[23] Inoue, "Asakura shimatsuki," 360–361.   [24] Inoue, "Asakura shimatsuki," 361–364.

On the day of the ceremony, Yoshikage positioned vassals along the route between An'yōji where Yoshiaki was staying and the Asakura palace. At each of the three gates of the palace, he similarly stationed two guards. Nijō Haruyoshi arrived at the Asakura palace two hours before the official start of the event, presumably to verify that all arrangements were in order according to court protocol. Around noon, Yoshiaki set out from An'yōji in a lacquered palanquin, born amid a large procession of more than 100 people that included pages (*komono*), shogunal guards (*hashirishū*), attendants (*otomoshū*), and advisors (*dōbō*). When Yoshiaki arrived at the main residence, a brief ceremonial exchange of three drinks (*sankon*) and gifts occurred.[25] Yoshikage presented to the Ashikaga lord a sword, bow, arrows, and armor set; and from the garden to the south of the residence, Yoshikage's son brought forth a palomino horse to present to Yoshiaki. From here, they moved to the palace's formal gathering room (*kaisho*) for the main banquet that served as the heart of the visitation. On this occasion, seventeen rounds of drinks were consumed, with different food courses served throughout and with waves of vassals and family members entering to present an astonishing quantity of gifts, mostly swords and horses. The event was thus an elaborate celebration of Yoshiaki's coming of age and also a unique opportunity for Yoshikage to bring the most loyal and long-serving members of his administration, military organization, and family into the presence of the shogunal heir. Yoshiaki reportedly returned to An'yōji at 10 a.m. the next morning.[26] In the days following this elaborate banquet, Yoshikage continued to provide entertainment for his distinguished guests, hosting, for example, a performance of Noh plays. For the Asakura lord and the elites of Ichijōdani, it is hard to image a more politically affirming and culturally pleasurable series of events.

The elation of this moment of centrality for the Asakura and Ichijōdani was short-lived, and indeed can be seen as the high point before an extraordinarily rapid collapse of the fortunes of both the ruling family and their domain. Late in the sixth month, rumors spread that a member of Yoshiaki's entourage from Kyoto intended harm to the Asakura, and Yoshikage quickly canceled any further banquets or similar rituals of sociability. On 6/25 tragedy struck, and Yoshikage's son Kumagimimaru, who was still a toddler, died of poisoning. "Yoshikage's grief was a terrible thing," according to the historian Suitō Makoto. The boy's two wet nurses

---

[25] For more on the *sankon* ceremony, see Rath, *Food and Fantasy in Early Modern Japan*, 67.

[26] The entire event is also recorded in "Asakura Yoshikage tei onari-ki," transcribed in *Fukui-shi-shi*, vol. 2, 808–814.

took the Buddhist tonsure in despair, and a couple identified as the culprits were executed, though we lack further details about them or their crime.[27] Within a matter of weeks, Ashikaga Yoshiaki had left Echizen, headed to a rendezvous with Oda Nobunaga that would change the course of Japanese history. In a letter to Uesugi Kenshin, Yoshiaki wrote that Nobunaga had promised to join him in the effort to retake Kyoto and that Asakura Yoshikage had "no other affairs to attend to" and would likely cooperate with their efforts; in light of the recent death of Yoshikage's son, this seems like a disingenuous account of the state of the Asakura leader's interests at the moment.[28] Instead, it seems probable that Yoshiaki and Yoshikage actively disagreed on the best course for the Ashikaga lord to embark on and that Yoshiaki was hiding this from other powerful warlords like Kenshin to create the appearance that his alliance with Nobunaga was part of a broad coalition. We do not know what Yoshikage's position was regarding the plans of Yoshiaki, or indeed the terms of their parting, though Yoshikage did order a force to accompany Yoshiaki and his men to the border with Ōmi Province as a courtesy.[29]

For Ashikaga Yoshiaki, the departure from the hospitality of the Asakura and the comforts of Ichijōdani was of course the launching point for his campaign to become shogun and to reestablish his family as the military rulers of all of Japan. To accomplish this, he needed Nobunaga to act as his protector and champion, which the brash Oda lord initially seemed willing to do. The key first step was simply to ensure that Yoshiaki could safely enter Kyoto. After failed negotiations with Rokkaku Jōtei, who controlled southern Ōmi Province and had allied himself with the warlords dominating Kyoto, Nobunaga marshaled his forces to accomplish on the battlefield what he had been unable to execute via diplomacy. Over the course of less than a month, his armies toppled the defensive positions and castles of the Rokkaku and their allies, taking many hostages as well as many heads along the way. Yoshiaki followed step by step, until he was able in the middle of the tenth month of 1568 to enter Kyoto itself. "On the 22nd of the Tenth Month, Yoshiaki went to the imperial palace and, at a ceremony held in formal attire, was installed as Seii Shōgun [sic], Barbarian-Conquering General. Having established the shogun securely in the capital city, Nobunaga enjoyed glory unparalleled in the Precincts of the Sun. He deserved to be honored until the end of times, to be held up as an

---

[27] Inoue, "Asakura shimatsuki," 365, 379.

[28] Suitō, *Asakura Yoshikage*, 81. See also Suitō Makoto, "Setchōki no Asakura Yoshikage," in *Asakura Yoshikage no subete*, 57.

[29] Inoue, "Asakura shimatsuki," 366.

example to his descendants."[30] Yoshiaki had found his champion, and his long period of wandering, looking for support from provincial warlords like the Asakura, was, for the time being at least, forgotten.

Urban Destruction

The newly reestablished shogunate issued a directive to Asakura Yoshikage to travel to Kyoto and serve Yoshiaki as a commissioner in the new government. According to one war chronicle, Yoshikage brought this demand to a counsel of his vassals, seeking their advice. Those assembled were unable to reach a consensus, and in the end two primary positions emerged. One side was in favor of agreeing to the shogunate's demand, arguing that serving as part of the administration of a newly reinvigorated warrior government would represent the fulfillment of obligation (*giri*); furthermore, Nobunaga was already putting together a wide coalition of powerful allies, and it would be hard for the lord of a single province, like Yoshikage, to resist him. The other side argued that Nobunaga showed little sign of being truly interested in service or loyalty to the shogunate, but in all likelihood wanted to appropriate the authority of the legitimate warrior government and gradually take control of the armies of all the provinces in the name of his own family's glory. Destroying Nobunaga would be a true display of loyalty to the government. Since Nobunaga's accomplishments to date amounted to very little, an Asakura alliance with the Azai, Rokkaku, Wakasa Takeda, the forces of Ishiyama Honganji, and the monks of Enryakuji on Mt. Hiei, as well as coordination with the Kitabatake of Ise and Takeda Shingen of Kai and Shinano, could easily surround and destroy Nobunaga. Yoshikage listened carefully to both sides, and then declared that the demand to proceed to Kyoto and join the government represented not the will of the shogun but a trap laid by Nobunaga, and that he would refuse the request.[31]

The gradual decay of the relationship between Ashikaga Yoshiaki and Nobunaga is well documented, and Asakura Yoshikage's decision not to

---

[30] Ōta, *The Chronicle of Lord Nobunaga*, 124; Ōta, *Shinchō kōki*, 89.

[31] This account is found in only one version of the war chronicles, a text known as *The Record of the Asakura House (Asakura-ke ki)*, a variant of the better-known *Asakura shimatsuki*, and its uncanny accuracy in describing the actions that Nobunaga would ultimately take has led historians to treat it as a later account and largely discount this passage as an accurate description of a debate within the Asakura leadership. However, it is indisputable that Yoshikage did face the two choices outlined in this narrative – collaborate with Nobunaga and his puppet shogun or resist, and the Asakura lord chose the second path, which ultimately led to the destruction of his house. Suitō Makoto summarizes the account in *Asakura-ke ki* in "Setchōki no Asakura Yoshikage," 61–63.

serve in the shogunate's government must have seemed like the right course in light of Nobunaga's increasingly belligerent actions toward Yoshiaki in early 1570. Nobunaga had taken on the role of chief military leader, issuing directions to high and low "for the sake of the state, for the sake of Nobunaga."[32] The Asakura, meanwhile, seem to have anticipated the possibility of invasion, and worked to strengthen extant defenses and add some new fortresses.[33] In the fourth month of 1570, Nobunaga indeed launched his armies out of Kyoto and began his first invasion of Echizen. Yoshikage responded by sending a force of 3,000 soldiers to Tsuruga to fortify defensive positions. Oda men proceeded directly north out of Kyoto and into Asakura territory, assaulting the fortress on Mt. Tezutsu (near Tsuruga) and reportedly taking 1,370 heads.[34] Nobunaga's armies attacked Kanegasaki Castle, whose defenders withdrew, and then Hikida Castle, with similar results. Nobunaga seemed bound for a victory. However, he was taken completely by surprise when his ally and brother-in-law Azai Nagamasa, a warlord based in northern Ōmi Province, suddenly turned against him and began attacking Oda forces, effectively cutting off a clear line of retreat for Nobunaga back to his home in Gifu. It seems that the historical alliance between the Azai and the Asakura triumphed over the more recent Oda affiliation with the Azai through marriage. Nobunaga was apparently so unprepared for the possibility of Nagamasa's defection that he initially believed it to be a false rumor, "but from all sides it was reported to be true. 'What's done is done,' Nobunaga concluded."[35] The Oda lord ordered an immediate retreat from Echizen and pulled his forces back to Kyoto, and a week later, he decamped to Gifu to reconsider his strategy.

Yoshikage now turned to the support of his new allies and sent troops to cooperate with the Azai as well as the Rokkaku in attacks on Oda positions in Ōmi and Mino Provinces. Nobunaga, in turn, responded by preparing his troops for a counter-assault on this anti-Nobunaga league. He also convinced several leaders in the Azai forces to switch sides and join his forces, taking over two fortresses in the process.[36] He then led an attack on the Azai headquarters, Odani Castle (present-day Nagahama City, Shiga Prefecture), which was extremely inaccessible and well defended, before shifting to an assault with his ally Tokugawa Ieyasu on forces in Yokoyama Castle, to the southeast (in present-day Maibara city).

---

[32] See Lamers's helpful discussion of Nobunaga's use of the term *tenka* and his escalating actions in 1570 in *Japonius Tyrannus*, 70–72.

[33] Inoue, "Asakura shimatsuki," 373.

[34] Ōta, *The Chronicle of Lord Nobunaga*, 142–143; Ōta, *Shinchō kōki*, 106.

[35] Ōta, *The Chronicle of Lord Nobunaga*, 143; Ōta, *Shinchō kōki*, 107.

[36] Ōta, *The Chronicle of Lord Nobunaga*, 145; Ōta, *Shinchō kōki*, 109.

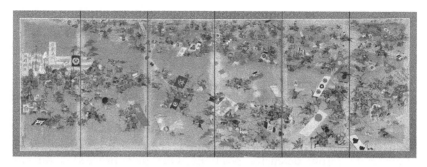

Figure 6.3 *Battle of Anegawa*, folding screen, 1837.
Used with permission of the Fukui Prefectural History Museum.

The Azai and the Asakura saw this as their opportunity to counterattack Nobunaga; combining the Asakura army of 8,000 men with the Azai force of 5,000, they positioned themselves along the northern bank of the nearby Ane River. Facing them across the water were the forces of Nobunaga and Ieyasu, with some support from the forces of the Mino samurai Inaba Ittetsu. Few accurate records of the battle exist, though *The Chronicle of Lord Nobunaga* paints a lively picture of the conflict unfolding in the early morning hours of 6/28: "A terrible, confused man-to-man battle ensued. They crossed swords and slashed away amid black clouds of dust. Blades splintered, sword guards were cleft in two; on all sides everyone fought for all he was worth."[37] In some later accounts of what became known as the Battle of Anegawa (Figure 6.3), tales of meritorious duels between particular warriors from each side emerge, but are impossible to verify.

What is widely reported is that the Oda and Tokugawa forces were victorious, killing many "warriors of standing," which implies that numerous Asakura and Azai samurai and foot soldiers died in the battle. The historian Suitō Makoto suggests that the wildly divergent reports of the results of the battle that appear in a few otherwise reliable texts from the time indicates that no one really had a clear grasp of what exactly had happened. Nobunaga claimed the victory and seemed to have recovered his equilibrium after the earlier betrayal of the Azai, but this was hardly an overwhelming defeat of his enemies.[38] The Asakura and Azai leaders survived the conflict and retreated to fight another day, while Oda Nobunaga directed his forces back to attack Odani Castle, but found that it would require a lengthy siege and thus withdrew to Kyoto and later

[37] Ōta, *The Chronicle of Lord Nobunaga*, 147–148; Ōta, *Shinchō kōki*, 110–111.
[38] Suitō, "Setchōki no Asakura Yoshikage," 68.

back to Gifu. In the eighth month, he turned his attention to an attack on enemies in Kawachi and Settsu Provinces (present-day Osaka and Hyogo prefectures).

In the ninth month of 1570, Asakura Yoshikage made contact with the headquarters of the Single-Mind league (*ikkō ikki*), the religious uprising that had emerged as a major power in late sixteenth-century politics and that had become one of the major centers of opposition to Nobunaga's campaigns.[39] The parties agreed to collaborate in an attack on Nobunaga's forces, and Yoshikage therefore launched his armies out of Echizen toward Ōmi Province, where they joined up with Azai forces and league forces to form a substantial army of almost 30,000 men. They advanced around Lake Biwa toward Kyoto and on 9/20 attacked Oda units stationed in Sakamoto (present-day Otsu). Two of Nobunaga's trusted commanders were killed, including his younger brother Oda Nobuharu. Yoshikage wrote a series of letters several weeks later in which he congratulated various warriors on the many heads they took in this conflict, which he called the Battle of Lower Sakamoto.[40] Yoshikage and his allies now turned their attention to Kyoto and planned what they hoped would be their final push to retake the capital from Nobunaga. The next day their forces invaded Yamashina and the area around Daigoji, putting them just to the east of the city; perhaps they were loath to invade Kyoto itself for fear of causing damage to the capital city.

Nobunaga responded rapidly and decisively, pulling back his armies from their campaigns in Settsu Province to the south and traveling quickly back to the capital with Shogun Yoshiaki. On 9/24, just four days after the Asakura and Azai victory at Sakamoto, Nobunaga moved his forces toward Onjōji, with the goal of blocking the Asakura and Azai from entering Kyoto, and perhaps forcing them back north. The Asakura and Azai responded, however, by moving their men up the slopes of Mt. Hiei, where they took a string of small fortresses and dug in, secure in their easily defendable positions. Nobunaga summoned monks from Enryakuji, the sprawling Buddhist temple complex that had long occupied the summit of the mountain, and offered to restore various historical estates to the temple (thereby increasing their wealth) if they would assist him. He added a threat, noting that "if the monks were to violate Nobunaga's conditions, he would burn down the whole Enryakuji."[41] The monks gave no response, effectively throwing their support behind

[39] *Asakura karoku*, 103. Accessed at www.lib.pref.toyama.jp/gallery/collection/pageintro .aspx.
[40] See Fukui, *Asakura shi godai no hakkyū monjo*, 201–202.
[41] Ōta, *Chronicle of Lord Nobunaga*, 155; Ōta, *Shinchō kōki*, 117.

the Asakura and the Azai. Nobunaga surrounded Mt. Hiei but did not attempt to send his own men up into the forested slopes, where they would be easy targets for their fortified enemies.

The two sides largely held these positions until the onset of winter, with occasional skirmishes but little substantial movement. As the weather deteriorated and it became more difficult to maintain supply lines back to Echizen, outside observers began calling for the two sides to make peace. First Shogun Yoshiaki, then the chief imperial advisor (*kanpaku*) Nijō Haruyoshi, and finally Emperor Ōgimachi (1517–1593) all issued orders for a truce to be declared, bringing to an end the constant threat of war that was causing widespread anxiety in the capital city.[42] After some haggling, the Asakura and Azai agreed to withdraw from Mt. Hiei on the condition that Nobunaga retreat across Lake Biwa and take his forces all the way back to Gifu. Nobunaga did so on 12/14, and the Asakura and their allies then withdrew from Mt. Hiei the following day.[43] If the Battle of Anegawa had represented a clear victory for Nobunaga, and the Battle of Lower Sakamoto was an obvious win for Yoshikage, this protracted occupation of Mt. Hiei, which reportedly raised the specter of previous periods of devastating civil war for the residents of Kyoto, was a stalemate for all involved. Indeed, it would prove to be a damaging incident for Enryakuji and the monks of Mt. Hiei most of all.

It is worth examining Nobunaga's next move – an assault on Mt. Hiei – in some detail for two reasons. First, it is not well known that this famous event was caused, in effect, by the initial attempt of the Asakura and the Azai to challenge Nobunaga. Second, the audacity of Nobunaga's actions served as a vivid foreshadowing of his treatment of enemies like the Asakura and sites of resistance like Ichijōdani. True to his word, in the ninth month of 1571, Nobunaga returned to Mt. Hiei with an army said to number 30,000 and ordered a full-scale attack on the various Enryakuji sub-temples and temples.[44] Indiscriminate violence was in some sense the currency of warfare in Japan during this Age of Warring States, and the slaughter of enemies in the hundreds or even thousands marked by the taking and display of heads as a ritual articulation of victory was common. Yet a full-scale attack on noncombatants was somewhat unusual, perhaps showing us Nobunaga's intention to signal that nothing but complete compliance with his ambitions

---

[42] See Suitō, "Setchōki no Asakura Yoshikage," 71–72.

[43] Ōta, *The Chronicle of Lord Nobunaga*, 159; Ōta, *Shinchō kōki*, 122.

[44] This number comes from the report of Luis Frois. See Michael Cooper, ed., *They Came to Japan*, 98.

would be tolerated. According to the report of Portuguese missionary Luis Frois, the leaders of Enryakuji learned of Nobunaga's intentions and attempted to mollify him with gifts of gold, which he rebuffed. They still could not fathom his true intentions and in particular doubted that he would desecrate the chief shrine of the mountaintop complex, and thus gathered there along with their families as well as a large number of townspeople from Sakamoto. But on 9/12, Nobunaga first ordered the destruction of Sakamoto: the town was burned down and all its remaining inhabitants killed.

Next he ordered his men to destroy the temples around the base of the mountain as well as the major temple complexes of its slopes, which Frois refers to as "the seven universities" because of their role in training monks and in broader Buddhist education. It is hard to imagine the quantity of books, sutras, paintings, scrolls, ritual implements, and iconography that was lost in this act. Next, Nobunaga ordered his army to form a ring around the base of the mountain and march upward, gradually constricting their lines, killing all whom they encountered, and guaranteeing that none escaped. As the *Chronicle* notes:

One by one they cut off the heads of priests and laymen, children, wise men, and holy men alike. They presented the heads to Lord Nobunaga, saying: "Here is an exalted prelate, a princely abbot, a learned doctor, all the men of renown at the top of Mount Hiei." Moreover, they captured countless beautiful women and boys, and led them before Nobunaga. "We don't care about the evil monks," they shrieked, "but spare us!" Nobunaga, however, absolutely refused to reprieve them. One by one, they had their heads chopped off, a scene horrible to behold. Thousands of corpses lay scattered about like so many little sticks, a pitiful end.[45]

The next day, according to Frois, Nobunaga commanded his gunners, who bore arquebuses (*teppō*), to go into the woods and hunt any surviving stragglers. Although the Jesuit observers seem to have seen this act in positive terms because they understood Buddhist institutions to be a barrier to the spread of Christianity, Kyoto elites and indeed most Japanese observers appear to have been horrified by an act they had never imagined to be possible. Diarists in the imperial court expressed their despairing stupefaction in unusually bald expressions, referring to the "ruin of the Buddhist law" and "disaster for the realm."[46] The destruction of the temple complexes of Mt. Hiei and the neighboring town of Sakamoto was a preview of Nobunaga's plans for his enemies. We do not know how the Asakura, or their allies the Azai, learned of Nobunaga's

[45] Ōta, *The Chronicle of Lord Nobunaga*, 165–166; Ōta, *Shinchō kōki*, 126–127.
[46] See Lamers's excellent account in *Japonius Tyrannus*, 75–76.

actions or what they made of them, but we can speculate that their intention to resist was redoubled even as some perhaps began to question if resistance to the Oda lord was even possible.[47]

At the start of 1572, the forces arrayed against Nobunaga were impressive, including the Asakura and the Azai, the Single-Mind league of the Ishiyama Honganji and their confederates across the region, and, perhaps most importantly, the warlord Takeda Shingen. The previously subjugated Miyoshi and Matsunaga clans rose up against Nobunaga in this year as well. And though he seemed powerless at times, the shogun, Ashikaga Yoshiaki, also continued to resist Nobunaga to a limited degree throughout this period. Yet Nobunaga soldiered on, invading Ōmi province again in the third month to keep pressure on the Azai and Asakura, and then returning in the seventh month with his son Nobutada at his side.[48] His forces attempted to gain control of boat traffic on Lake Biwa, and attacked a range of positions across northern Ōmi, including some sites close to the Echizen border. In anticipation of an assault, the Azai sent messages to Asakura Yoshikage asking for reinforcements, and Yoshikage responded by sending out an advanced army and then following in person at the head of the main Asakura army. According to *The Chronicle of Lord Nobunaga*, the Azai message to Yoshikage claimed that Nobunaga's position had been weakened by various attacks and that it would be a simple matter to destroy his forces in the region. One wave of Asakura men arrived to reinforce the Azai in the middle of the seventh month, and Yoshikage and his forces arrived at the beginning of the eighth month; Yoshikage set up camp on a nearby hill. It soon became clear that the Azai account of the situation had been inaccurate. The Oda army had successfully pushed through northern Ōmi toward the Azai's well-situated mountain fortress of Odani Castle. Nobunaga had attacked the town beneath the fortress, burning and destroying it completely in a repeat of his army's destruction of the temples and residences of Mt. Hiei, and had begun the construction of a fortress on a nearby hill while his generals led attacks on nearby castles. Thus, Yoshikage had been lured into a somewhat vulnerable position and seemed unwilling to engage Nobunaga's forces. The two camps then settled in for a long siege, punctuated by skirmishes resulting in small victories for both sides: for example, several important vassals of the Asakura defected to the Oda side, a major blow for Yoshikage;[49] not long after, some Asakura men snuck into the Oda camp under cover of a

---

[47] See Berry, *Hideyoshi*, 46–47.
[48] Ōta, *The Chronicle of Lord Nobunaga*, 168, 171; Ōta, *Shinchō kōki*, 131, 134.
[49] Ōta, *The Chronicle of Lord Nobunaga*, 173–174; Ōta, *Shinchō kōki*, 136.

storm and set fire to supplies, which caused fighting to break out among Nobunaga's own men, reportedly with significant loss of life.[50] Still, Nobunaga himself returned to Gifu, perhaps because he couldn't force a decisive confrontation with the Asakura and Azai, or perhaps because of news that Takeda Shingen was moving against Tokugawa Ieyasu in Mikawa Province to the east, bringing the fearsome old warlord closer to the action in central Japan.

In the twelfth month of 1572, after four months spent away from Ichijōdani, Yoshikage decided to pull out of northern Ōmi and return to Echizen. The increasingly frigid temperatures of winter must have been one factor in this decision. By retreating, however, he was not only leaving the Azai somewhat exposed, but also acting counter to the wishes of Takeda Shingen, who had repeatedly entreated the Asakura and the Azai to maintain their pressure on Oda armies in Ōmi, allowing him to drive across central Japan toward the capital. Shingen had in fact just enjoyed a significant victory against Nobunaga and his allies by overrunning the domain of Tokugawa Ieyasu. In the tenth month of 1572, Shingen had invaded Tōtōmi, driving a huge force of 25,000 across the province. One by one he toppled the outer fortifications of the Tokugawa domain. Next, he feinted toward Kakegawa Castle and Takatenjin Castle, which would have largely isolated Ieyasu at his headquarters in Hamamatsu. Ieyasu fell for the bait and launched his army to the field, where Shingen's men easily defeated his forces. Ieyasu, however, cleverly assigned his fierce and experienced vassal Honda Tadakatsu to the position of rear guard, to slow down the pursuing enemy and allow Ieyasu to reach the safety of Hamamatsu Castle.

Shingen proceeded cautiously in his pursuit of Ieyasu, who had received a few reinforcements from Nobunaga. Ieyasu fielded his army to meet Shingen and his men north of Hamamatsu. He reportedly spread his forces in a formation known as "crane's wing" (*kakuyoku*) with the goal of enclosing the much larger Takeda force (though the use of these Chinese techniques may be later glosses). This was, however, a strategy that Shingen knew well, having used it on several occasions, and he reportedly arranged his men in the "fish scale" (*gyōrin*) formation, which easily penetrated the opposing lines. The Takeda forces routed the combined Oda and Tokugawa armies, and Ieyasu fled to Hamamatsu Castle while the remaining Oda soldiers escaped north to Owari. That evening Ieyasu's vassals Ōkubo Tadayo and Amano Yasukage gathered together all the arquebuses (*teppō*) to be found and launched a night

---

[50] Inoue, "Asakura shimatsuki," 383.

assault on the encamped Takeda forces, but to little effect.[51] He was completely vulnerable, and could have been eliminated by Shingen.

However, the Takeda lord opted not to destroy Ieyasu, but instead turned his army to the west, and wrote on 12/28 to Yoshikage of his disappointment that the Asakura had failed to maintain pressure on Nobunaga in Ōmi and had instead withdrawn to Echizen.[52] Shingen's anger was understandable; by attacking Nobunaga from the north and the east, and with the assistance of the Single-Mind league forces, the Takeda, Azai, and Asakura could have surrounded Nobunaga, and with a military mastermind like Shingen coordinating the attack, perhaps they could have destroyed him. Instead, the anti-Nobunaga forces found themselves once again in disarray, and Nobunaga, now in open conflict with Shogun Yoshiaki, continued his quest to pacify the realm.

Asakura Yoshikage opened 1573 with the rituals of any other new year, including the drafting of letters to allies near and far. One of those was Kennyo, chief abbot of the Ishiyama Honganji, headquarters of the True Pure Land uprising and one of the primary enemies of Nobunaga.[53] In a response dated 1/27, Kennyo thanked Yoshikage for his New Year's greetings, and reported to the Asakura lord on the various activities of his confederates across the provinces. Although the Asakura had fought against religious uprisings in the past, in 1573 Kennyo and his enormous network represented a vital partner in the movement to oppose Nobunaga. As the year progressed, however, this broad coalition began to collapse with surprising speed. In the fourth month, Shingen, on whom many had pinned their hopes, died of an illness while bogged down in Mikawa Province, having made very little progress after his defeat of Tokugawa Ieyasu; the man most likely to triumph over Nobunaga was now removed from the stage. Also in the same month, Shogun Yoshiaki once again turned against Nobunaga, and found himself driven out of Kyoto. Nobunaga's armies invaded the capital city and, over the course of two days, burned down huge swaths of the upper city and its surrounding districts, causing enormous loss of life and property. In a final gambit, Yoshiaki stationed some of his loyal warriors in Nijō

---

[51] Many historians have narrated this battle and its context. One useful summary can be found in Morita Kōji, "Mikatagahara no tatakai," in *Tokugawa Ieyasu jiten*, ed. Fujino Tamotsu et al. (Shinjinbutsu Ōraisha, 1990), 200–207. It is also worth noting that this battle was the object of more scrutiny in contemporaneous documents than most battles in this period. See, for example, the many excerpts in Tokyo Daigaku Shiryō Hensanjo, ed., *Dai Nihon shiryō*, beginning with the entry on Genki 3/12/22 in ser. 10, vol. 11, p. 8.

[52] Suitō, "Setchōki no Asakura Yoshikage," 83.

[53] Uematsu Torazo, ed., *Ishiyama Honganji nikki* (Seibundō Shuppan, 1966–1968), 608–610.

Castle in Kyoto and then moved to Makinoshima Castle (near present-day Uji city) to the south of Kyoto, a formidable fortress partially protected by the Uji River. From here, he would attempt to direct the final assault on Nobunaga. Instead, the Oda lord, no longer anxious about a possible assault by Takeda Shingen, unleashed his full army on Nijō Castle on 7/18, taking it with almost no resistance, and then toppled Makinoshima in just one day. "Nobunaga ... considered making Yoshiaki commit suicide. But Heaven's Will is terrible, and the repercussions were sure to be undesirable. So Nobunaga spared the shogun's life and exiled him. 'Let future generations be my judge,' Nobunaga said. He kept Yoshiaki's infant son as a hostage," and sent the shogun into exile with his ladies-in-waiting, "barefooted and head over heels."[54] Although Yoshiaki would live until 1597 as a monk, he never again entered the main stage of politics.

The Asakura anticipated an assault from Nobunaga and, as their allies disappeared, must have felt increasing trepidation. Yoshikage in the third month of 1573 moved his army out of Ichijōdani and to Tsuruga, where he would be better able to meet an Oda invasion launched out of Kyoto.[55] Nobunaga, however, was occupied with his pursuit of Yoshiaki and his assault on Kyoto, and Yoshikage returned to Ichijōdani after two months of waiting. In the seventh month he led his armies into northern Ōmi to reinforce the Azai. Finally, in the eighth month of 1573, with neither Takeda Shingen nor Ashikaga Yoshiaki to concern him, Nobunaga turned to the elimination of the Asakura and the Azai. On 8/8, one of the key Azai generals defected to Nobunaga's cause, and the Oda lord used this as the opportunity to reignite the conflict, launching his army out of Gifu and renewing his assault on Azai and Asakura positions in northern Ōmi. When Nobunaga's forces arrived in the region of Odani Castle on 8/10, they positioned themselves to the north to cut off access to the road back to Echizen. Yoshikage, in turn, spread out his forces in an attempt to surround the Oda army. These two armies were of roughly similar size, according to later accounts, with around 20,000 men each, though some estimate that the Oda force may have numbered closer to 30,000. Little action occurred for two days, until a tumultuous storm hit the area on 8/12, and Nobunaga reportedly used the cover of the rain to lead an attack on an Asakura defensive garrison built on a nearby peak. The Asakura forces, taken by surprise and quickly overwhelmed, surrendered to Nobunaga. Rather than take their heads, the Oda lord opted to send them to Yoshikage to report on

[54] Ōta, *The Chronicle of Lord Nobunaga*, 189–190; Ōta, *Shinchō kōki*, 151–152.
[55] Inoue, "Asakura shimatsuki," 384.

their defeat and the loss of this important defensive position, estimating that this would force the Asakura into a hasty retreat to Echizen. The plan worked, and Yoshikage decided to retreat to Tsuruga, while more and more of his men defected to Nobunaga.[56]

What followed was a disastrous rout. The Asakura forces fled first to Hikida Castle, and then Yoshikage and many of his remaining guards and advisors continued on to Tsuruga. The Oda armies, pursuing them through forty kilometers of forests, hills, and low mountains, cut down all the Asakura soldiers who attempted to halt their advance or who simply were caught. "Nobunaga's men took more than three thousand heads. They made a list of those they knew by sight." The grisly ledger that follows includes the names of various Asakura samurai, vassals, and stalwarts of the Echizen army. According to *The Chronicle*, one captured Echizen soldier admitted to feeling great resentment against the Asakura, but that in light of the death of so many of his comrades, he could not in good standing join Nobunaga's forces. So, he took his own life through ritual suicide. Such acts were extolled in the war tales: "His heroism was unprecedented, and his glory beyond dispute."[57]

Nobunaga arrived in Tsuruga and set up camp there on 8/14, while Yoshikage fled from Fuchū to Ichijōdani. The Asakura lord stayed in the city that his family had established generations ago and patronized for almost a century for just one day, and then fled to the east on 8/16, leaving his family behind. His cousin Asakura Kageakira had suggested that he hide in Heisenji, a Tendai Buddhist temple in Ono.[58] Meanwhile, on 8/17 Nobunaga readied his forces and launched a full-scale assault on central Echizen, setting up camp in Fuchū where Yoshikage had been just days previously. It seems they encountered little organized resistance. On 8/18, Nobunaga's armies began to burn the buildings of the city of Ichijōdani, and this process continued for three days. "They burned every structure and every house without sparing a single temple or even the Buddhist priests' residences."[59] Even the dogs and birds fled the burning city, with only a few winter crows flying above the valley.

What happened to the people of Ichijōdani? Any who hid or fought must have died, and a range of human remains has been excavated from various sites across the city. Many also must have fled, of course, which is supported by both the scant documentary evidence and the existence in

---

[56] Ōta, *The Chronicle of Lord Nobunaga*, 192–194; Ōta, *Shinchō kōki*, 154–156; Suitō, "Setchōki no Asakura Yoshikage," 88.

[57] Ōta, *The Chronicle of Lord Nobunaga*, 195–196; Ōta, *Shinchō kōki*, 156–157. See also the account of the battle and rout in Inoue, "Asakura shimatsuki," 387.

[58] Inoue, "Asakura shimatsuki," 398.   [59] Inoue, "Asakura shimatsuki," 393.

later years of refugee communities in nearby urban centers. *The Chronicle* provides two melancholy accounts of women, in particular, fleeing the destruction of the city. The first account follows a literary trope of noblewomen forced to escape their homes in the wake of the defeat of their ruler; the victimization of high-ranking women in these narratives functions as a critique of the power and authority of the male head of the family or in this case the warlord Asakura Yoshikage himself. The author of the war tale is mostly interested in the implication that the patriarch has failed in his Confucian duties, demonstrating a lack of virtue and a kind of withdrawal of the mandate of heaven: "That ladies of exalted rank, their litters and carriages but a memory, should have had to flee barefooted and head over heels, struggling desperately not to lag behind in following Yoshikage's traces! The eyes could not bear to witness such a sight; mere words could never express it."[60] The suffering of these wealthy women is a synecdoche for the suffering of the province of Echizen, with the blame falling at the feet of the Asakura. Although this representation of people fleeing is perhaps disingenuous in its attempt to use the romanticized figure of the noblewoman fallen low to generate sentiment, it is a reminder of how difficult escape from the burning city must have been. In addition to the rush to escape the fires, Nobunaga sent out his forces with explicit instructions to eliminate stragglers and refugees. "Every day a hundred, two hundred captured confederates were brought, bound with ropes .... Nobunaga gave his pages orders to kill every single one, a sight too horrible to see."[61]

The second account, by contrast, is unusual in its attention to an oft-overlooked characteristic of the experience of war in sixteenth-century Japan: the weaponization of sexual violence. According to *The Chronicle*, a group of soldiers caught up with a woman fleeing the devastation of the city, a high-ranking woman – perhaps a member of the Asakura family – who was desperately seeking to escape on her own. They "held her prisoner some three or five days" before she was able to quietly escape and commit suicide by throwing herself into a well. The assailants are referred to as "ruffians" (*yajin*) and "immature bastards" (*itaranu yatsubara*),[62] in contrast to her status as a "court lady" (*nyōbō*) and a "unique person" (*yuiitsujin*). We might read this anecdote as yet another trope of the high-ranking women suffering because of the poor leadership of the ruler. Certainly, *The Chronicle* as a whole exhibits what Hitomi Tonomura has called masculinist constructions that demonstrate little

---

[60] Ōta, *The Chronicle of Lord Nobunaga*, 196; Ōta, *Shinchō kōki*, 158.
[61] Ōta, *The Chronicle of Lord Nobunaga*, 197; Ōta, *Shinchō kōki*, 159.
[62] Elisonis and Lamers translate these terms as "boors" and "rogues," respectively.

attention to or interest in the experience of women or even the idea that women had a point of view.[63] Yet the unusual consideration in the narrative of these men's imprisonment of the woman against her will, however, and the trauma expressed by her brave but tragic death suggest that she was not simply captured but rather raped over a series of many days. And unlike many of the tales of the Heian and early medieval period, in which "the violation of the female body" is treated "simply as a consequence of male passion," here the act of subjugating and violating this woman from Ichijōdani is narrated as a crime.[64] Yet the literary intent of the account is still clear. Before drowning herself, the woman somehow managed to find an inkstone and to write a death poem on a paper handkerchief:

> Were I to remain,
> My existence would always
> Be clouded. Let me
> Be gone, vanish like the moon
> At the edge of the mountain.

How should we read this poem? Is this a sincere expression of trauma by a survivor of imprisonment and rape? Or is the war chronicle reducing the experience of the woman to a kind of embodiment of the sentiment of grief for the fallen Asakura and the devastated city of Ichijōdani? Is the tale's account of the woman's suicide an accurate and faithful narration of the response of a victim of sexual violence? These are difficult questions to answer.[65] Regardless of the intent of the narrative, the situation it describes unquestionably occurred in the wars of this era, seen in a range of sources. Women's bodies were treated as a kind of currency within warrior society, with women exchanged as hostages, taken as prisoners and even as a kind of booty after a battlefield victory, and exchanged alongside ceramics, swords, and horses as trophies. And as we can see in various war tales and battlefield screens from the period, male soldiers participated in the dangers of war in part because of the lure of significant rewards: treasures stolen from storehouses, clothes confiscated from dead bodies, and women's lives either violated or snuffed out completely in the name of profit and male samurai empowerment.

---

[63] Hitomi Tonomura, "Black Hair and Red Trousers: Gendering the Flesh in Medieval Japan," *The American Historical Review* 99.1 (February 1994): 151.

[64] Tonomura, "Black Hair," 153.

[65] Tonomura wrestles with the challenge of imagining the "subjective experience of rape" in premodern Japan in her essay "Sexual Violence against Women: Legal and Extralegal Treatment in Premodern Warrior Societies," in *Women and Class in Japanese History*, ed. Hitomi Tonomura, Anne Walthall, and Wakita Haruko (University of Michigan, 1999), 146–147.

Ichijōdani was destroyed. Asakura Yoshikage still lived, having fled to the township of Ono with the hope of finding support from the priests of Heisenji. However, according to *The Chronicle*, the Buddhist leadership of the temple "pledged loyalty to Nobunaga," making Yoshikage's last gambit as unsuccessful as his stand against the Oda army.[66] His cousin Asakura Kageakira invited him to take refuge at a temple in Ono known as Kenshōji, but betrayed him and sent soldiers to take his life. Yoshikage had been comprehensively defeated, and now faced treachery by a member of his own family. He committed ritual suicide on 8/20 with the assistance of two vassals, who then also took their own lives.[67] The traitor Kageakira captured the family members who had accompanied Yoshikage, took hold of Yoshikage's head, and traveled to Fuchū to offer his gratitude to Nobunaga for invading Echizen. Yoshikage's family – including his wife and remaining son – were killed, and Kageakira was rewarded for his actions, although *The Chronicle* claims he "had done something unheard-of in previous generations."[68] The main line of the Asakura, and their city of Ichijōdani, were no more. Because Yoshikage had refused to join Nobunaga's drive to pacify the realm in his own name, and perhaps because of some tactical errors along the way, the Asakura – like dozens of similar warlords, tens of thousands of soldiers, and countless noncombatants and their communities – were systematically eliminated.

To mark the start of the New Year after this victory, Nobunaga held a huge, public banquet in Gifu, followed by a private party with his Horse Guards, the elite soldiers who were his closest aids and companions. To demonstrate his complete dominance over his enemies, Nobunaga had arranged for the lacquered and gilt skulls of Asakura Yoshikage and his former allies Azai Hisamasa and Azai Nagamasa to be passed around the celebration, grotesquely transformed into sake vessels. It was not enough to raze Ichijōdani to ashes and to topple the castle of the Azai and kill all of their soldiers. A greater degree of humiliation was apparently required to satiate Nobunaga's desire for power.[69]

The Aftermath

Nobunaga's work was of course far from finished. He appointed an Asakura vassal, Maeba Nagatoshi, who had defected to the Oda side,

---

[66] Ōta, *The Chronicle of Lord Nobunaga*, 197; Ōta, *Shinchō kōki*, 159.
[67] Inoue, "Asakura shimatsuki," 395–396.
[68] Ōta, *The Chronicle of Lord Nobunaga*, 198; Ōta, *Shinchō kōki*, 160.
[69] Ōta, *The Chronicle of Lord Nobunaga*, 204; Ōta, *Shinchō kōki*, 165.

as the new administrator of Echizen province. Nagatoshi's tenure was short-lived, as the province became enveloped in a Single-Mind league religious uprising, successfully pushing Nobunaga's troops out of Echizen for several years. Many who had allied themselves with Nobunaga were killed, including the traitorous Asakura Kageakira. Yet this conflict, too, ended with the scale of bloodshed that was increasingly becoming Nobunaga's signature form of problem-solving. In 1575, Nobunaga launched his second full-scale invasion of Echizen, this time to attack the religious league that had taken over the province and fortified a string of castles and defensive positions. His armies spared no prisoners, and reportedly killed between 30,000 and 40,000 men and women during the eighth month alone.[70] As Lamers reports in his study of Nobunaga, the warlord proudly wrote to his representative in Kyoto: "The town of Fuchū is littered with corpses, and there is not an empty space left; I would like to show it to you. Today I will search the mountains and the valleys and kill [everybody]."[71] Here is embodied the core political policy of Nobunaga – *tenka fubu*, or "rule the realm by force."

The destruction of Ichijōdani, with its elimination of a century of urban growth and the untimely death of thousands of city residents, unfortunately is obscured by this larger narrative of violence in the name of "unification," a teleological tale that inevitably leads us to the ostensibly positive outcome of a modern and monolithic Japan. Nobunaga's distinctive brand of "take no prisoners" violence seems like a transitional phase before Toyotomi Hideyoshi's more measured policies of castle-smashing and sword-hunting, and both are preludes to Tokugawa policies of political control through social containment and compulsory pageantry. And, of course, it is also undeniable that Ichijōdani was hardly alone as a community destroyed in the late sixteenth century. Countless late medieval castle towns were eliminated in this period of widespread warfare, and even mercantile and port cities were destroyed as side effects of the clash of warlord armies. Hakata, for example, reportedly lost 7,000 out of 10,000 homes in the early 1570s as a result of military conflict in the region.[72] In the broader flow of Japanese history as understood in conventional historiography, the late medieval period is simply and unquestionably marked by violence, a kind of ritual offering before the glory of unification and resulting national togetherness under the Tokugawa settlement of 1603 (and 1615).

---

[70] Ōta, *The Chronicle of Lord Nobunaga*, 237; Ōta, *Shinchō kōki*, 195–196.
[71] Lamers, *Japonius Tyrannus*, 115–116.   [72] Toyama, *Ōtomo Sōrin*, 212.

Yet this paradigm is dissatisfying in light of the rich history of urban life in Ichijōdani explored in the preceding chapters. The lives of the Asakura, their family members and vassals, and the merchants, artisans, and assorted city dwellers who surrounded them cannot be reduced to some sort of meaningless transition between stable warrior governments. The city of Ichijōdani thrived in this age of warfare, even when faced by the threat of uprisings, invasions, and other forms of military conflict. Although the city was born of military necessity, flourishing beneath a mountaintop castle in an isolated and defensible valley that was surely chosen with warfare in mind, its dyers and bead-makers, monks and doctors, and even its samurai families lived meaningful lives and died and were mourned and memorialized in the city for multiple generations. How does the rich archaeological record of their lives, legible to us only as ruins, relate to the idea of "Sengoku," the Age of Warring States or provinces, when central authority failed and regional conflict reigned supreme? Did life flourish in Ichijōdani despite the political instability of late medieval Japan, or because of it? In addition to these questions, we need to ask what the legacy of this unrestrained violence is for Japanese politics and society in the early modern and modern periods. I provide some answers in the Epilogue that follows, but one conclusion is absolutely clear: Hideyoshi and Ieyasu unquestionably inherited the habit of tyrannical militarism that Nobunaga pioneered on an early modern scale.

Epilogue
The Excavated Nation on Display

> Castles continue to serve as tools for crafting identities, often in contested processes. One of the most fraught issues remains the historical relationship of castles to the military, which was largely erased and ignored in the second half of the twentieth century. Very few castle sites deal with their military history, although many artifacts attest to this past.   —Oleg Benesch and Ran Zwigenberg, *Japan's Castles: Citadels of Modernity in War and Peace*

In 2017, on one of my regular visits to Ichijōdani, I picked up a pamphlet of upcoming events associated with the museum and research center that is now the primary custodian of the site, the Ichijōdani Asakura Family Site History Museum. Ichijōdani is considered an important prefectural tourist destination, and is well advertised at travel agencies and in the tourist information booths in the Fukui train station. Sitting on the bus headed to what is now a rural site tucked into the hills on the edge of the prefectural capital, I was struck by the rich variety of historical activities available to visitors, and the layers of meaning inscribed in the labeling and framing of the site.

The special exhibition at the History Museum at the time, titled "Narrating Important Cultural Properties: Life in Warrior Residences and Merchants' Houses" (these translations are my own), appeared first in the pamphlet, an indication that the primary draw of Ichijōdani is the rich collection of excavated and collected historical materials housed and studied in the museum. This exhibition lasted two months, and three other exhibitions were advertised in the pamphlet, showcasing the scholarly range of the museum: "The Asakura Vassal Band," organized around a historic document; "Wooden Objects and Daily Life in the Sengoku Period," highlighting the unusual fact that even wooden objects survived and were excavated by archaeologists; and "Excavating and Researching Ichijōdani: The Work of a Curator." Indeed, the History Museum and its associated archaeological research center is widely seen as one of the most important and productive late medieval research sites in Japan, and a number of prominent historians and archaeologists have worked there over the decades, including Satō Kei, Ono Masatoshi, and Mizuno Kazuo.

This exhibition announcement was followed in the pamphlet by "May 21: Study Trip to the Site," accompanied by a picture of the excavated ruins of the Asakura palace. The seasonality and chance to encounter rural nature was prominently highlighted: "Welcome the beautiful season of fresh green leaves." Visitors to Ichijōdani thus could look forward to the familiar pleasures of a history museum but additionally the excitement of a site visit, particularly the opportunity to walk across the entire valley and experience a huge variety of ruins and remains. Regular buses run up and down the valley for those unwilling or unable to trek back and forth across many kilometers, but in my visits to the valley, I have always noted how many domestic and foreign tourists are committed to walking the long distances and even taking the serious hikes up the mountain required to see all the major sites, despite the difficulty of some of the paths and trails.

Another Sunday event, this time a "seminar," foregrounded an equally powerful draw for tourists: "Medieval Townhouses," in which the dwellings of "medieval city residents" would be explained using "archaeological remains." Yet the picture that accompanied this item was not of an archaeological site, but what appeared to be a new construction in the style of a medieval dwelling. In fact, one of the primary attractions in Ichijōdani is the existence of a major complex of newly constructed medieval urban townhouses, which serves as the stage for a startling range of performances and pseudo-educational experiences. This "Reconstructed Town," as it is known in the park's literature, extends for approximately 200 meters alongside the river and prefectural highway in central Ichijōdani (Figure E.1).

The structures were built using traditional methods of carpentry and stone masonry, and include a cluster of samurai residences, numerous wooden gates, a group of townspeople's houses, and appropriate (if underdecorated) interiors. Constructed wells and toilets are also present in both the samurai's and townspeople's residences, and the small differences in size and scale provide a useful visual guide to the distinctions in status and power of the residents of the town. The goal of the construction is of course public education. As one Ichijōdani pamphlet produced by the History Museum notes, the objectives are

to preserve the numerous and excellent archaeological artifacts in the form of an historical park. One step in achieving this is to display historical remains in a manner that is easy for the general public to understand by providing a three-dimensional recreation of the town, just as it was unearthed in the archaeological survey. In this way, this project aims to offer visitors an opportunity to re-live an

Figure E.1 Ichijōdani reconstructed town.
Photograph by the author.

historical experience, and to create a deeper appreciation of the historical remains.

In addition to the life-size, full-scale construction, a 50:1 scale model of the neighborhood is also on display in the visitor's entrance building.

Perhaps, as Stephen Greenberg has noted, "Reconstruction provides a simulacrum of a past: it may not be the actual past, but it triggers our imagination."[1] Yet nearby, you will also find pictures of the Reiwa Emperor visiting Ichijōdani in 2005 (when he was Crown Prince) and an amusing picture of the Japanese superhero Ultraman walking through town during the filming of a television commercial in 2011. The tension between the serious archaeological research that continues to occur in Ichijōdani and the tourist-focused pageantry of the construction as a kind of medieval theme park is one of the defining characteristics of this site.

Another recurring series described in the pamphlet is an event known as "Kids Museum," with a variety of educational activities aimed at

[1] Stephen Greenberg, "Place, Time and Memory," in *Museum Making: Narratives, Architectures, Exhibitions*, ed. Suzanne Macleod et al. (Routledge, 2012), 102.

younger visitors. The first, "Sengoku Calligraphy Cram School," is described as follows: "Let's try writing the favorite words of Sengoku warlords using brush and ink on traditional Echizen paper!" The use of the phrase "cram school" (*juku*) is meant to be humorous, deliberately contrasting a festive trip to a countryside historic site with the grueling after-school and weekend studying that is all too common in Japan today; if you are visiting Ichijōdani, by definition you are not in cram school, though this approach to labeling educational activities seems more likely to appeal to parents than to children. Another similar offering is titled "Make 'drunken elephant' pieces for a game of *shogi* [chess]," and is described as follows: "'Drunken elephant' *shogi* pieces were excavated from the Asakura residence site. Let's make 'drunken elephant' pieces and actually play *shogi*!" The goals of these activities are thus mixed and not always completely coherent; the serious scholarly work of the archaeologists and historians is displayed in the museum's exhibitions, most prominently, while the general attractiveness of the site and the opportunity to "connect" with the famous figures of the Sengoku era are used to draw visitors to the model Ichijōdani neighborhood and the educational facilities at the museum. The larger strategy is surely to attract visitors of all ages with a variety of offerings aimed at their broad interests.

Ichijōdani is clearly a key historic and tourist site in the contemporary prefecture of Fukui. It also plays a major role in national narratives of Japan's medieval period, and is frequently put on display in exhibitions at museums such as Rekihaku, the National Museum of Japanese History, located in Sakura, Chiba Prefecture, outside Tokyo. The museum's galleries of course have undergone numerous reinstallations over the years, but after its opening in 1983, it has consistently had a least one major gallery devoted to the medieval period, and from the late 1990s up until the 2010s (and perhaps beyond?), Ichijōdani has enjoyed pride of place as one of the few locations to be singled out as a nationally significant site. In 2013, for example, the medieval gallery was divided into six major sections: (1) daily life and culture of the common people, (2) Japan during the Age of Exploration, (3) print culture, (4) imperial culture (of the Heian period), (5) the eastern provinces and the western provinces (the Kamakura period), and (6) warlords and uprisings. This final section was built around a display of materials from Ichijōdani and a scale model of the town, referred to as "the excavated archaeological site of the Echizen Asakura family." The museum thus posits Ichijōdani as a representative example of the rule of warlords over a thriving urban center. However, the complete destruction of the city and the elimination of the Asakura as rulers of Echizen is elided. It is as though the meaning of this picture of thriving urban life is not changed in any way by its elimination, perhaps because it occurred within the context of "unification," which is presumed to be a necessary and natural preface to the formation of the modern nation. The implications of this erasure are disturbing, and I will consider them further below.

Also in 2013, Rekihaku hosted a special exhibition titled "Techniques That Made the Age: The Medieval Revolution in Production" (*Jidai o tsukutta waza: chūsei no seisan kakumei*), with an accompanying catalogue. Here, too, Ichijōdani was prominently featured as one of the key sites for understanding the range of medieval tools and production technologies in Japan. First in a section in the catalogue on utensils and tools associated with the application of makeup (pp. 26–27), and then again in a chapter devoted to different technologies for producing the objects of daily life (pp. 38–39), the Ichijōdani site and its rich range of excavated objects are featured prominently. Similarly, in an overview of medieval ceramics, the production and distribution of Echizen wares are highlighted (pp. 60–65) as one of the better understood traditions that was both part of a long regional pottery lineage and also national in scope, with many of the excavated shards coming from Ichijōdani. A chapter on craftspeople used objects excavated from Ichijōdani to explain the domestic tools and daily life of the medieval period, exhibiting kitchen utensils, tableware, stone braziers, and beads before introducing the Akabuchi neighborhood in the city and its range of excavated ateliers and workers' residences (pp. 106–112). In a subsequent section examining luxury goods commissioned by powerful patrons such as warlords, Ichijōdani is cited as a source of technically sophisticated metal goods with fine detail (pp. 154–156). In a chapter on foreign technologies, a set of locks and keys excavated in Ichijōdani is displayed and discussed, with the suggestion that they may have been used to lock Chinese cabinets or other forms of imported furniture (p. 176). Ichijōdani is thus deployed in this exhibition and catalogue as a kind of synecdoche for medieval Japan itself. Yet again, however, the complete destruction of the city is erased both as a defining feature of its place in history and as a reason for the survival, in a sense, of so many materials in the archaeological site.

In fact, the other city that appears prominently in the "Techniques That Made the Age" exhibition and catalog is Kusado Sengen, one of the first medieval sites to be excavated in the postwar era, beginning in the 1960s. This market town thrived in present-day Fukuyama city in Hiroshima prefecture, on the Seto Inland Sea near the mouth of the Ashida River. It was gradually abandoned by the late sixteenth century, and floods in the seventeenth century actually helped to preserve in mud a range of pottery, accessories, cooking utensils, farming and fishing tools, and craft tools used to produce lacquer and metalwork. Over eight excavations have produced a wealth of objects and indications of their distribution, demonstrating a thriving commercial center that was primarily active in local and regional trade, and which was led by wealthy merchants, but which is largely unknown in the documentary records. Furthermore, researchers have also located what appears to be a larger, better fortified residence of a proprietor of some sort, though the identity of the family that occupied it – a particularly wealthy merchant household? a warrior lineage? – is unknown. Kusado Sengen and Ichijōdani are often paired as model examples of urban settlements from medieval Japan, but the profound difference in how these communities came to an end – one seemingly through an organic process of out-migration and environmental change, the other through a profoundly violent and sudden act of war – is effaced, implying that both endings are somehow "natural."[2]

In a symposium held in 2011, the comparison between Ichijōdani and Kusado Sengen was made directly by one of the most highly regarded scholars of Ichijōdani, the archaeologist Ono Masatoshi. The occasion was the fortieth anniversary of the designation of the Ichijō valley as a special archaeological site and the thirtieth anniversary of the opening of the History Museum. In his keynote speech, later published in the symposium proceedings, Ono argued that the excavation and analysis of these two sites represented the genesis of an entirely new field, medieval archaeology, after most of the attention of archaeologists in Japan to that point had been focused on prehistoric and early Japan. By "medieval archaeology," Ono explained, he meant not simply the excavation of medieval sites, but a new vision of the period, "making archaeological findings the subject of our consideration about the medieval."[3] The thrust of this new vision was not to emphasize specific excavations of "castles or graves or kilns" but to focus on the regular places of daily life: neighborhoods (chō), small towns (mura), and cities (toshi). Careful consideration of excavated materials such as ceramics in the context of excavated structures such as the palace of a warlord, warrior residences,

---

[2] Ichijōdani and Kusado Sengen both appear as free-standing volumes in the series *Yomigaeru chūsei*, which can be translated as "Restoring the Medieval." For more recent scholarship on Kusado Sengen, see Shōji, *Kusado Sengen* and Suzuki Yasuyuki, *Chūsei Setonai no minatomachi: Kusado Sengen chō iseki* (Shinsensha, 2007).

[3] Ono Masatoshi, "Ichijōdani wa nani o nokoshita no ka? Chūsei daikibo iseki no kinō/kyō/ashita," in Fukui Kenritsu Ichijōdani Asakura Shi Iseki Shiryōkan, *Sengoku jōkamachi Ichijōdani no miryoku o saikō suru* (Fukui Kenritsu Ichijōdani Asakura Shi Iseki Shiryōkan, 2011), 1.

and commoner townhouses allows analysis of the space of the city in terms of social class and political power, fundamental themes in the study of medieval Japan. Kusado Sengen and Ichijōdani were in effect perfect sites to launch this new phase in the study of medieval Japan because of the size and scope of the sites themselves, which allowed holistic analysis of topics such as urban life and urban space. Yet Ono ignores the context that makes the two sites profoundly different: Ichijōdani's story, as I have attempted to show in this book, is at the very center of the narrative of the end of the medieval period and the beginning of the "unification" of Japan and the establishment of the Tokugawa settlement. Kusado Sengen, on the other hand, is largely unknown in extant documentary evidence, and stands out as a kind of surprise discovery, a reminder of how much detail from the past is still buried, effectively hidden from our view entirely.

Like Ichijōdani, Kusado Sengen is prominently represented to tourists, schoolchildren, and other visitors in a museum format. Unlike Ichijōdani, however, where part of the attraction is the combination of both natural beauty and historical authenticity in the choice of location for the townhouse construction, Kusado Sengen's original location – now a small island in the middle of a river – is not an appropriate site for an exhibition.

Instead, in the Hiroshima Prefectural Museum of History in Fukuyama City, you will find a life-size construction (Figure E.2) of five structures, a replica stream, and various features of a market based on excavation data, providing a kind of platform for the display of unearthed archaeological materials and creative visualization of daily life in this medieval port town.

When you enter the display room, which is indoors but constructed to create the appearance of an outdoor scene, you immediately cross onto a bridge that extends across artificial water, leading to a shore marked by patches of reeds and grasses. On the right of the path through the display is a small boat, its stern still "floating," filled with bales of grain and two bamboo poles for pushing the vessel through shallow water. Beyond the boat is an orderly pile of these same grain bales, as well as a rough shelter for a stockpile of large ceramic jars wrapped in straw rope. On the opposite side of the path are two large ceramic vats next to a single-story, thatched-roof structure displaying unearthed archaeological materials, mostly ceramics, and modern reconstructions of wooden containers and baskets on stands and platforms. The back and side walls of this structure are covered by hanging, hand-woven bamboo blinds (*sudare*), and two bamboo poles prop up another shade at the front of the building, creating an open and inviting atmosphere, a kind of

Figure E.2 Kusado Sengen gallery, Hiroshima Prefectural Museum of History.
Public domain photograph, by carpkazu, 2007.

"open-for-business" signal. Indeed, the low containers, mostly baskets, are filled with replicas of dried and fresh fish, shellfish, fowl, and salt, to show how a storefront might have been arranged. The second structure similarly has bamboo blinds rather than walls, and on the ground is a collection of baskets holding replicas of various vegetables as well as several larger wooden containers holding dried grains and cereals. Farther down the path is a well, followed by two additional structures that display excavated and newly made replica objects from the lives of workers. The studio space of a lacquerer is on display, as well as the workshop of a wooden clog maker and the home and atelier of a blacksmith. At the far end of the exhibition, a religious hall containing a statue of the bodhisattva Jizō stands to represent the religious life of the town, as well as a small replica graveyard with a handful of stone stupas.

The experience of entering the main Kusado Sengen exhibition room in the Hiroshima Prefectural Museum of History can be disconcerting. The ceiling is arched and painted flat white, and lights are projected upward to create the illusion, which is not particularly successful, that you are outdoors and that the sky is perhaps overcast, bright but gray. Great care was taken in the production of the buildings in an authentic fashion, using wood, thatch, and stone, yet this contrasts with the cement floors off the main path and the occasional intrusion of modern museum features such as the barriers and ropes erected around the well. And of course unlike the townhouses in Ichijōdani, which are built over the fully excavated neighborhood that they represent, the exhibition of the Kusado Sengen replica is in a large modern museum, part of a park built on the former castle grounds of Fukuyama Castle, headquarters of the Bingo-Fukuyama domain during the Tokugawa period. The Fukuyama Art Museum and Fukuyama Castle Museum are located nearby, as is Fukuyama Station, a stop on the San'yo line of the bullet train. The original archaeological site of Kusado Sengen is located two kilometers away, in the Ashida River, meaning that the display of Kusado Sengen's materials is divorced from the natural environment that shaped its history (as well as its destruction).[4] What is concerning about the approach to presenting the remarkable archaeological materials from Kusado Sengen is the sense of stasis, as though the work of analyzing and interpreting the Kusado Sengen site and its implications in the history of medieval Japan is somehow a completed project. We are presented with what scholars of archaeological replicas refer to as "a far more static past, or tableau, that often lacks the educational excitement of ever-present discovery and, more worryingly, [is] more easily open to the abuse of deliberate or accidental misinterpretation."[5]

The use of replicas and new constructions (or reconstructions, or *fukugen*, as they are usually called in Japanese) at important historic and archaeological sites is quite common in Japan. In 1966, the precursor to today's Agency for Cultural Affairs, the Committee for the Protection of Cultural Properties, issued the *Handbook for Archaeological Investigation* (*Maizō Bunkazai hakkutsu chōsa no tebiki*), which includes specific provisions to guide archaeologists in the whole trajectory of an archaeological excavation, "including explanation of the Law, notification procedures, planning excavations, excavation techniques for the major kinds of archaeological features, survey and recording procedures, artifact processing and reconstruction methods,

---

[4] I visited the Hiroshima Prefectural Museum of History, as well as the original excavation site of Kusado Sengen in Fukuyama City, in 2012, and took extensive photographs. My descriptions here are based on that field work, as well as materials provided by the museum: www.pref.hiroshima.lg.jp/site/rekishih/kusado-1.html

[5] Peter G. Stone and Philippe G. Planel, "Introduction," in their edited volume *Experimental Archaeology, Education and the Public* (Routledge, 1999), 7.

report writing and exhibition."[6] The act of reconstruction – which could range from the simple piecing together of ceramic shards with plaster filling to reassemble the shape of a vessel to the much more elaborate new architectural (re)constructions seen at many sites – is thus posited as one of the core practices of the discipline of archaeology as outlined by a government agency, and it is thus not surprising to see sites like Kusado Sengen and Ichijōdani display reproduced townhouses and markets as one of their primary means of communicating with the public. Yet the context in which replicas and reproductions are presented transforms their educational message and phenomenological effect. Kusado Sengen's mock market town is locked in a stuffy indoor room, conveying the unfortunate message that the small universe of the town is perfectly understood and forever captured by its own museumification.[7] Ichijōdani's model warrior residences and commoner townhouses allow visitors to experience something of the ontology of the medieval place of the city, drawing on the forests and surrounding hills as well as the size and dimensions of the structures to allow a less alienating feeling of being in the historic site than in Kusado Sengen. Likewise, the ongoing excavations around the valley serve as an important reminder that the research of understanding the site is ongoing, and not locked up behind glass. However, the disturbing lack of attention to the actual mechanism and politics of the city's destruction banishes Ichijōdani to a kind of historical purgatory in which the violence of the late sixteenth century never happened and the "thriving Sengoku castle town" fantasy enjoys a fictitious immortality.

It may be that public exhibitions have omitted the destruction of Ichijōdani and Kusado Sengen from displays of their remarkable material culture because of the methodological orientation of the discipline of archaeology, as Brian Ayers has argued. "Much of archaeological

[6] Gina Barnes, "The Origins of Bureaucratic Archaeology in Japan," *Journal of the Hong Kong Archaeological Society* 12 (1986–1988): 190.
[7] See Peter G. Stone and Phillipe G. Planet, "Introduction," in *The Constructed Past: Experimental Archaeology, Education and the Public* (Routledge, 1999), 6: "There is 'something for everyone' on the most successful construction sites, and those that have survived the longest and maintained their integrity the most seem to have achieved a balance between scientific, educational and presentational aims. The archaeologists feel that they are performing a valuable service by submitting their discipline to the scrutiny of the general public; teachers (and hence their students) have direct access to the most recent research without the customary fifteen- to twenty-year gap between specialist report and (frequently inaccurate) school textbook; the public has a glimpse of a different world which, thanks to ongoing research, has at least the possibility of change, and thus of avoiding becoming a static theme park image. By presenting an active, 'hands-on' approach, construction sites engage their visitors more easily than traditional museum displays."

research, because it is concerned with material culture, is heavily linked to human construction, whether it be in the form of houses, fortifications, drains, shipping or pottery vessels." Ayers makes the point that to effectively engage with the public, archaeologists need to consider who their audiences are and then to highlight not just "outputs" (meaning material culture) but also "outcomes," such as social and economic changes that are legible through archaeological excavations. Similarly, Ayers notes that archaeologists often lack agency in terms of the "management of the historic environment." In publicly funded organizations such as the Ichijōdani Asakura Family Site History Museum and the Hiroshima Prefectural Museum of History, national and prefectural politics, trends in heritage management, and the concerns of a range of competing professionals including museum curators, historians, and exhibition designers surely influence the display of these sites and their excavated materials as much as or probably more than the hermeneutic objectives of the archaeologists who managed the excavations.[8]

Still, surely what matters most about both of these sites is the relationship between the liveliness of their communities at their zenith and the destruction of those same communities for particular reasons and in a particular historical period. These and other examples of medieval urban life represent what Ono calls a "microcosm" (*shō'uchū*) of the medieval, or to more literally and pedantically translate the Japanese word, a "small universe." I would propose that the medieval provincial city represents a small universe that is distinct and worth our consideration. These cities help us to better understand the diversity of mentalities and experiences of premodern people and also to apprehend nation-building and elite power agglomeration as, in a sense, an institutionalized erasure of these small worlds in the name, literally, of one ruling family. From the perspective of the small universes that were destroyed along the way, "unification" is not a form of progress toward stability but a weaponization of unconstrained violence. The small universe of the medieval provincial city is vitally necessary in the narrative of Japanese history, as it reveals a past that is contested yet not always moving toward the Pax Tokugawa, not always subservient to the imperial court and the vision of Kyoto as the center of Japan.

Yet the erasure of the everydayness of medieval urban life is itself constitutive of the political processes of the early modern Tokugawa

---

[8] B. Ayers, "'Have you found anything?' Archaeology and Public Engagement in the Urban Historic Environment," in *Lübecker Kolloquium zur Stadt Archäologie im Hanseraum XI: Archäologie im Hier und Jetzt*, ed. D. Rieger and M. Schneider (Lübeck, 2021).

settlement and the modernization that followed it.[9] In accepting the teleological periodization of Japanese history and its subsumption of diverse medieval universes of experience into a metanarrative of unification, we tacitly accept the modern nation-state's erasure of the infinite possibilities of the past. We lose sight of ways of being and knowing that defy the definition of Japaneseness naturalized in Meiji and its afterlives. The erasure of places like Ichijōdani may seem like a kind of necessary precondition for the modern. But we must push back against this erasure by excavating the distinctive medieval ontology of the interconnected medieval urban spaces, as well as the stories of their destruction. As Arturo Escobar has noted, "our ontological stances about what the world is, what we are, and how we come to know the world define our being, our doing, and our knowing – our historicity."[10]

Learning to respect what Jane Bennett calls the vital materialism of objects such as those excavated in Ichijōdani, as well as the environment that shaped the city and the ontology of the people who lost their lives there, is part of a larger moral and philosophical step. We must overcome the hubris of the binaristic separation of animate from inanimate, culture from nature, and human from nonhuman in order to confront the challenges of anthropocentric destruction. Otherwise, we run the risk of going the way of the Asakura, with Nobunaga's predatory violence replaced now by the insatiable consumptive needs of modern human societies. The interlinked urban spaces of sixteenth-century Japan, each of them a small universe of material life, together form a medieval multiverse that has gone ignored for too long.

---

[9] This process is perhaps a precursor to the flattening of daily life through the banality of everyday experience, as explored in the writings of Walter Benjamin, Gerorg Simmel, and Georg Lukacs, the totalization of being under the modern capitalist system.

[10] Arturo Escobar, "Notes on the Ontology of Design" (unpublished manuscript), 23.

Bibliography

Abe Akinori. "Echizen ni okeru 15 seiki kōhan – 16 seiki chūyō no doki/tōjiki." In *Hokuriku ni miru kinsei seiritsuki no doki/tōjiki no yōsō: jōkamachi to sono shūhen iseki no hajiki zara (kawarake) o chūshin ni*. Ishikawa Ken Maizō Bunkazai Sentaa, 2019.

Abe Yōsuke. *Sengoku daimyō ronshū, vol. 9: Uesugi shi no kenkyū*, ed. Nagahara Keiji. Yoshikawa Kōbunkan, 1984.

Adolphson, Mikael S., and Anne Commons, eds. *Lovable Losers: The Heike in Action and Memory*. University of Hawai'i Press, 2015.

Amino Yoshihiko. *Amino Yoshihiko chōsakushū, vol. 13: Chūsei toshi ro*. Iwanami Shoten, 2007.

Amino Yoshihiko chōsakushū. 19 volumes. Iwanami Shoten, 2007–2009.

Nihon chūsei toshi no sekai. Chikuma Shobō, 1996.

Amino Yoshihiko and Ishii Susumu. *Chūsei toshi to shōnin shokunin*. Meicho Shuppan, 1991.

Arntzen, Sonja. *Ikkyū and the Crazy Cloud Anthology: A Zen Poet of Medieval Japan*. University of Tokyo Press, 1986.

Asakura Hisashi. "Gesshū Jukei shōron–kaken no gakufū." *Chūsei bungaku kenkyū* 17 (1991): 34–52.

Auslander, Leora, Amy Bentley, Leor Halevi, H. Otto Sibum, and Christopher Witmore. "AHR Conversation: Historians and the Study of Material Culture." *American Historical Review* 114.5 (2009): 1355–1404.

Ayers, B. "'Have you found anything?' Archaeology and Public Engagement in the Urban Historic Environment." In *Lübecker Kolloquium zur Stadt Archäologie im Hanseraum XI: Archäologie im Hier und Jetzt*, ed. D. Rieger and M. Schneider. Lübeck, 2021.

Barnes, Gina. "The Origins of Bureaucratic Archaeology in Japan." *Journal of the Hong Kong Archaeological Society* 12 (1986–1988): 183–196.

Batten, Bruce. *Gateway to Japan: Hakata in War and Peace, 500–1300*. University of Hawai'i Press, 2006.

Bell, Catherine. *Ritual Theory, Ritual Practice*. Oxford University Press, 1992.

Bender, John Elijah. "Wind, Forest, Fire, and Mountain: The Evolution of Environmental Management and Local Society in Central Japan, 1450–1650." PhD dissertation, University of California at Santa Barbara, 2017.

Bennett, Jane. *Vibrant Matter: A Political Ecology of Things*. Duke University Press, 2009.

Berry, Mary Elizabeth. *The Culture of Civil War in Kyoto*. University of California Press, 1994.

Birmingham Museum of Art. *Echizen: Eight Hundred Years of Japanese Stoneware*. University of Washington Press, 1994.

Birt, Michael Patrick. "Warring States: A Study of the Go-Hojo Daimyo and Domain, 1491–1590." PhD dissertation, Princeton University Press, 1983.

Butler, Lee. *Emperor and Aristocracy in Japan, 1467–1680: Resilience and Renewal*. Harvard University Asia Center, 2002.

Carson, Barbara. *The Governor's Palace: The Williamsburg Residence of Virginia's Royal Governor*. Colonial Williamsburg Foundation, 1987.

Carter, Stephen D. *The Columbia Anthology of Japanese Essays: Zuihitsu from the Tenth to the Twenty-First Century*. Columbia University Press, 2014.

Householders: The Reizei Family in Japanese History. Harvard University Asia Center, 2007.

Ching, Dora C. Y., Louise Allison Cort, and Andrew M. Watsky, eds. *Around Chigusa: Tea and the Arts of Sixteenth-Century Japan*. Princeton University Press, 2017.

Christy, Alan S. "Translator's Introduction: A Map to Amino Yoshihiko's Historical World." In Amino Yoshihiko, *Rethinking Japanese History*. University of Michigan Center for Japanese Studies, 2012.

Cleveland Museum of Art. *Handbook of the Cleveland Museum of Art*. Cleveland Museum of Art, 1966.

Collcutt, Martin. *Five Mountains: The Rinzai Zen Monastic Institution in Medieval Japan*. Harvard Asia Center Press, 1981.

"Zen and the *Gozan*." In *The Cambridge History of Japan, vol. 3: Medieval Japan*, ed. Kozo Yamamura. Cambridge University Press, 1990. 583–652.

Cooper, Michael. *João Rodrigues's Account of Sixteenth-Century Japan*. Hakluyt Society, 2001.

Cort, Louise Allison. "Disposable but Indispensable: The Earthenware Vessel as Vehicle of Meaning in Japan." In *What's the Use of Art? Asian Visual and Material Culture in Context*, ed. Jan Mrazek and Morgan Pitelka. University of Hawai'i Press, 2007. 46–76.

Cort, Louise Allison, and Andrew M. Watsky, eds. *Chigusa and the Art of Tea*. Smithsonian Institution, 2014.

Creighton, Oliver. "Overview: Castles and Elite Landscapes." In *The Oxford Handbook of Later Medieval Archaeology in Britain*, ed. Christopher Gerrard and Alejandra Gutiérrez. Oxford University Press, 2018. 355–370.

DeSilvey, Caitlin, and Tim Edensor. "Reckoning with Ruins." *Progress in Human Geography* 37.4 (2012): 465–485.

Dobbins, James C. "Editor's Introduction: Kuroda Toshio and His Scholarship." *Japanese Journal of Religious Studies* 23.3–4 (1996): 217–232.

"Portraits of Shinran." In *Living Images: Japanese Buddhist Icons in Context*, ed. Robert H. Sharf and Elizabeth Horton Sharf. Stanford University Press, 2001.

Doi Tadao, Morita Takeshi, and Chōnan Minoru, trans. *Hōyaku Nippo jisho*. Iwanami shoten, 1980.

Drott, Edward R. "Gods, Buddhas, and Organs: Buddhist Physicians and Theories of Longevity in Early Medieval Japan." *Japanese Journal of Religious Studies* 37.2 (2010): 247–273.

Eason, David. "The Culture of Disputes in Early Modern Japan, 1550–1700." PhD dissertation, University of California at Los Angeles, 2009.

Erdmann, Mark Karl. "Azuchi Castle: Architectural Innovation and Political Legitimacy in Sixteenth-Century Japan." PhD dissertation, Harvard University, 2016.

Escobar, Pablo. "Postconstructivist Political Ecologies." *The International Handbook of Environmental Sociology*, 2nd ed., ed. Michael Redclift and Graham Woodgate. Edward Elgar Publishing, 2010. 91–105.

Frank, Ronald K. "Battle for Minds: Regulating Buddhism in Sixteenth-Century Japan." *Asia Pacific: Perspectives* 5.1 (December 2004): 12–17.

Fujitani, T., Geoffrey M. White, and Lisa Yoneyama, eds. *Perilous Memories: The Asia-Pacific War(s)*. Duke University Press, 2001.

Fujiwara Takeji. "Ichijōdani Asakura shi iseki no shūkei ni tsuite." In *Sengoku jōkamachi Ichijōdani ni kan suru gaisetsu/ronshū*. Fujiwara Takeji, 2014.

Fukui Ken. *Shiryō hen: chūsei, vol. 2: Fukui kenshi*. Fukui, 1986,

Fukui Ken Kyōiku Iinkai. *Ichijōdani Asakura shi iseki: Gosho/An'yōji*. 1971.

Tokubetsu shiseki: Ichijōdani Asakura shi iseki VII. Fukui Ken Kyōiku Iinkai, 1976.

Fukui Ken Kyōiku-cho Maizō Bunkazai Chōsa Sentaa. *Tokubetsu shiseki: Ichijōdani Asakura shi ikseki hakkutsu chōsa hōkoku 13*. 2016.

Fukui Kenritsu Ichijōdani Asakura Shi Iseki Shiryōkan. *Asakura shi godai no hakkyū monjo*. Fukui Kenritsu Ichijōdani Asakura Shi Iseki Shiryōkan, 2004.

Asakura shi no kakun. Fukui Kenritsu Ichijōdani Asakura Shi Iseki Shiryōkan, 2008.

Hana saku jōkamachi Ichijōdani. Fukui Kenritsu Ichijōdani Asakura Shi Iseki Shiryōkan, 2005.

Ichijōdani no ishi. Fukui Kenritsu Ichijōdani Asakura Shi Iseki Shiryōkan, 2010.

Ichijōdani no shūkyō to shinkō. Fukui Kenritsu Asakura Shi Iseki Shiryōkan, 1999.

Sengoku jidai uchi to soto: Echizen Asakura shi to sono jidai no taigai kōryū. Fukui Kenritsu Ichijōdani Asakura Shi Iseki Shiryōkan, 2013.

Sengoku no manabiya: Asakura bunka, bunbu o kimeru. Fukui Kenritsu Ichijōdani Asakura Shi Iseki Shiryōkan, 2013.

Tokubetsu shiseki: Ichijōdani Asakura shi iseki hakkutsu chōsa hōkoku 6. Fukui Kenritsu Asakura Shi Iseki Shiryōkan, 1988.

Tokubetsu shiseki: Ichijōdani Asakura shi iseki hakkutsu chōsa hōkokusho, vols. 1–16. Fukui Kenritsu Ichijōdani Asakura Shi Iseki Shiryōkan, 1979–2017.

Waza: shutsudo ibutsu ni miru chūsei tekōgei no sekai. Fukui Kenritsu Ichijōdani Asakura Shi Iseki Shiryōkan. 2007.

Fukui Shi. "Asakura shimatsuki." Transcribed in *Shiryō hen 2: kodai, chūsei*. In *Fukui shishi*. Fukui Shi, 1983–2008. 816–978.

"Asakura Yoshikage tei onari-ki." *Shiryō hen 2: kodai, chūsei*. In *Fukui shishi*. Fukui Shi, 1983–2008. 808–814.

Futaki Ken'ichi. *Chūsei buke girei no kenkyū*. Yoshikawa Kōbunkan, 1985.

Buke girei kakushiki no kenkyū. Yoshikawa Kōbunkan, 2003.

Gay, Suzanne. "Muromachi Bakufu Rule in Kyoto: Administrative and Judicial Aspects." In *The Bakufu in Japanese History*, ed. Jeffrey P. Mass and William P. Hauser. Stanford University Press, 1985. 49–65.

The Moneylenders of Late Medieval Kyoto. University of Hawai'i Press, 2001.

Gerhart, Karen M. *The Material Culture of Death in Medieval Japan*. University of Hawai'i, 2009.

ed. *Women, Rites, and Ritual Objects in Premodern Japan*. Brill, 2018.

Gesshū Jūkei. "Gen'un bunshū." In *Zoku gunsho ruijū*. Vol. 13-1. Zoku Gunsho Ruijū Kanseikai, 1959. 287-439.

Glassie, Henry. *Folk Housing in Middle Virginia: Structural Analysis of Historic Artifacts*. University of Tennessee Press, 1975.

Pattern in the Material Folk Culture of the Eastern United States. University of Pennsylvania Press, 1969.

Goble, Andrew Edmund. *Confluences of Medicine in Medieval Japan: Buddhist Healing, Chinese Knowledge, Islamic Formulas, and Wounds of War*. University of Hawai'i Press, 2011.

"Rhythms of Medicine and Community in Late Sixteenth Century Japan: Yamashina Tokitsune (1543–1611) and His Patients." *EASTM* 29 (2008): 13–61.

Goodwin, Janet R. "Shooting the Dead to Paradise." *Japanese Journal of Religious Studies* 16.1 (1989): 64–68.

Greenberg, Stephen. "Place, Time and Memory." In *Museum Making: Narratives, Architectures, Exhibitions*, ed. Suzanne Macleod et al. Routledge, 2012. 95–104.

Gunji, Naoko. "Amidaji: Mortuary Art, Architecture, and Rites of Emperor Antoku's Temple." PhD dissertation, University of Pittsburgh, 2007.

Hall, John Whitney. "The Castle Town and Japan's Modern Urbanization." In *Studies in the Institutional History of Early Modern Japan*, ed. John Whitney Hall and Marius B. Jansen. Princeton University Press, 1968. 182–201.

"Foundations of the Modern Japanese Daimyo." *The Journal of Asian Studies* 20.3 (1961): 324–325.

Government and Local Power in Japan, 500 to 1700: A Study Based on Bizen Province. Princeton University Press, 1966.

Hanawa Hokinoichi, ed. *Gunsho ruijū*, vol. 12. Keizai Zashisha, 1905.

Hanawa Hokinokichi, ed. *Oyudono no ue no nikki, Zoku gunsho ruiju*. Suppl., vol. 8. Taiyō Shinsha, 1943.

Hanley, Susan. *Everyday Things in Premodern Japan: The Hidden Legacy of Material Culture*. University of California Press, 1997.

Harada Tomohiko. *Nihon hōken toshi kenkyū*. Tokyo Daigaku Shuppankai, 1957.

Hasebe Gakuji. "An Introduction to Song Ceramics" (trans. Maiko Behr). In *Sōjiten*. Asahi Shinbunsha, 1999. 30–35.

Henare, Amiria, Martin Holbraad, and Sari Wastell, eds. *Thinking through Things: Theorising Artefacts Ethnographically*. Routledge, 2007.

Herman, Bernard L. *Architecture and Rural Life in Central Delaware, 1700–1900*. University of Tennessee Press, 1987.

Town House: Architecture and Material Life in the Early American City, 1780–1830. University of North Carolina Press, 2005.

Hiroshi Kaneaki. *Kaneaki kyōki*. National Museum of Japanese History diary database.

Hiroshima Kenritsu Rekishi Hakubutsukan. *Umi kara chūsei o miru: chūsei no minatomachi*. Hiroshima Kenritsu Rekishi Hakubutsukan, 1996.

Hirota, Dennis. *Wind in the Pines: Classic Writings of the Way of Tea as a Buddhist Path*. Asian Humanities Press, 1995.

Horton, H. Mack. *The Journal of Sōchō*. Stanford University Press, 2002.

"Sanjonishi Sanetaka." In *Dictionary of Literary Biography, vol. 203: Medieval Japanese Writers*, ed. Steven D. Carter. Gale Group, 1999.

Song in an Age of Discord: The Journal of Sōchō and Poetic Life in Late Medieval Japan. Stanford University Press, 2001.

Idemitsu Bijutsukan. *Echizen kotō to sono saigen: Kuemongama no kiroku*. Idemitsu Bijutsukan, 1994.

Iimura Hitoshi. "Jobun: Ikō to shite no 'michi,' 'michi' kare mieru iseki." In *Chūsei no michi to hashi*, ed. Fujiwara Yoshiaki. Kōshi Shoin, 2005. 3–22.

Ikegami Hiroko. "Sengoku daimyō ryōkoku ni okeru shoryō oyobi kashindan hensei no tenkai." In *Sengoku daimyō ronshū, vol. 1: Sengoku daimyō no kenkyū*, ed. Nagahara Keiji. Yoshikawa Kōbunkan, 1983. 377–388.

Inoue Kikuo. "Medieval Japanese Ceramics: The Six Old Kilns and Their Contexts." In *Kotō no fu, chūsei no yakimono: Rokukoyō to sono shūhen*, ed. Miho Museum. Miho Museum, 2010. 456–473.

Inoue Toshio, Kuwatana Kōnen, and Fujiki Hisashi, eds. "Asakura shimatsuki, Kaetsutō jōki, Esshū gunki." In *Nihon shisō taikei, vol. 17: Rennyo Ikkō-ikki*, ed. Inoue Toshio and Kasahara Kazuo. Iwanami Shoten, 1972. 325–426.

Ishibashi Shinji. "Katsuno jōkamachi iseki ni okeru Sengoku ki jōkan no shoyōsō." In *Kōwan toshi to taiga kōeki*, ed. Ōba Kōji et al. Shinjinbutsu Ōraisha, 2004. 130–164.

Ishii, Miho. "Acting with Things: Self-Poiesis, Actuality, and Contingency in the Formation of Divine Worlds." *HAU: Journal of Ethnographic Theory* 2.2 (2012): 371–388.

Ishii Susumu. *Chūsei bushi dan*. Shōgakkan, 1974.

Kōkogaku to chūseishi kenkyū. Meicho Shuppan, 1991.

Ishii Susumu and Suitō Makoto. *Sekibutsu to sekitō*. Yamakawa Shuppansha, 2001.

Itoh Ikutaro. "Korean Ceramics of the Koryo and Choson Dynasties" (trans. Morgan Pitelka). In Itoh Ikutaro, *Korean Ceramics from the Museum of Oriental Ceramics, Osaka*. Metropolitan Museum of Art, 2000. 9–27.

Iwamoto Shōji. *Kusado Sengen*. Kibito Shuppan, 2000.

Iwata Takashi. "Ichijōdani Asakura Shi iseki no benjo ikō ni tsuite." In *Kiyō 1999*. Fukui Kenritsu Ichijōdani Asakura Shi Iseki Shiryōkan, 2000.

"Ichijōdani no shōhi to ryūtsū." In *Sengoku daimyo Asakura shi to Ichijōdani*, ed. Mizuno Kazuo and Satō Kei. Kōshi Shoin, 2002. 206–232.

"Jōkamachi Ichijōdani no seiritsu to hen'yō." In *Toshi o tsukuru*, ed. Chūsei Toshi Kenkyūkai. Shinjinbutsu Ōraisha, 1998. 49–61.

"Sengoku ki o aruita geta." In *Jitsuzō no Sengoku jōkamachi Echizen Ichijiodani*, ed. Ono Masatoshi. Heibonsha, 1990. 128–132.

Izutsu Gafu. *Genshoku Nihon fukushoku shi*. Kōrinsha Shuppan, 1989.

Johnson, Matthew. *Behind the Castle Gate: From Medieval to Renaissance*. Routledge, 2002.

Kakiuchi Kōjirō. "Seki no anka." In *Jitsuzō no Sengoku jōkamachi Echizen Ichijiodani*, ed. Ono Masatoshi. Heibonsha, 1990. 137–138.

Kamei Nobuo, ed. *Shiro to jōkamachi*. No. 402. *Nihon no Bijutsu*. Tōbundō, 1999.

Kanda Chisato. "Echizen Asakura shi no zaichi shihai no tokushitsu." In *Sengoku daimyō ronshū, vol. 4: Chūbu daimyō no kenkyū*, ed. Katsumata Shizuo. Yoshikawa Kōbunkan, 1983. 179–223.

Shūkyō de yomu Sengoku jidai. Kōdansha, 2010.

Kaner, Simon, Brian Ayers, Richard Pearson, and Oscar Wrenn, eds. *The Archaeology of Medieval Towns: Case Studies from Japan and Europe*. Archaeopress, 2020.

Kawamoto Keiko. *Nihon byōbue shūsei*, 18 vols. Kōdansha, 1977–1982.

Keene, Donald. *Yoshimasa and the Silver Pavilion: The Creation of the Soul of Japan*. Columbia University Press, 2003.

Kerr, Rose. *Song Dynasty Ceramics*. V & A Publications, 2004.

Kesao Ihara. "Historical Materials about Jigekanjin Officials in the Medieval Imperial Palace." *REKIHAKU* 156 (2009): 1–5.

Kikuchi Tetsuo and Fukuda Toyohiko, eds. *Yomigaeru chūsei, vol. 4: Kita no chūsei: Tsugaru, Hokkaidō*. Heibonsha, 1989.

Kim, Wondong. "Chinese Ceramics from the Wreck of a Yuan Ship in Sinan, Korea; with Particular Reference to Celadon Wares." PhD dissertation, University of Kansas, 1986.

Kojima Michihiro. *Shiseki de yomu Nihon no rekishi, vol. 7: Sengoku no jidai*. Yoshikawa Kōbunkan, 2009.

Sengoku/shokuhōki no toshi to chiiki. Seishi Shuppan, 2005.

Kojima Michihiro and Senda Yoshihiro. "Shiro to toshi." In *Iwanami Kōza Nihon tsūshi, vol. 10: Chūsei 4*, ed. Asao Naohiro et al. Iwanami Shoten, 1994. 193–232.

Kokuritsu Rekishi Minzoku Hakubutsukan, ed. *Chusei toshi Tosaminato to Ando shi*. Kokuritsu Rekishi Minzoku Hakubutsukan, 1994.

Jidai o tsukutta waza: chūsei no seisan kakumei. Kokuritsu Rekishi Minzoku Hakubutsukan, 2013.

Nihon shutsudo no bōeki tōji, 5 vols. Kokuritsu Rekishi Minzoku Hakubutsukan, 1994.

Tōjiki no bunkashi. Kokuritsu Rekishi Minzoku Hakubutsukan, 1998.

Kosoto Hiroshi. "Volumes of Knowledge: Observations on Song-Period Printed Medical Text." In *Tools of Culture: Japan's Cultural, Intellectual, Medical, and Technological Contacts in East Asia, 1000s–1500s*. Association for Asian Studies, 2009. 212–227.

Koyama Masato. "Jukō chawan no kyomō." In *Kyoto-fu Maizō Bunkazai Ronshū*, vol. 6. Kyoto-fu Maizō Bunkazai Chōsa Kenkyū Sentaa, 2010.

Kurashige, Jeffrey Yoshio. "Serving Your Master: The Kashindan Retainer Corps and the Socio-economic Transformation of Warring States Japan." PhD dissertation, Harvard University, 2011.

Lamers, Jeroen. *Japonius Tyrannus: The Japanese Warlord Oda Nobunaga Reconsidered*. Hotei Publishing, 2001.

Treatise on Epistolary Style: Joao Rodriguez on the Noble Art of Writing Japanese Letters. University of Michigan Center for Japanese Studies, 2002.

Latour, Bruno. *Reassembling the Social: An Introduction to Actor-Network-Theory*. Oxford: Oxford University Press, 2007.

Li Baoping and Li Jianan. "Chinese Storage Jars in China and Beyond." In *Chigusa and the Art of Tea*, ed. Louise Allison Cort and Andrew M. Watsky. Freer Gallery of Art and Arthur M. Sackler Gallery, Smithsonian Institution, 2014.

Lillehoj, Elizabeth. "Reconsidering the Identity of Ri Shūbun." *Artibus Asiae* 55.1–2 (1995): 99–124.

Lippit, Yukio. *Painting of the Realm: The Kano House of Painters in 17th-Century Japan*. University of Washington Press, 2012.

Lu, Hui-Wen. "A Forgery and the Pursuit of the Authentic Wang Xizhi." In *Visual and Material Cultures in Middle Period China*, ed. Patricia Buckley Ebrey and Shih-shan Susan Huang. Brill, 2017. 193–225.

Masanori Fujii. *Asakura shimatsuki*. Benseisha, 1994.

Mass, Jeffrey P. *Antiquity and Anachronism in Japanese History*. Stanford University Press, 1992.

  Lordship and Inheritance in Early Medieval Japan: A Study of the Kamakura Soryō System. Stanford University Press, 1989.

Matsubara Nobuyuki. "Asakura Yoshikage no seiko Kōtokuin to Wakasa Takeda shi." In *Asakura Yoshikage no subtete*, ed. Matsubara Nobuyuki. Shinjinbutsu Ōraisha, 2003.

  ed. *Asakura Yoshikage no subtete*. Shinjinbutsu Ōraisha, 2003.

Matsui Akira. "Sakan datta nikushoku." In *Yomigaeru chūsei, vol. 8: Umoreta minato machi Kusado Sengen/Tomo/Onomichi*, ed. Matsushita Masao. Heibonsha, 1994.

Matsuyama Hiroshi. *Nihon chūsei toshi no kenkyū*. Daigakudō Shoten, 1973.

  Shugo jōkamachi no kenkyū. Daigakudō Shoten, 1982.

Mayo, Christopher Michael. "Mobilizing Deities: Deus, Gods, Buddhas, and the Warrior Band in Sixteenth-Century Japan." PhD dissertation, Princeton University Press, 2013.

McClain, James L. "Castle Towns and Daimyo Authority: Kanazawa in the Years 1583–1630." *The Journal of Japanese Studies* 6.2 (Summer 1980): 267–299.

  Kanazawa: A Seventeenth-Century Japanese Castle Town. Yale University Press, 1982.

McCormick, Melissa. "Genji Goes West: The 1510 *Genji Album* and the Visualization of Court and Capital." *Art Bulletin* 85.1 (March 2003): 54–85.

McKelway, Matthew Philip. *Capitalscapes: Folding Screens and Political Imagination in Late Medieval Kyoto*. University of Hawai'i Press, 2006.

Miho Museum, ed. *Kotō no fu, chūsei no yakimono: Rokukoyō to sono shūhen*. Miho Museum, 2010.

Miller, Daniel. *Stuff*. Polity Press, 2009.

Minami Echizen Machi. "Koku shitei shiseki Somayama jōato." 2013; accessed November 7, 2016, www.town.minamiechizen.lg.jp/kurasi/103/128/p001165.html.

Miura Keiichi. *Nihon chūsei no chiiki to shakai*. Shibunkaku Shuppan, 1993.

Miyanaga Kazumi. "Asakura shi to Echizen Sarugaku." *Ichijōdani Asakura Shi Iseki Shiryōkan kiyō* (1995).

  "Tenji gaisetsu." In *Sengoku no manabiya: Asakura bunka, bunbu o kimeru*. Fukui Kenritsu Ichijōdani Asakura Shi Iseki Shiryōkan. 2013. 14–20.

Mizuno Kazuo and Satō Kei, eds. *Sengoku daimyo Asakura shi to Ichijōdani*. Kōshi Shoin, 2002.

Mizuno Kazuo. "Ichijōdani Asakura shi iseki shutsudo ibutsu." In *Sengoku daimyo Asakura shi to Ichijōdani*, ed. Mizuno Kazuo and Satō Kei. Kōshi Shoin, 2002. 253–270.

"Ichijōdani no bunka." In *Sengoku daimyo Asakura shi to Ichijōdani*, ed. Mizuno Kazuo and Satō Kei. Kōshi Shoin, 2002. 135–158.

"Ichijōdani no kurashi." In *Sengoku daimyo Asakura shi to Ichijōdani*, ed. Mizuno Kazuo and Satō Kei. Kōshi Shoin, 2002. 233–250.

"Kodomo no asobi: koma to hagoita to." In *Jitsuzō no Sengoku jōkamachi Echizen Ichijiodani*, ed. Ono Masatoshi. Heibonsha, 1990. 116–120.

Morita Kōji. "Mikatagahara no tatakai." In *Tokugawa Ieyasu jiten*, ed. Fujino Tamotsu et al. Shinjinbutsu Ōraisha, 1990. 200–207.

Morohashi Tetsuji. *Daikanwa jiten*, 13 vols. Taishūkan, 1955.

Morse, Edward Sylvester. *Japanese Homes and Their Surroundings*. Ticknor and Company, 1886.

Moto-Sanchez, Milla Micka. "Jizō, Healing Rituals, and Women in Japan." *Japanese Journal of Religious Studies* 43.2 (2016): 307–331.

Murai Ryōsuke. *Sengoku daimyō kenryoku kōzō no kenkyū*. Shibunkaku Shuppan, 2012.

Murai Yasuhiko. *Chanoyu no koten, vol. 1: Kundaikan sōchōki, Okazarinosho*. Seikai Bunkasha, 1983.

Murata Shūzō. "Jō ato chōsa to Sengoku shi kenkyū." In *Tenbō Nihon rekishi, vol. 12: Sengoku shakai*, ed. Ikegami Hiroko and Inaba Tsuguharu. Tōkyōdō Shuppan, 2010. 246–266.

Nagashima Fukutarō, annot. *Chadō koten zenshū, vol. 9: Matsuya kaiki*, ed. Sen Sōshitsu, Tankōsha, 1977.

Nihon Kōkogaku Kyōkai, ed. *Shugosho kara Sengoku joka e*. Meichō Shuppan, 1994.

Niki Hiroshi and Ishii Nobuo. *Shugosho/Sengoku jōkamachi no kōzō to shakai: Awa no kuni Shōzui*. Shibunkaku Shuppan, 2017.

Nishida Hiroko. "Tenmoku: The World of Iron-Black Glazed Ceramics Preserved in Japan" (trans. Martha J. McClintock). In *Sōjiten*. Asahi Shinbunsha, 1999. 214–217.

Ōhira Kei'ichi. "Kyokusui no en saikō: Ō Gishi ga Rantei de kyokusui no en o moyōsu made, soshite sono go." *Hyōfū* 41 (November 15, 2004): 97–110.

Okada Tetsu. *Nabemono kigen jiten*. Chikuma Shobō, 2013.

Okuno Takahiro. "Shoki no Oda shi." In *Sengoku daimyō ronshū, vol. 17: Oda seiken no kenkyū*, ed. Fujiki Hisashi. Yoshikawa Kōbunkan, 1985.

Omote Akira and Masayoshi Itō. *Konparu kodensho shūsei*. Wanya Shoten, 1969.

O'Neal, Halle. "Inscribing Grief and Salvation: Embodiment and Medieval Reuse and Recycling in Buddhist Palimpsests." *Artibus Asiae* 79.1 (2019): 5–28.

Ono Masatoshi. "Hakkutsu sareta Sengoku jidai no machiya: Echizen no rei o chūshin ni." In *Chūsei toshi to shōnin shokunin: kōkogaku to chūsei shi kenkyū 2*, ed. Amino Yoshihiko and Ishii Susumu. Meichō Shuppan, 1992. 93–128.

"Hibi no kurashi." In *Jitsuzō no Sengoku jōkamachi Echizen Ichijiodani*, ed. Ono Masatoshi. Heibonsha, 1990. 103–115.

"Ichijōdani wa nani o nokoshita no ka? Chūsei daikibo iseki no kinō/kyō/ ashita." In *Fukui Kenritsu Ichijōdani Asakura Shi Iseki Shiryōkan. Sengoku jōkamachi Ichijōdani no miryoku o saikō suru.* Fukui Kenritsu Ichijōdani Asakura Shi Iseki Shiryōkan, 2011.

Sengoku jōkamachi no kōkogaku: Ichijōdani kara no messeiji. Tankōsha, 1997.

"Shōfuku no shakushi." In *Jitsuzō no Sengoku jōkamachi Echizen Ichijiodani*, ed. Ono Masatoshi. Heibonsha, 1990. 168–169.

Ono Masatoshi and Suitō Makoto, ed. *Yomigaeru chūsei, vol. 1: Jitsuzō no Sengoku jōkamachi, Echizen Ichijōdani.* Heibonsha, 1990.

Ono Masatoshi, Gomi Fumihiko, and Hagihara Mitsuo, eds. *Chūsei no taiga kōryū: ba, hito, gijutsu.* Kōshi Shoin, 2006,

Ooms, Herman. *Tokugawa Ideology: Early Constructs, 1570–1680.* Princeton University Press, 1985.

Ōta Gyūichi. *The Chronicle of Lord Nobunaga*, ed. Jurgis S. A. Elisonas, and Jeroen P. Lamers Brill, 2011.

Ōta Gyūichi, Okuno Takahiro, and Iwasawa Yoshihiko, eds. *Shinchō kōki.* Kadokawa Shoten, 1969.

Ōzeki Kunio. "Shinryō." In *Encyclopedia of Shinto*, accessed November 18, 2019, http://k-amc.kokugakuin.ac.jp/DM/dbSearchList.do;jsessionid= A0BA4F8FB9EC495A13E343380954F59C?class_name=col_eos&search_ condition_type=1&db_search_condition_type=0&View=0&focus_type=0& startNo=1&searchFreeword=shinryo&searchRangeType=0.

Phillips, Quitman E. *The Practices of Painting in Japan, 1475–1500.* Stanford University Press, 2000.

Pickering, Andrew. "Material Culture and the Dance of Agency." In *The Oxford Handbook of Material Culture Studies*, ed. Dan Hicks and Mary C. Beaudry. Oxford University Press, 2010. 191–208.

Pitelka, Morgan. "Chinese Ceramics and Warrior Sociability in Sixteenth-Century Japan." In *Around Chigusa: Tea and the Arts of Sixteenth-Century Japan*, ed. Dora C. Y. Ching, Louise Allison Cort, and Andrew M. Watsky. Princeton University Press, 2017. 53–70.

Handmade Culture: Raku Potters, Patrons, and Tea Practitioners in Japan. University of Hawai'i Press, 2005.

"A Melodramatic Age." In *Letters from Japan's Sixteenth and Seventeenth Centuries: Correspondence of Warlords, Tea Masters, Zen Priests, and Aristocrats*, ed. Morgan Pitelka, Reiko Tanimura, and Takashi Masuda. Institute of East Asian Studies, 2021.

Spectacular Accumulation: Material Culture, Tokugawa Ieyasu, and Samurai Sociability. University of Hawai'i Press, 2016.

Rambelli, Fabio. *Buddhist Materiality: A Cultural History of Objects in Japanese Buddhism.* Stanford University Press, 2007.

Ramirez-Christensen, Esperanza. *Murmured Conversations: A Treatise on Poetry and Buddhism by the Poet-Monk Shinkei.* Stanford University Press, 2008.

Ratcliff, Christian Doran. "The Cultural Arts in Service: The Careers of Asukai Masaari and His Lineage." PhD dissertation, Yale University, 2007.

Rath, Eric. *Food and Fantasy in Early Modern Japan.* University of California Press, 2010.

Rollason, David. *The Power of Place: Rulers and Their Palaces, Landscapes, Cities, and Holy Places.* Princeton University Press, 2016.

Roth, Gustav, Franz-Karl Ehrhard, Kimiaki Tanaka, and Lokesh Chandra. *Stupa: Cult and Symbolism.* International Academy of Indian Culture and Aditya Prakashan, 2009.

Ruppert, Brian O. "Beyond Death and the Afterlife: Considering Relic Veneration in Medieval Japan." In *Death and the Afterlife in Japanese Buddhism,* ed. Jacqueline I. Stone and Mariko Namba Walter. University of Hawai'i Press, 2008. 102–136.

Saeki Kōji. "Chinese Trade Ceramics in Medieval Japan" (trans. Peter Shapinsky). In *Tools of Culture: Japan's Cultural, Intellectual, Medical, and Technological Contacts in East Asia, 1000s–1500s,* ed. Andrew Edmund Goble, Kenneth R. Robinson, and Haruko Wakabayashi. Association for Asian Studies, 2009. 163–182.

Saitō Shin'ichi. *Chūsei bushi no shiro.* Yoshikawa Kōbunkan, 2006.

Sakamoto Yoshihiro. "Bungo Funai no tatemono ikō." In *Ōuchi to Ōtomo: cūsei Nishi Nihon no nidai daimyō,* ed. Kage Toshio. Bensei Shuppan, 2013. 219–225.

——— "Bungo 'Funai' no Toshi kōzō to gaikokujin no kyoju." In *Chūsei no taiga kōryū: ba, hito, gijutsu,* ed. Ono Masatoshi, Gomi Fumihiko, and Hagihara Mitsuo. Kōshi Shoin, 2006. 36–39.

Sakurai Eiji. "Enkai to kenryoku." In *Utage no chūsei: ba, kawarake, kenryoku,* ed. Ono Masatoshi, Gomi Fumihiko, and Hagihara Mitsuo. Kōshi Shoin, 2008. 219–240.

Sasaki Kensaku. "Chūsei Odawara no machiwari to keikan." In *Chūsei no michi to hashi,* ed. Fujiwara Yoshiaki. Kōshi Shoin, 2005. 169–192.

Satō Kei. "Asakura shi no seisui to Ichijōdani." In *Sengoku daimyo Asakura shi to Ichijōdani,* ed. Mizuno Kazuo and Satō Kei. Kōshi Shoin, 2002. 11–34.

——— "Asakura shi to Muromachi bakufu: orei shinjō o chūshin to shite." In *Sengoku daimyo Asakura shi to Ichijōdani,* ed. Mizuno Kazuo and Satō Kei. Kōshi Shoin, 2002. 35–58.

——— *Asakura Takakage: Sengoku daimyō Asakura shi no ishizue kizuita mōshō.* Ebisu Kōshō, 2014.

——— "Kiyohara no Nobukata no Echizen gekō to Asakura shi." In *Sengoku no manabiya: Asakura bunka, bunbu o kimeru,* ed. Fukui Kenritsu Ichijōdani Asakura Shi Iseki Shiryōkan. Fukui Kenritsu Ichijōdani Asakura Shi Iseki Shiryōkan, 2013. 10–13.

——— "Shiryō shōkai, 'Echizen Ichijōdani kyokusui no en shika.'" *Ichijōdani Asakura Shi Iseki Shiryōkan kiyō* (1993): 1–9.

Satō Shin'ichi. "Imagawa kana mokuroku." In *Chūsei hōsei shiryō shū,* vol. 3, ed. Satō Shin'ichi, Ikeuchi Yoshisuke, and Momose Kesao. Iwanami Shoten, 1965.

Scheid, Bernhard. "Shinto as a Religion for the Warrior Class: The Case of Yoshikawa Koretaru." *Japanese Journal of Religious Studies* 29.3–4 (Fall 2002): 299–324.

Schlereth, Thomas J. *Artifacts and the American Past.* American Association for State and Local History, 1980.

Material Culture: A Research Guide. University Press of Kansas, 1985.
"Material Culture and Cultural Research." In *Material Culture: A Research Guide*, ed. Thomas J. Schlereth. University Press of Kansas, 1985. 1–34.
Schweizer, Anton. *Ōsaki Hachiman: Architecture, Materiality, and Samurai Power.* Reimer, 2016.
Shiga Tarō. "Muromachi shōgunke no shihō o saguru." In *Muromachi shōgunke no shihō o saguru*, ed. Tokugawa Bijutsukan. Tokugawa Bijutsukan, 2008. 158–169.
Shinmura Taku, ed. *Nihon iryōshi.* Yoshikawa Kōbunkan, 2006.
Shirane, Haruo, ed. *Early Modern Japanese Literature: An Anthology, 1600–1900.* Columbia University Press, 2008.
Japan and the Culture of the Four Seasons: Nature, Literature, and the Arts. Columbia University Press, 2012.
Skord, Virginia. "Monogusa Tarō: From Rags to Riches and Beyond." *Monumenta Nipponica* 44.2 (Summer 1989): 171 –198.
Soga Takashi. *Sengoku bushō to nō.* Yūzankaku, 2006.
Soranaka, Isao. "Obama: The Rise and Decline of a Seaport." *Monumenta Nipponica* 52.1 (Spring 1997): 85–102.
Spafford, David. "An Apology of Betrayal: Political and Narrative Strategies in a Late Medieval Memoir." *Journal of Japanese Studies* 35.2 (2009): 321–352.
A Sense of Place: The Political Landscape in Late Medieval Japan. Harvard Asia Center, 2013.
"The Language and Contours of Familial Obligation in Fifteenth- and Sixteenth-Century Japan." In *What Is a Family? Answers from Early Modern Japan*, ed. Mary Elizabeth Berry and Marcia Yonemoto. University of California Press, 2019. 23–46.
Stavros, Matthew. "Building Warrior Legitimacy in Medieval Kyoto." *East Asian History* 31 (June 2006): 1–28.
Kyoto: An Urban History of Japan's Premodern Capital. University of Hawai'i Press, 2014.
Stavros, Matthew, with Norika Kurioka. "Imperial Progress to the Muromachi Palace, 1381: A Study and Annotated Translation of *Sakayuku hana.*" *Japan Review* 28 (2015): 3–46.
Steenstrup, Carl. "Hojo Soun's Twenty-One Articles: The Code of Conduct of the Odawara Hojo." *Monumenta Nipponica* 29.3 (Autumn 1974): 283–303.
Stoler, Ann Laura. *Imperial Debris: On Ruins and Ruination.* Duke University Press, 2013.
Stone, Peter G., and Philippe G. Planet. "Introduction." In *The Constructed Past: Experimental Archaeology, Education and the Public*, ed. Peter G. Stone and Phillipe G. Planet. Routledge, 1999. 1–14.
Sue Tomoko. "Girei sahō to shite no keshō." In *Nihon no keshō bunka.* Shiseidō, 2007.
Suegara Yutaka. "Ichijōdani ni bunka o tsutaeta hitobito." In *Sengoku no manabiya: Asakura bunka, bunbu o kimeru*, ed. Fukui Kenritsu Ichijōdani Asakura Shi Iseki Shiryōkan. Fukui Kenritsu Ichijōdani Asakura Shi Iseki Shiryōkan. 2013. 5–9.
Suitō Makoto. *Asakura Yoshikage.* Yoshikawa Kōbunkan, 1981.

"Ichijōdani no shinkō sekai." In *Jitsuzō no Sengoku jōkamachi Echizen Ichijiodani*, ed. Ono Masatoshi. Heibonsha, 1990. 142–161.

"Setchōki no Asakura Yoshikage." In *Asakura Yoshikage no subtete*, ed. Matsubara Nobuyuki. Shinjinbutsu Ōraisha, 2003. 26–57.

Suzuki Yasuyuki. *Chūsei Setonai no minatomachi: Kusado Sengen chō iseki.* Shinsensha, 2007.

Takagi Hisashi. "Chūsei ni okeru Echizenyaki no seisan to ryūtsū." In *Tōsetsu* (2002–2008): 25–30.

Takahashi Shin'ichirō. *Buke no koto, Kamakura.* Yamakawa Shuppansha, 2005.

Chūsei no toshi to bushi. Yoshikawa Kōbunkan, 1996.

Chūsei toshi no chikara: Kyō, Kamakura, to jisha. Kōshi Shoin, 2010.

Takahashi Yasuo, ed. *Chūsei no naka no Kyōto.* Shinjinbutsu Ōraisha, 2006.

Takahashi Yasuo with Matthew Stavros. "Castles in Kyoto at the Close of the Age of Warring States: The Urban Fortresses of the Ashikaga Shoguns Yoshiteru and Yoshiaki." In *Japanese Capitals in Historical Perspective: Place, Power and Memory in Kyoto, Edo and Tokyo*, ed. Nicolas Fiévé and Paul Waley. RoutledgeCurzon, 2003. 41–66.

Takemoto Chizu. *Shokuhōki no chakai to seiji.* Shibunkaku Shuppan, 2006.

Takeuchi Rizō, ed. *Daijōin jisha zōjiki.* In *Zōho zoku shirō taisei*, vol. 7. Rinsen Shoten, 1978.

Tamamura Takeji. *Gozan zensō denki shūsei.* Shibunkaku Shuppan, 2003.

Tamanaga Mitsuhiro and Sakamoto Yoshihiro. *Ōtomo Sōrin no Sengoku toshi, Bungo Funai.* Shinsensha, 2009.

Tanabe, George J., Jr. "Merit and Merit-Making." In *Encyclopedia of Buddhism*, vol. 2, ed. Robert E. Buswell, Jr. Macmillan Reference, 2004. 532–534.

Tanaka Naoko. *Muromachi no gakumon to chi no keisho: ikoki ni okeru seito e no shiko.* Bensei Shuppan, 2017.

Toda Hiroyuki. "Soga ha no kaiga." In *Sengoku daimyo Asakura shi to Ichijōdani*, ed. Mizuno Kazuo and Satō Kei. Kōshi Shoin, 2002. 185–205.

Tōkai Maizō Bunkazai Kenkyūkai. *Kiyosu: Shokuhōki no shiro to toshi.* Tōkai Maizō Bunkazai Kenkyūkai, 1988.

Tokugawa Yoshinobu. *Chatsubo.* Tankōsha, 1982.

Tōkyō Daigaku Shiryō Hensanjo, ed. *Dai Nihon shiryō.* Tōkyō Daigaku Shuppankai, 1964.

Tōkyō Kokuritsu Hakubutsukan. *Shinan kaitei hikiage bunbutsu.* Chūnichi Shinbunm Shinbunsha, 1983.

Tonomura, Hitomi. *Community and Commerce in Late Medieval Japan: Corporate Villages of Tokuchin-ho.* Stanford University Press, 1986

"Black Hair and Red Trousers: Gendering the Flesh in Medieval Japan." *The American Historical Review* 99.1 (February 1994): 129–154.

Community and Commerce in Late Medieval Japan: The Corporate Villages of Tokuchin-ho. Stanford University Press, 1992.

"Sexual Violence against Women: Legal and Extralegal Treatment in Premodern Warrior Societies." In *Women and Class in Japanese History*, ed. Hitomi Tonomura, Anne Walthall, and Wakita Haruko. University of Michigan, 1999. 135–152.

Toyama Mikio. *Ōtomo Sōrin.* Yoshikawa Kōbunkan, 1975.

Toyoda Takeshi. *Nihon no hōken toshi.* Iwanami Shoten, 1952.
Toshi oyobi za no hattatsu. Chūō Kōronsha, 1948.
Tsang, Carol Richmond. *War and Faith: Ikkō Ikki in Late Muromachi Japan.* Harvard East Asian Center, 2007.
Tsutsui Hiroichi. "Seigan meibutsuki." In *Chadō gaku taikei, vol. 10: Cha no koten,* ed. Tsutsui Hiroichi. Tankōsha, 2001. 373–402.
Tyler, Royall, trans. *The Tale of the Heikei.* Penguin, 2012.
Uematsu Torazo, ed. *Ishiyama Honganji nikki.* Seibundō Shuppan, 1966–1968.
Von Verschuer, Charlotte. *Rice, Agriculture, and the Food Supply in Premodern Japan.* Routledge, 2016.
Wakita Haruko. "Muromachi ki no keizai hatten." In *Iwanami Kōza Nihon rekishi, vol. 7: Chūsei 3.* Iwanami Kōza, 1976. 51–98.
Nihon chūsei toshiron. Tokyo Daigaku Shuppankai, 1981.
Taikei Nihon no rekishi, vol. 7: Sengoku daimyō. Shogakkan, 1993.
Wakita Haruko with Susan B. Hanley. "Dimensions of Development: Cities in Fifteenth-and Sixteenth-Century Japan." In *Japan before Tokugawa: Political Consolidation and Economic Growth, 1500–1650,* ed. S. Hall, Nagahara Keiji, and Kozo Yamamura. Princeton University Press, 1981. 295–326.
Walley, Akiko. "Inscribing and Ascribing Merit: Buddhist Vows and the Hōryūji Shaka Triad." *Harvard Journal of Asiatic Studies* 73.2 (2013): 299–337.
Walthall, Anne. "The Life Cycle of Farm Women in Tokugawa Japan." In *Recreating Japanese Women 1600–1945,* ed. Gail Lee Bernstein. University of California Press, 1991.
Watsky, Andrew M. *Chikubushima: Deploying the Sacred Arts in Momoyama Japan.* University of Washington Press, 2004.
Wert, Michael. *Meiji Restoration Losers: Memory and Tokugawa Supporters in Modern Japan.* Harvard University Asia Center, 2013.
Winfield, Pamela D., and Steven Heine, ed. *Zen and Material Culture.* Oxford University Press, 2017.
Wu, Marshall P. S. *The Orchid Pavilion Gathering: Chinese Painting from the University of Michigan Museum of Art.* University of Michigan, 2000.
Yano Tamaki. *Kundaikan sōchōki no sōgō kenkyū.* Bensei Shuppan, 1999.
"Meibutsuki no seisei kōzō: Jikken to henshū no hazama." In *Chadō gaku taikei, vol. 10: Cha no koten,* ed. Tsutsui Hiroichi. Tankōsha, 2001. 66–108.
Yazaki, Takeo. *Social Change and the City in Japan: From Earliest Times through the Industrial Revolution,* trans. David Swain. Japan Publications, 1968.
Yiengpruksawan, Mimi Hall. *Hiraizumi: Buddhist Art and Regional Politics in Twelfth-Century Japan.* Harvard University Asia Center, 1998
Yonehara Masayoshi. *Sengoku bushi to bungei no kenkyū.* Ōfū, 1994.
Yoshioka Yasuhide, "Ichijōdani no toshi kōzō." In *Sengoku daimyo Asakura shi to Ichijōdani,* ed. Mizuno Kazuo and Satō Kei. Kōshi Shoin, 2002. 59–82.
Yoshioka Yasunobu. *Nihon kaiiki no doki/tōji, chūsei hen.* Rokkō Shuppan, 1989.
"Tōhoku Nihon kaiiki ni okeru chūsei tōki no seisan to ryūtsū." In *Chūsei Sueki no kenkyū.* Yoshikawa Kōbunkan, 1994.
Zhu Boqian. *Longquanyao Qingci.* Yishujia Chubanshe, 1998.

Index

Oda Nobunaga, 14, 29, 104, 111, 117–118,
146
and Ashikaga Yoshiaki, 133, 174, 192
assassination of, 42
destruction of Ichijōdani, 2, 23, 102, 113,
135, 180–181, 195–207, 209–211, 223
and unification, 3–6, 21, 93–95, 108, 185
Odawara, 35, 66
Ōmi province, 191, 195, 197, 199,
202–203, 205
onari. See visitation ceremonies
Ōnin War, 5, 8, 21–22, 29, 98–105, 109,
114, 117, 146, 151, 153, 158, 165,
172, 187
Ōtomo, 33–36, 42, 104, 119
Ōtomo Yoshinao, 103
Ōtomo Yoshishige, 33
Ōuchi, 105, 115

palace city, 7, 13–15, 17, 21, 52, 57, 65, 78,
95, 116, 149, 185
pestle (*surikogi*), 54, 74
plaster-wall (*nurikabe*) specialist, 50
porcelain, x, 2, 51, 55, 70, 75, 77–80, 83,
91, 170, 174–175
provincial city, 3, 5, 22, 34, 43, 222
provincial codes (*bunkokuhō*), 108–112
Provincial Office (*kokufu*), 27

Reconstructed Town of Ichijōdani, 23, 213
Reconstructed Town of Kusado Sengen,
216–222
*Record of Praiseworthy Famous Objects
(Seigan meibutsuki)*, 175
Records about All Countries in the Eastern Sea
(K: *Haedong jegukgi*; J: *Kaitō
shokokuki*), 182
ritual, 15, 19, 36–42, 49, 70, 77, 113,
120–124, 139, 143–144, 148, 150,
154, 188
and earthenware ceramics, 55
and the environment, 178
and material culture, 3
suicide, 206, 209
theories of, 18
roads, 2, 23, 27, 36, 44, 57, 62, 132–133,
151–152
of Akabuchi, 47–50
of Bungo Funai, 34
of Echizen, 90
of Hirai, 46–47
of Ichijōdani, 30–33
of Odawara, 35
Rokkaku, 102, 105, 109, 196–197

Rokkaku Jōtei, 195
Rokkaku Yoshikata, 192
ruins, 2, 6, 20, 51, 176, 182, 201, 211, 213
scholarship on, 22–25

Saigōji, 47, 56, 84, 126–127, 131, 148, 175
Saiokuken Sōchō, 152
Sakai, 7, 10, 64, 92, 172, 175, 183
Sakamoto, 199–201
samsara, 124, 139
samurai sociability. *See* gift exchange; tea
culture; visitation ceremonies
sarugaku. See Noh
Scroll of Fukutomi (Fukutomi zōshi),
54, 75
Sea of Japan, 30, 91
Seishun, 131
Sengoku. *See* Age of Warring States
sexual violence, 207
Shiba, 4–5, 29, 95, 98–105, 107, 117, 146,
152, 165
Shiba Takatsune, 97
Shiba Yoshitoshi, 100
Shimazu, 183–185
shogunal deputy (*kanrei*), 98
shugo. See governor
shugosho. See governors' residences
Sinan shipwreck, 63
Single-Mind religious leagues (*ikkō ikki*),
93, 102, 146, 199
six old kilns theory, 87–89
small universe (*shō'uchū*), 180, 221–223
Sōami, 169, 173
Soga school of painting, 161–165
Sōtetsu, 152
stone Buddhas (*sekibutsu*), 3, 126, 133,
136–147
stone pagodas (*sekitō*), 126, 133,
136–147
stone warmers (*bandoko*), 86
surrogate parent, surrogate child (*yorioya
yoriko*) system, 106

Takeda, 5, 94, 104–105, 109, 175
of Wakasa, 45, 149, 186, 196
Takeda Shingen, 93, 196, 202–204
Takeda Yoshimune, 192
Tanino Ippaku, 53
tax reports (*sashidashi*), 107
tea culture, 19, 39, 41, 63–64, 76, 80,
83–84, 92, 119, 126, 128, 131–132,
151, 153, 177–178, 180
and the Asakura, 173–176
tea diary (*chakaiki*), 175

For EU product safety concerns, contact us at Calle de José Abascal, 56–1°,
28003 Madrid, Spain or eugpsr@cambridge.org.

www.ingramcontent.com/pod-product-compliance
Ingram Content Group UK Ltd.
Pitfield, Milton Keynes, MK11 3LW, UK
UKHW020354140625

459647UK00020B/2466